POLITICAL DISAPPOINTMENT

POLITICAL DISAPPOINTMENT

A CULTURAL HISTORY

from

RECONSTRUCTION

to the

AIDS CRISIS

SARA MARCUS

THE BELKNAP PRESS OF HARVARD UNIVERSITY PRESS

Cambridge, Massachusetts | London, England   2023

First printing

Cataloging-in-Publication Data is available from the Library of Congress

ISBN 9780674248656

For Roy

CONTENTS

INTRODUCTION

Loss and American Culture

A t key moments in history, profound transformation seems close enough to touch. The foundations of the present order are crumbling; the ruling figures totter and sway. The structures and conditions of suffering—capitalism, patriarchy, white supremacy—are finally on the defensive, and in these moments, it's possible to believe that a better collective life may at last be within reach.

This book is not about those moments. It is, instead, about what comes next.

Windows of possibility have a habit of closing without delivering on utopian promises. Yet people often persist in their desires for a different political life, a better world, even after the time for possibly attaining those objects has passed—for how long, it is difficult to say for certain, but it has passed for now. Such desires do not survive unchanged, though: shifting conditions reshape them, reorient them, and alter their temporalities and moods. Desire lives on as disappointment.

Let's begin, then, with a conception of political disappointment as untimely desire: a longing for fundamental change that outlasts a historical moment when it might have been fulfilled. To keep longing for a lost future is evidence of survival. The loss may have undone a dream of a more just and peaceful existence, but the dreamer nonetheless goes on existing and aspiring. There is more at stake than mere survival, though, because disappointment shapes practices and forms that extend desire's reach beyond the inner arena or immediate scene of loss. In acknowledging loss, disappointment ushers shared desire actively into the world.[1] And since we are all, at different times and in variously constitutive ways, undone by loss and grief, disappointment allows us to recognize thwarted and untimely desire as grounds for solidarity.[2]

This book will argue that disappointment was the defining political experience of the United States in the twentieth century, that it shaped many of the century's most important works of literature and art, and that by confronting shared loss directly, writers and artists produced new collectivities and political possibilities. As with perhaps any project founded on an ideal, America has been disappointing people from the beginning. But in the history of this country, the experience of a possible transformation's failure to arrive becomes particularly salient beginning with the failure of Reconstruction and its aftermath. From that point forward, the experience of outdated and unfulfilled desire predominates throughout the twentieth century. The end of Reconstruction in 1877, and the decades of racial retrenchment that followed, marked the decisive end of postwar experiments in reassembling the United States as a multiracial democracy.[3] Rather than a multiracial democracy, in fact, America at the turn of the twentieth century began its transformation into a global empire, and this new level of international ambition dovetailed with a redoubled domestic investment in white supremacy.[4] Accordingly, this book takes the end of Reconstruction as its starting point and goes on to trace disappointment throughout the century.

It was at this moment of post-Reconstruction retrenchment, domestically and globally, that W. E. B. Du Bois famously declared, "The problem of the Twentieth Century is the problem of the color line." At its initial appearance in the "Forethought" of Du Bois's 1903 book *The Souls of Black Folk,* this sentence argues for the book's relevance to any "Gentle Reader," whether white or Black: a shared location in the new century, and the centrality of racial division to that century, makes racism a concern for everybody. The line reappears at the opening of the book's second essay, "Of Our Spiritual Strivings," immediately after a searingly personal account of experiencing double consciousness as an African American and an examination of "the shadow of a deep disappointment" that has "rest[ed] upon the Negro people" since the end of the Civil War, and especially since the end of Reconstruction.[5] Taken together, Du Bois's three opening concepts—a new century characterized by stark racial division, an experience of the self as similarly divided, and a collective historical condition of "deep disappointment" likewise based in ongoing racial injustice— set forth a foundational role for disappointment in the shaping of the post-Reconstruction era and the twentieth century as a whole, while also indicating that disappointment can be both rooted in particular experiences and important for a wide range of people inhabiting a shared moment in history.

Indeed, throughout *Souls,* and especially in "Of Our Spiritual Strivings," Du Bois offers a rich theory of political desire and disappointment that is so crucial for my project in this book that it is worth taking a moment to look closely at it now. The passage from "Of Our Spiritual Strivings" about the "shadow of a deep disappointment" begins with a description of a desire so enveloping that it seems to organize a whole community's yearning with religious force:

> Away back in the days of bondage they thought to see in one divine event the end of all doubt and disappointment; few men ever worshipped Freedom with half such unquestioning faith as did the American Negro for two centuries. To him, so far as he thought and dreamed, slavery was indeed the sum of all villainies, the cause of all sorrow, the root of all prejudice; Emancipation was the key to a promised land of sweeter beauty than ever stretched before the eyes of wearied Israelites. In song and exhortation swelled one refrain—Liberty; in his tears and curses the God he implored had Freedom in his right hand.[6]

Du Bois describes the expectation of freedom as an all-encompassing orientation expressed initially as a sonic unison, spanning oratory and music. But upon its arrival, juridical emancipation falls short of expectations. "At last it came,—suddenly, fearfully, like a dream," he writes, and what follows bears little resemblance to the initial object of desire: "The freedman has not yet found in freedom his promised land."[7]

Du Bois writes here of how disappointment entails a changed experience of historical time, where the posture of expectant waiting for a singular event—the anticipation of being able to someday say, "At last it came"—gives way to a stretched-out temporality of nonarrival in which fulfillment "has not yet" been found. Unlike the concept of the "not yet" that the Frankfurt School philosopher of hope Ernst Bloch and his utopian heirs would soon enshrine—a temporality that inclines toward the ever-present possibility of a better future—the present perfect tense in Du Bois's phrase "has not yet found" highlights the ongoing experience of nonfulfillment that cannot be erased by appeals to a utopian horizon that beckons forever in the distance.[8]

Du Bois uses the word *disappointment* to describe this experience, in which an object that seemed both an ideal and a proximate actuality remains unexpectedly out of reach: "Whatever of good may have come in these years of change, the shadow of a deep disappointment rests upon the Negro people,—a disappointment all the more bitter because the unattained ideal was unbounded save by the simple ignorance of a lowly people."[9] This passage bears a striking similarity to the language Sigmund Freud would use fourteen years later to describe a subject who has failed to mourn correctly: when one cannot properly get over a loss, Freud would write, one instead castigates oneself, turning any criticism of the lost object (which, Freud stipulates, could be either "a loved person" or "some abstraction . . . such as one's country, liberty, an ideal, and so on") inward in an effort to keep the lost object pristine, an operation that casts a melancholic mood over the mourner: "Thus the shadow of the object fell upon the ego."[10] For Du Bois, in contrast, disappointment is not so much a matter of a melancholic mood descending on the disappointed, let alone one of pathologizing a refusal to accept the nonarrival of "liberty, an ideal, and so on"; it concerns, rather, a historical alteration in the relation to one's objects, and even a transformation in those objects themselves.

Du Bois writes that a procession of seemingly new objects arose sequentially in the wake of freedom: first the right to vote, then liberal education, then industrial training. "All these in turn have waxed and waned," he writes, "until even the last grows dim and overcast. Are they all wrong,—all false?" But this multiplicity, this splintering of the initial object after disappointment, is just a moment on the road to synthesis: "Each alone was over-simple and incomplete,—the dreams of a credulous race-childhood, or the fond imaginings of the other world which does not know and does not want to know our power. To be really true, all these ideals must be melted and welded into one."[11]

The ongoing investment in changing yet continuous ideals, pursued in necessarily partial "dreams" and "imaginings," can effect such a fusion, opening new access to the universal via the particular:[12]

> Freedom, too, the long-sought, we still seek,—the freedom of life and limb, the freedom to work and think, the freedom to love and aspire. Work, culture, liberty,—all these we need, not singly but together, not successively but together, each growing and aiding each, and all striving toward that vaster ideal that swims before the Negro people, the ideal of human brotherhood, gained through the unifying ideal of Race; the ideal of fostering and developing the traits and talents of the Negro, not in opposition to or contempt for other races, but rather in large conformity to the greater ideals of the American Republic, in order that some day on American soil two world-races may give to each those characteristics both so sadly lack.[13]

4

The disappointment Du Bois describes in this essay is a desire rendered polyphonic, and potentially transformative, precisely through nonfulfillment. Desire's past efforts continue in an ongoing present: "The long-sought, we still seek." The continuation is far from simple, though, since disappointment transmutes an initial monophony into a choral arrangement, whose ensemblic profusion Du Bois conveys with the liltingly rhythmic phrases "the freedom of life and limb, the freedom to work and think, the freedom to love and aspire," all of these sounding "not singly but together"—not as a solo voice but in the melded harmony of a chorus.

Having begun *The Souls of Black Folk* with a reflection on a deep disappointment founding the twentieth century, Du Bois concludes his book with an analysis of the Sorrow Songs, those choral songs out of slavery that he calls "the music of an unhappy people, of the children of disappointment."[14] A fuller discussion of the music in *Souls* will have to wait until Chapter 1, but it's worthwhile to stay one beat longer with the significance Du Bois grants to sound and transcriptions of sound, especially choral music. The Sorrow Songs are for Du Bois the paradigmatic expression of African American experience and a key expression of disappointment; they are also a distinctively *American* cultural practice, "the sole American music" as well as "the most beautiful expression of human experience born this side the seas."[15] *Political Disappointment* aims to understand more thoroughly this intimate connection between sound, disappointment, African American art, and American experience.

It is in writing about music, and in reproducing musical scores, that Du Bois conveys most capaciously both human experiences within the color line and the political desires that extend beyond it: how it feels not only to be produced as a problem but also to sense and aspire to the possibility of an existence beyond such constriction. In Du Bois's transcriptions of music and discussions of musical effects, the potential for something beyond what materially *is* becomes an object for consciousness while still remaining out of reach. This is not unique to Du Bois, and a discussion of it will help explain the role of music and sound in this study of disappointment.

Sonic Expansiveness and Transcriptive Practices

A deep affinity between sound and the exceeding of constraint is a common theme in musicology and philosophy, literature and social sciences.[16] Sound traverses vast cosmological and anthropological chasms: in our aural imaginary, human cries rise to heaven, divine voices descend to earth, and listeners imagine that otherwise unknowable others become accessible through their music.[17] In literature, sound regularly passes through solid walls, between prison bars, from a village street to a cramped attic garret above, or around city-block corners.[18] A golden record on which Louis Armstrong and His Hot Seven amble through "Melancholy Blues" is currently drifting toward possible listeners in another star system to show nearly unthinkable beings what it is like to live and listen on Earth.[19]

This intuitively understood expansiveness of sound exists in paradoxical relation to its inevitable mediation through form, technique, and matter.[20] To be heard or otherwise sensed, sound has to resonate through some external substance, setting molecules into motion in waves that eventually reach a perceiving body; and to endure in time, to be replayable and available for contemplation, sound has to be recorded, written, or inscribed into forms that are not, themselves, sound. Some medium—a page of sheet music, a written or spoken recollection, an inscription into wax or vinyl or code, an expanse of air or resonator of bone—always intervenes, transferring the pulse along. Sound simultaneously spurs and frustrates dreams of immediacy and intimacy.

It's just this paradox—that an intuitively perceived possibility of surpassing constraint is accessible only via mediation that keeps the dreamed-of transcendence out of reach—that helps explain the prominent role sound and music, and especially transcriptions of sound and music, occupy in this study of disappointment. *Political Disappointment* was initially conceived as a literary study, but sound seeped in from the beginning, first at the corners and seams, then as a suffusing, resonant presence. Repeatedly I encountered instances where writers transcribed sound to index untimely desires for elusive futures. At the outset of Ralph Ellison's *Invisible Man,* his underground protagonist, hibernating in preparation for some future action, uses Armstrong's music to conjure the sense of time's "nodes, those points where time stands still or from which it leaps ahead."[21] At the conclusion of Toni Cade Bambara's *The Salt Eaters,* perhaps the novel that treats post–civil rights exhaustion and disappointment most explicitly, a ferocious bolt of thunder, "cracking the air as if the very world were splitting apart," arrives as a portent of a new existence being born, "the thunderous beginning of the new humanism."[22] That sound, which Bambara renders "Damballah" in reference to a Beninese deity and Vodou *lwa* of the same name, echoes the thunder whose Sanskrit voice at the end of T. S. Eliot's *The Waste Land* indexes a yearned-for peacefulness that contrasts sharply with the poem's portrait of alienated modern life.[23]

Such instances look and sound different from one another, and from the stately staves of Du Bois's choral transcriptions, but they all draw some of their dynamic force from the tension between oral tradition and literary form. This tension has been especially consequential for the history of African American literature; Black authors have long innovated textual practices capable of mediating between, as Henry Louis Gates Jr. puts it in a discussion of African American writers, "a profoundly lyrical, densely metaphorical, quasi-musical, privileged Black oral tradition on the one hand, and a received but not yet fully appropriated standard English literary tradition on the other hand."[24] Many canonical works of African American literature theorize this oral/literate binary, and mediations between the two terms, while also conducting concerted engagements with elements that are not just "quasi-musical," as Gates proposes, but *musical,* full stop.

Yet all literature bears the marks of a relation to the sound of human communication, even where the engagement with any particular oral tradition may be more attenuated. In this book, I will bring our attention to transcriptive practices—by which I mean the array of practices that aspire to render sound in writing, as well as writing's attempts to encompass or approximate sound—and I will argue that transcriptive practices enact sonic destabilizations of deceptively settled literary forms, turning up the volume on writing's ancient and ongoing aural inclinations while amplifying literature's aspiration to approach sound's apparent powers of escape.[25]

Transcriptions are both records and scores, remains of past performances and invitations to future ones. Ever inexact, transcriptive practices introduce alterations and mutations with each new writing, securing both the persistence and the evolution of their sonic objects. Du Bois's transcriptive practices in *Souls* are exemplary in this regard, as he reproduces existing musical transcriptions—transcriptions that already registered substantial acts of rewriting in their redactions from the oral—but he alters them still further by removing the lyrics, turning vocal scores into more abstracted contours of harmony and rhythm. Many of the transcriptions that feature centrally in the history of American disappointment are likewise choral transcriptions in that they inscribe group vocal performance as a means of marking paths from and leaving possible trails back to contingently audible alliances that erratically coalesce, fade out, and go on reverberating. Indeed, all the transcriptive practices to be discussed here, even those that do not register group song as such, are choral in one important sense: they record ongoing desires whose future activation, in whatever altered form, will necessarily be a collective undertaking in which performers or writers collaborate with those who came before.

In *Political Disappointment*, I propose links between broad historical forces and comparatively minor or passing moments in literature and sound: an uneven stack of fermatas in a transcribed spiritual, an old woman's prolonged cough in a short story, three gnomic words proclaimed by a civil rights leader at the side of a Mississippi road, a two-and-a-half-minute audiotaped duet between an artist driving through the desert and a singer he hears on the radio. This method may strike some readers as exceptionally detailed. It is also deliberate. Inspired by Alexandra Vazquez's method of "listening in detail," I embrace an investment in the fleeting or easily overlooked moment, especially as I argue that political disappointment for much of the twentieth century was difficult to express directly and thus often found its way into minute fissures in official discourses. Vazquez's elaboration of listening in detail articulates a link between granular listening and the kind of incompletable yearning that characterizes desire amid loss. Listened-to details, Vazquez writes, may be "all that is left behind from" one's immigrant parents' former home: "They remind us that that place is always partial, that we will never have a fullness of a past picture or sound." Yet for all that partiality, she goes on, "details are things that we learn to live on, imagine off, and use to find other kinds of relationships" to a home that stands as an inherited source to which it is impossible to fully return: "To listen in detail is . . . to listen closely to and assemble that inherited lived matter that is both foreign and somehow familiar into something new."[26] Listening in detail is a transcriptive practice through which we find new forms for historical experience, and its generative care for audible details is central to this book's method.

In developing an account of political disappointment, then, this book attends closely to sound and literature in tandem, and especially to the transcriptive practices through which these two realms interact. I am guided in this approach by sonic-literary research by scholars and writers including Hanif Abdurraqib, Daphne Brooks, Brent Hayes Edwards, Emily Lordi, Carter Mathes, Fred Moten, Ronald Radano, Anthony Reed, and Jennifer Stoever. The richness of their work demonstrates that tuning to sound and music as a literary scholar can yield important insights about sonic and literary texts. Such intermedial conversations are especially robust in African American studies, owing in part to the central importance of sound and music in the archive of Black cultural production, as well as to the role of the sonic in the African American literary tradition, as discussed earlier; accordingly, *Political Disappointment* owes a great deal to the theorizing of links between sound and literature that not only scholars of Black culture but also its creators have been pursuing for centuries.

I read and hear in their work an exhortation to attend to the long history of pathbreaking scholarship on literature and sound in African American studies, and I also endeavor to chart such resonances and their ramifications across multiple strains of cultural history.

"I Do Want *Something*"

Political Disappointment, with its deliberately interracial archive, grows out of my attempts to understand the changing fortunes, over the course of the twentieth century, of an aspirationally multiracial Left. It is also grounded in my personal acquaintance with political disappointment, which long predates my academic interest in the topic. In the summer of 2000, as a recent college graduate, I worked coordinating legal support for people arrested for protesting at the Republican National Convention in Philadelphia.[27] The previous few years had seemed exceptionally promising for the activist Left. In 1999 and 2000, labor unions had joined with environmental groups, anarchist collectives, and Indigenous activists to nonviolently disrupt meetings of the World Trade Organization, World Bank, and International Monetary Fund in Seattle and Washington, DC. These mobilizations had been especially popular among mostly white countercultural radicals, but the Republican National Convention protests in Philadelphia broke from that model, with people of color leading some of the strongest organizing efforts and with white activists recognizing the urgent necessity of building resilient multiracial coalitions. "Another world is possible" was a common tagline in those days, and it felt entirely true.

Possible, perhaps; but for me and many people I knew, the sense of a different world's being proximate shut down abruptly in the summer of 2000. Hundreds of protesters were jailed for weeks; nonviolent activists and organizers were held on inflated bails, up to $1 million, and groundlessly charged with serious felonies.[28] And the following year, the September 11 attacks and their aftermath—missile strikes overseas, resurgent xenophobia domestically—made victory for the global justice movement, so recently a sensed possibility, seem unimaginable. Demoralized and drained, I pulled back from the activist community in Philly and eventually left town altogether. I turned my attention instead to the slow labors of grassroots community organizing—I was hired by a foundation that supported such work—and of writing, trying to think my way through the promises and letdowns of the political projects that had defined the past few years in my life and the lives of my communities. I had longed for, and sometimes even expected, large-scale changes in the economic and political order; I still longed for them, but in the aftermath of the Philadelphia protests and everything that had followed, I could no longer see how to bring them about.

Looking to literature to help me make sense of this situation, I found refuge in Grace Paley's fiction. Earlier, when vast changes had seemed within reach, her wry humor, the bemused arm's length from which she considered radical dreams, had struck me as misplaced; her irreverence had clashed with my sense of self-importance. But now, the way her characters inhabited political commitment as one strand in a long and braided lifetime, the way she treated high stakes with a light touch, struck me as the only way to survive the world. In "Wants," the opening story in Paley's celebrated 1974 collection *Enormous Changes at the Last Minute*, the narrator sums up the scheduling conflicts of a twenty-seven-year marriage this way: "First, my father was sick that Friday, then the children were born, then I had those Tuesday-night meetings, then the war began."[29] The interwoven scales of relation and care spur a telescoping of temporalities, in which a single night, a weekly meeting, and a yearslong war fold up into the same timeline of attachment and foreclosure.

Paley's fiction, I started to understand, gave form to desires that had outlasted their windows of possibility. "Wants," as its title suggests, thematizes this issue directly. In this story, a woman runs into her ex-husband on the steps of the public library, the two discuss why their marriage failed, and at the conversation's apex, the man suggests that it all comes down to a question of desire:

> I wanted a sailboat, he said. But you didn't want anything.
>
> Don't be bitter, I said. It's never too late.
>
> No, he said with a great deal of bitterness. I may get a sailboat. As a matter of fact I have money down on an eighteen-foot two-rigger. I'm doing well this year and can look forward to better. But as for you, it's too late. You'll always want nothing.[30]

The woman has encountered him on her way to pay an eighteen-year-old library fine and to turn in, then check out again, two Edith Wharton novels. As her ex-husband rehashes old arguments, the narrator tries to smooth things over, but his final accusation about wanting nothing, combined with his triumphant report of material progress, strikes a nerve. "I looked through *The House of Mirth*, but lost interest. I felt extremely accused. Now, it's true, I'm short of requests and absolute requirements," the narrator tells her reader, still conciliating even as she reels from the attack. "But I do want *something*. I want, for instance, to be a different person."

She then lists off several specific desires having to do not with concrete items like a sailboat but with her own involvement in civic and political structures. These ascend from the mundane (wanting to be someone who returns library books on time) to the modestly municipal ("I want to be the effective citizen who changes the school system") and finally to the unattained geopolitical: "I *had* promised my children to end the war before they grew up." (The italics are Paley's; the story was published the year before the Vietnam War ended.)[31]

By crowning a list of present-tense desires with an emphatically pluperfect vow that has manifestly not been kept, the narrator casts that unmet intention as another form of ongoing desire. Unlike the other desires on the list, this last one can no longer even be worked toward. The children have presumably grown up, and the war drags on. Notwithstanding the narrator's assertion to the contrary, it is, in fact, too late. Yet her desire persists—albeit in altered form, as signified by the changed verb and verb tense, from "I want" to "I *had* promised." This promise also stands alone as a one-sentence paragraph, giving it extra emphasis.

The promise form marks this desire as having initially taken shape under conditions of apparent attainability—one generally only makes promises one expects to be able to keep. Meanwhile, the italicized pluperfect tense registers the now-eclipsed attainability yet declines to spell it out. Leaving the failure implicit establishes a shared understanding between Paley and her readers. In other words, the withheld explicit statement of disappointment, the focus on its status as historical vow and its position among other clearly ongoing desires, operates not to isolate the speaker in a deluded state of suspended wishing or cruel optimism but rather to connect the speaker with an implied collective of others who understand and might even share this ongoing, untimely desire.[32]

The narrator's matter-of-fact admission of nonfulfillment, devoid of both bravado and self-pity, sets the stage for her to recognize, at the story's conclusion, the slow fulfillment of other aspirations: "Just this morning I looked out the window to watch the street for a while and saw that the little sycamores the city had dreamily planted a couple of years before the kids were born had come that day to the prime of their lives."[33] It also permits her to appreciate her own modest steps toward change, such as bringing two overdue books back to the library. She immediately checks these books out again, suggesting that what's past its time can still be encountered anew.

Paley's story illustrates a particular disappointment that's often seen as the defining political letdown of the twentieth century in the United States, especially on the left: the aftermath of the 1960s. This theme is at the heart of much post-1960s American literature, from Alice Walker's *Meridian* and Toni Cade Bambara's *The Salt Eaters* to Thomas Pynchon's *Vineland*. And the general mood of the US Left contexts I joined as a teenager at the end of the twentieth century—entering by way of majority-white queer and feminist punk scenes, a primarily white-led labor movement in the Northeast, and a Jewish Left profoundly shaped by Freedom Summer memories and Exodus mythographies—was dominated by lament for the unfulfilled passing of the 1960s social movements and for instances of interracial solidarity throughout the twentieth century.

But political disappointment didn't come into being when Martin Luther King Jr. and Fred Hampton were assassinated or when Richard Nixon was elected president. Nor did it have its genesis in the Red Scare of the 1950s that cut short the midcentury efflorescence of Popular Front–influenced culture and gave rise to a genre of ex-radical writings based less in disappointment than in disillusionment: bitter or sheepish pronouncements that one's desires, misbe-gotten from the start, were suitable only for disavowal.[34] Far from being uniquely tied to the 1960s or 1950s, political disappointment pervades the twentieth century from its earliest moments. Its history in the United States goes back much further than that, of course: from the first instances of settler contact, thwarted desires and derailed expectations plagued Indigenous inhabitants and Puritan settlers, enslaved Africans and optimistic immigrants, albeit in very dif-ferent ways and to very different degrees. As discussed earlier, the aftermath of Reconstruction inaugurates a period of particularly intense disappointment, born of the failure to remake America as a multiracial democracy in the wake of slavery. Post-Reconstruction disappointment landed with particular force on African Americans, but its effects were broadly felt: the idea that America had not yet fulfilled its potential as a land of justice and equality persisted throughout the twentieth century and cut across multiple demographics. This book bears at its heart an argument that common ground can be mapped among diverse experiences of disappointment, despite the admitted risks of doing injustice to the specificities of each.

That said, my approach here is grounded in key insights from Black studies. In addition to the intellectual debt to Du Bois I've outlined, this book's approach to political disappointment as a historical and temporal experience rather than a purely affective one owes a great deal to Saidiya Hartman's formulation of enslavement's ongoing effects as "the afterlife of property" rather than melancholia; Christina Sharpe's mapping of a multivalent wake of Atlantic slavery; and Rinaldo Walcott's exploration of contemporary Blackness as existing in a time of juridical emancipation that marks the continual nonarrival of freedom.[35]

There's another lineage I'm claiming here too, of a strain of American studies and Americanist literary studies that has long aspired to being "multiracial" in the same sense that many have aspired to actualize America itself as a "multiracial" project, a strain that has often tried to tell a story—a multiple, centrifugal story that is always threatening to disaggregate—about America overall. It's a foolhardy ambition at best, perhaps, and certainly a violent and dangerous one at worst, which may be why it sounds so woefully dated as I invoke it here. But just as there's still some life left in the stubborn aspiration that the tenacious catchphrase "multiracial democracy" indexes, at once modestly liberal and counterfactually utopian, without which it's hard to envision a properly coalitional approach to salvaging any possibility of forging a shared life on this chunk of stolen land, I will try in these pages to do multiracial Americanist cultural studies that steers clear of imperial arrogance or liberal boosterism, taking my cues and foundations from the constitutive margins of "America."

My decision to proceed in this way grows directly out of my argument that disappointment can furnish grounds for affective solidarity capable of fueling and spurring powerful collective and coalitional practices. It has done so in the past, as this study will detail. In addition, I am guided by Hartman's insight that telling "a narrative of defeat [can] enable a place for the living or envision an alternative future": that rehearsing and tarrying with defeat (Hartman's term) or nonfulfillment (mine) are useful both in "establishing who we are in relation to who we have been" and in "animat[ing] our desire for a liberated future."[36] In other words, discussing and being awake to nonfulfillment itself, not only to the redemptive and utopian practices or hopes that often accompany it (though of course those too), can paradoxically keep desire for something else alive and moving in the world. This is the work of disappointment.

Possible Object-Worlds

The world as we inhabit it is not the only possible world; the conditions that envelop us are not the only conditions that could exist. Present arrangements of individual and collective life are particular, contingent, and changeable, rather than eternally ordained and unmovable. And there exist, if only in potential form, other possible organizations of collective life, past, present, and future.

These modest convictions, whose truth is borne out every time our circumstances change in a way that takes us by surprise, amount to the conditions of possibility for political desire, a wish for a different arrangement of political life. "All humans deep down, whether they admit this or not, know that it would be possible or it could be different," Theodor Adorno said in a 1964 conversation with Ernst Bloch, keeping the referent of *it* vague.[37] Bloch, for his part, worked throughout his career to plumb yearnings for *everything* to be different, yearnings that could be satisfied only by reaching a utopian horizon "where freedom would be, where everything would be right or together in a much deeper sense"—which is to say, yearnings that could not ever be truly satisfied. Fulfillment is not, for Bloch, the point: the point is instead the yearning, the open-ended longing for an arrangement of the world where all troubles are far behind us. If this object is definitionally unattainable—as Adorno persuasively proposes in pointing out that any time an ideal is enacted in reality, it necessarily falls short of our wishes for it—that again redirects our attention to the yearning itself, the continued orientation toward a more or less indeterminate utopian horizon that Bloch writes about as hope, that José Esteban Muñoz associates with queerness, that Ashon Crawley describes as otherwise thinking.[38]

I share these visionary thinkers' interest in and care for such inclination toward the possibility of an unbounded "otherwise." Not all political desires, though, incline only toward that utopian horizon. Utopian thinkers acknowledge this—Bloch wrote of the difference between "the kind of hope that consists only of dreams," on the one hand, and, on the other, educated or concrete hope, which is characterized by "specific disappointability" while nevertheless refusing to be "mediated by solid facts."[39] This paradox, in which Bloch seems to endorse a hope that is concretely grounded but rejects "facts" as "merely subjectively reified moments or objectively reified stoppages within a historical course of events," complicates any mobilization of Bloch as an avatar of historically specific political desire.[40] Muñoz, for his part, works at moments to right this imbalance, stating in an expansion on Bloch that "Concrete Utopianism is rooted in a kind of objective possibility," yet ultimately the question of objective possibility remains relatively sidelined both in Bloch's overall schema and in most contemporary mobilizations of his thought.[41]

Although open-ended yearning is a key component of political desire, such desire also always takes shape in relation to particular objects, whether these objects are as specific as rat abatement or as amorphous as freedom, and against the backdrop of particular arrangements of historical conditions. The disappointments that populate this book proceed from desires that are more determinate than pure utopian yearning, desires that incline toward objects more or less specific and whose possible fulfillment varies across history.

Discussions of the possibility of fundamental political change frequently magnetize around two poles, which we can loosely figure as utopian and pessimistic. Approaches associated with pessimism, especially Afro-pessimism, diagnose structural and conceptual foreclosures of political possibility. To Afro-pessimist thinkers such as Frank B. Wilderson III and Jared Sexton, certain strains of oppression and dehumanization, especially those having to do with the concept and position of Blackness, are fundamental elements of the modern world, written into Western structures of thought and governance from their foundation and thus basically impossible to eradicate by any means short of ending the current civilization and replacing it with something else.[42] In the utopian framework, by contrast, profound change is always possible, with boundless potential separated from our present by the merest scrim. This presumption may not always be laid out as explicitly as it is in Muñoz's work, but when scholars analyze art, music, performance, and other cultural practices as opening up present spaces where a wholly different world can be imagined, touched, or experienced, there is a presupposition at work that understands historical conditions to be almost infinitely malleable, perennially open to the imaginative and aesthetic interventions of a groundbreaking song, say, or the experience of sitting together in a theater.[43] My own intellectual and aesthetic formation, and even the structure of my own political desires, owes a great deal to scholarship and criticism that thinks about art, literature, sound, and performance this way. If I seem to subject it to criticism in these pages, it's because I love and value this approach, and I want to figure out how much of it can credibly survive an encounter with deeply dispiriting historical realities.

Utopian and pessimistic approaches alike generate conceptually ambitious reflections on political transformation and the desire for it. They help frame questions about what cultural practices can and cannot accomplish in the face of constrained agency and how to tell whether a persistent pattern of exclusion is merely long-lasting or effectively permanent.[44] Both of these approaches, and the ongoing dialogue between proponents of each, inform my engagement with the concepts and texts addressed in this book.

I am less interested, though, in discerning an overall quality of fundamental change as being primarily possible *or* foreclosed than I am in tracking historical instances when people sensed possibility waxing and waning amid historical flux, in asking how people's political desires changed in such instances, and in noticing how the resulting disappointment shaped culture. In what follows, then, I take a historically rooted critical approach to literature, sound, and other creative practices.

Readers may note an affinity between what I'm describing and Lauren Berlant's conception of cruel optimism, in which people return to a scene of failed fantasy in ways that make the fulfillment of that fantasy impossible. Berlant's work on cruel optimism asks many of the same questions that I do in this work, and it's clear that instances of seeking personal solutions to systemic problems, and other forms of self-delusion and self-defeat Berlant so insightfully identifies, are among the possible responses to an ideal that has failed to deliver. I am most concerned here, however, with ongoing attachments to objects or ideals that, although disappointing, might not necessarily be responsible for a further decay of possibilities for flourishing. Berlant gestures toward this, especially in the discussion, toward the end of *Cruel Optimism*, of the "desire for the political"—a yearning for the scene and sense of shared political life that can in fact reopen political possibilities.[45] In this book I investigate cases of persistent unfulfilled desire that might be not (or not only) cruel but generative—aesthetically, conceptually, socially, and perhaps even politically.

Disappointment highlights the power of desire to serve as a critique of historical conditions. This stands in contrast to the related but quite distinct experiences of optimism or hope. For Bloch, hope is a way of smoothing out the peaks and valleys of historical attainability: "Hope still nails a flag on the mast, even in decline, in that the decline is not accepted."[46] Hope is, by Bloch's own admission, a way of clinging to a nonactuality, living in direct denial of specific facts and of facticity in general: it serves as "the determined negation of that which continually makes the opposite of the hoped-for object possible."[47] In disappointment, by contrast, we confront rather than negate the obstacles to fulfillment we encounter.

Utopian yearning and hope can never be adequately fulfilled, so they can never be finally disappointed. They can be subject to disillusionment, in which a yearner might come to believe that the yearning was mistaken from the outset, but as long as utopian yearning is active, it cannot be subject to disappointment, because its object, by being so open-ended, defined by its very remoteness, can never fail to deliver. This accounts, perhaps, for some of such yearning's appeal. But that very impossibility of disappointment also forecloses the productivity that only comes with acknowledgment of loss. Loss, and the generativity it spurs, is only possible when we permit ourselves to recognize our attachment to particular objects, actual or potential: objects that may vanish, or fail to materialize as expected, leaving disappointment in their wake.

The Productivity of Loss

Coming to terms with the loss of objects is an essential part of the production of selves and communities. Sigmund Freud's acknowledgment, in *The Ego and the Id,* of melancholic incorporation's key role in ego formation has been usefully amplified and developed by Judith Butler, who clarifies how the self is partially, and crucially, constituted by taking in elements of one's lost objects.[48] Melanie Klein, in her account of infant development, goes further, positing that an individual's habits of relating to others are fundamentally shaped by the experience of an even briefly disappointing object— namely the maternal breast, which intermittently fails to offer nourishment. Such early instances of nonfulfillment spur the infant to introject a version of its disappointing object within its internal object-world, instigating habits that never go away.[49]

For Klein, the introjected inner object at first appears alternately as all-providing (or "good") and all-denying (or "bad"). In rage against the "bad" breast, the infant imagines destroying it, or even destroying the mother. Since the infant could not survive if the mother were to be truly destroyed, though, this aggression quickly turns to "feelings of sorrow and concern for the loved objects, the fears of losing them and the longing to regain them," which in turn spur the infant to reconstitute the mother that it had previously fantasized about destroying. This sorrow and concern, the longing to regain the lost object, is what Klein calls "the 'pining' for the loved object."[50] Pining, in conjunction with a feeling of persecution by a "bad" object, constitutes the Kleinian depressive position that is, for her, the mark of healthy psychological development. It is introjection motivated by love rather than by aggression. And this combination of impulses—a wish to take an object into oneself, an impossibility of fully possessing it, an affect of love and care surrounding this incomplete operation—amounts to what we can recognize as a form of persistent desire conditioned by loss.

The Kleinian pattern of loss and reparation recurs later in life when irrevocable loss, such as the death of a loved person, comes to call. Successful mourning in such cases, Klein writes, requires the restoration of the lost object within one's inner object-world, a process she describes as a creative act: "The pining for the lost loved object also implies dependence on it," she writes in "Mourning and Its Relation to Manic-Depressive States," "but dependence of a kind which becomes an incentive to reparation and preservation of the object. It is creative because it is dominated by love."[51]

Utopian yearning would seem to close off the possibility of such productivity by defending the subject in advance against any admittance of loss. Political desire that allows itself to be disappointed, by contrast, lives on through transmutation, which I propose in this book we can understand as a sort of transcriptive practice. Intriguingly, Klein emphasizes the idea of mourning as productive, and not just internally:

> Thus while grief is experienced to the full and despair is at its height, the love for the object wells up and the mourner feels more strongly that life inside and outside will go on after all, and that the lost loved object can be preserved within. At this stage in mourning, suffering can become productive. We know that painful experiences of all kinds sometimes stimulate sublimations, or even bring out quite new gifts in some people, who may take to painting, writing or other productive activities under the stress of frustrations and hardships.... Such enrichment is in my view gained through processes similar to those steps in mourning which we have just investigated.[52]

The internally reparative work that can take place when loss is acknowledged but utter desolation is averted is not merely a metaphor for creative activity but actually fuels it.

The noted Kleinian Hanna Segal develops this line of thought, arguing that artists' aesthetic production is a direct outgrowth of the work of mourning.[53] Since what is created in the wake of such a loss is not the actual resurrection of the lost object but rather a stand-in for it, Segal specifically links the creation involved in mourning to the creation of symbols: "In this view symbol formation is the outcome of a loss, it is a creative act involving the pain and the whole work of mourning."[54]

This emphasis on symbolism anticipates the connection Nicholas Abraham and Marina Torok draw between introjection on the one hand and speech and metaphor on the other. For Abraham and Torok, speech arises directly from an experience of nonfulfillment. The infant, distraught to find its mouth not filled with its mother's breast, deals with this emptiness through "cries and sobs, delayed fullness, then as calling, ways of requesting presence, as language.... Finally, the early satisfactions of the mouth, as yet filled with the maternal object, are partially and gradually replaced by the novel satisfactions of a mouth now empty of that object but filled with words pertaining to the subject."[55] The first element I wish to underline here is Abraham and Torok's emphasis on the necessity of actually experiencing nonfulfillment as such: "The transition from a mouth filled with the breast to a mouth filled with words," they write, "occurs by virtue of the intervening experiences of the empty mouth."[56] Substitution does not entail a denial of nonfulfillment; indeed, it requires an experience of nonfulfillment in order for any productive transmuting to occur.

The second key element in Abraham and Torok's formulation is the role of others in making this substitution signify successfully, for filling the empty mouth with words effectively embeds the subject in a collective whose members are united by shared experience of nonfulfillment: "So the wants of the original oral vacancy are remedied by being turned into verbal relationships with the speaking community at large. Introjecting a desire, a pain, a situation means channeling them through language into a communion of empty mouths." Lest this be mistaken for mere correlation, Abraham and Torok almost immediately go further: "Since language acts and makes up for absence by representing, by *giving figurative shape* to presence, it can only be *comprehended* or *shared* in a 'community of empty mouths.'"[57] A shared experience of nonfulfillment is precisely what enables the ego's actions of substitution to acquire and convey meaning.

So, too, with political disappointment, wherein nonfulfillment acquires meaning through its being symbolized, shared, and transformed into other forms beyond those in which the desire for, and felt possibility of, a particular realignment had initially emerged. People need not be mourning precisely the same lost object as one another in order to be drawn—through symbols, substitution, and representation—into a "communion of empty mouths," a transformative collective held together by a shared experience of nonfulfillment.

Many scholars have found mourning, grief, and especially melancholia to be useful concepts in analyzing cultural responses to such disappointments, and I build on their work in this book.[58] Yet centering these as paradigmatic responses to political loss can risk sidelining key questions of flux and change. Mourning and melancholia are commonly understood as responses to a loss that is final, or that at best could be remedied only in an entirely other reality, whether that be an eschatological afterlife or its secular equivalent.[59] In cases of political loss, however, the finality of loss is itself a question, one that disappointment aims to address.

As all of this indicates, this book will discuss disappointment less as a single mood or clearly delineated affect than as a robust historical experience of persistent desire for an object that is less available than it previously had been, a generative experience that lends itself to transcription into different realms, forms, and practices. Political disappointment entails an understanding of loss and defeat as chronic, collective, historical problems and important drivers of cultural practice.

Disappointment in Politics

In one important sense, of course, all politics is marked by disappointment. In the process of organizing the living-together of beings with heterogeneous interests and desires, it is practically impossible to devise political structures that are not at any given moment failing to satisfy somebody, possibly everybody. When political scientists speak about disappointment, they're speaking about this: the inevitability of strategic compromises, ideological pendulum swings, broken campaign vows, vague slogans that permit multiple projected meanings, and so forth. Citizens who permit frustration with elected officials to threaten their faith in the political process, some scholars have argued, should cultivate a more realistic understanding of democratic systems, which might prevent this disappointment from ballooning into a permanent disaffection with politics as such.[60]

This book is not about that kind of disappointment, important though it is. Disappointment in representational politics occurs not periodically but perennially, and as long as this disappointment does not turn into disillusionment, there is always an outlet for it in the political realm. A desire to build a legislative majority for one's party can always be acted on politically—find a new candidate, strategize and regroup, start a lobbying firm—so although such a desire can also shape culture and aesthetics, it does so in tandem with concurrent political action.

With desires that depend for their possible fulfillment not on an orderly operation of a political system but on that system's transformation or supersession, though, disappointment is not perennial but erratic: actionability depends on temporary coalescences of conditions that often seem impossible to deliberately engineer, and these moments of actionability open and close over time. (One cannot join a march, for instance, if there is no mass movement for one's cause.) Certainly these desires, too, cannot but be disappointed in the quotidian sense, not just because all actually existing political arrangements entail trade-offs but because the realization of any ideal requires a demotion from that ideal. But different ideals fail differently, and to varying degrees. The disappointment that this book analyzes is the kind that arises in concert with transits in and out of the realm of politics, in and out of empirical conditions of possibility, in and out of there manifestly being something "political" to do.

This kind of disappointment warrants our attention because it does not counsel accommodation to existing structures or acceptance of their shortcomings. A potent critique is endemic to those disappointments that are so far-reaching that the frustrated desires cannot simply be plowed back into the present order. The more radical disappointments we'll be concerned with here are less constrained than their electoral counterparts by the conditions that produced their foreclosure.

Chapter Overview

When conditions do not support acting on a desire through "political" action, cultural practices such as literature and sound become particularly important as means of processing changed conditions and ensuring that desires for a profoundly altered collective reality find forms of survival.[61] These practices, and the forms they engender, produce durable records of untimely feelings, of affective experiences that might otherwise dissipate without a trace.

Piecing together transcriptive practices and traces of disappointment into a clarifying story about the twentieth century, the five chapters in this book proceed chronologically from the failure of Reconstruction through the AIDS crisis. In each chapter, a particular historical aftermath—a moment in the wake of potential transformation—comes into focus as a location of conceptual and aesthetic innovation. Chapter 1 deliberately grounds the entire project in African American disappointment, taking the failure to remake America as a multiracial democracy post–Civil War as the defining disappointment of the twentieth century, one whose ramifications persist to the present day. This chapter tells the story of how African American thinkers confronted Reconstruction's aftermath and proposed new theories of time, history, and progress to make sense of the dramatic regressions during what historian Rayford Logan terms the nadir of American race relations. In the work of W. E. B. Du Bois, Charles W. Chesnutt, and Fisk Jubilee Singers founding member Ella Sheppard, transcriptive practices mediating between sound and writing emerge as key means of staging conflictual ideas about historical change.

Further developing the possibilities and limitations of transcription, Chapter 2 of *Political Disappointment* tunes in to paramusical soundings—audible signals people create that travel alongside music—as a related practice of disappointment. This chapter looks to the 1930s to show how the trope of labored breath in Lead Belly's performances of worksongs, and representations of sound in Tillie Olsen's short-story collection *Tell Me a Riddle,* transcribe otherwise inexpressible desires for multiracial solidarity and immanent revolution amid Popular Front–era transformations of the American Left.

Chapter 3 turns to the soundscapes of 1960s activism as records of the disappointment that followed the passage of civil rights legislation. Here I focus on the 1966 March Against Fear, a march co-led by Martin Luther King Jr. and Stokely Carmichael, during which civil rights demonstrators outshouted each other with contesting chants and cast their disagreement over tactics as an argument about songs. Sound acted as both battleground and barometer throughout the monthlong March Against Fear, demonstrating the political uses of cacophony and quiet, not just as performative registers of refusal and resistance to transcription but also as collective aesthetic practices enabling people to engage in shared action amid disagreement.

In Chapter 4, I expand the book's acoustic archive to include not just material sounds and their transcriptions but also ideas about sound and voice, zeroing in on the figure of feminist voice in the late 1970s and early 1980s to clarify the role of disappointment in shaping feminist literature, theory, and practice. This chapter discusses performances, essays, and poetry by Pat Parker, Audre Lorde, and Adrienne Rich, in addition to feminist theory about sexuality and race by writers including Lorde and Hortense Spillers, to tell the story of a sea change in feminist thought—from the defining figure of "voice" in the early 1970s to a new focus, by the early 1980s, on vision and visibility. Here I explain how feminist thinkers theorized voicing and seeing as practices of disappointment in the face of backlash's reactive temporality. In particular, Parker's and Lorde's poetry surfaces a repeated practice of juxtaposing images of historical traumas with present-day concerns. I discuss this practice as a deliberate matter of seeing historically that the poets undertake in tandem with contemporaneous critical discussions about gender and visuality, and I show how such seeing then enables a more sonically and sensorially attuned approach to the question of voice.

This newly multisensory understanding of voice is further developed in Chapter 5, the book's final chapter, about art and sound produced during the AIDS crisis of the 1980s and 1990s. Here I think with Bernice Johnson Reagon's writing and music to discern listening, especially coalitional listening, as a practice of disappointment that forges bonds exceeding the boundaries of individual life-spans. Coalitional listening entails generosity, care, distanced intimacy, and attentive presence in the face of difference, even the seeming difference between living and dead; it is a practice capable not just of tuning in to voices generated within preexisting identities but of building new collectivities as well. I highlight such listening as it is enacted in the films and writing of Marlon Riggs and in David Wojnarowicz's visual art and audio diaries, where the artists variously listen to, imagine themselves being heard by, and engage in active listening on behalf of those who have gone before and those who have yet to come. The intimacies and care forged through such listening are not always comforting, but they are frequently transformative.

Political disappointment returns again and again throughout the twentieth century, marked by recurrent rhythms: Black thinkers in the 1960s are in direct conversation with the nadir-era writing of Chesnutt and Du Bois; feminist writers in the 1980s understand their moment as a repetition of post-Communist failure equally haunted by midcentury racial terror. Yet this history can be hard to see at a glance. When I started working on this project, Barack Obama's first presidential term was just ending. I completed the book's chapters during Donald Trump's catastrophic presidency; and as I wrote this introduction, Joe Biden had just taken office, spurring both relief and proleptic disappointment. Throughout the intervening years, with all their changing conditions, whenever I told people that I was writing about political disappointment, they always had the same response: "Oh, that's so timely!" People seem to think that our current moment—whenever that might be—is the most disappointed moment ever. But reading for disappointment in art, literature, sound, and the transcriptive practices where these overlap encourages us to take a longer view of things, helping us understand disappointment not merely as a reaction to failure but as a form of survival. By doing so, we can better understand the practices that help us live and persist through our own disappointed times.

CHAPTER 1

FAILURES OF THE RECONSTRUCTION

History and Disappointment

The story of the twentieth century in America is a story of disappointment, and the failure of Reconstruction is its first chapter. The Civil War had seemed to offer the possibility of remaking the United States as a multiracial democracy; during Reconstruction, those who longed for freedom sensed an opening, a partial advance that could be leveraged into more lasting developments.[1] Even whites recognized the redemptive potential in this moment, the possibility that, as W. E. B. Du Bois wrote in *Black Reconstruction in America*, "at last there could really be a free commonwealth of freemen."[2] But then Reconstruction ended, and the prospect of Black freedom, the possibility of American democracy, and the very notion of historical progress—the idea that the world would change for the better, if not evenly and steadily then at least reliably, as it moved forward in time—were all cast into serious doubt.

Du Bois attended college in the 1880s and 1890s, as the post-Reconstruction reversals were occurring. But those reversals were at odds with the prevailing ideology of the era, which he would later describe as "a day of Progress with a capital P." Looking back on the period, he wrote that as he embarked on his college education, "so far as I conceived, the foundations of present culture were laid, the way was charted, the progress toward certain great goals was undoubted and inevitable. There was room for argument concerning details and methods and possible detours in the onsweep of civilization; but the fundamental facts were clear, unquestioned and unquestionable."[3]

Indeed, most American intellectuals at the turn of the twentieth century believed humanity was on an inexorable upward trajectory.[4] The recently discovered laws of evolution, the rapid development of technology, the swift expansion in America's wealth and power: all seemed to promise unfailing ascent toward a better life. In Du Bois's retrospective account of the gospel of progress, he goes on to note the clear exception posed by the postbellum circumstances of Black life, an exception that left him well situated to ask questions about progress that most of his white contemporaries declined to consider. "Had it not been for the race problem early thrust upon me and enveloping me," he writes, "I should have probably been an unquestioning worshiper at the shrine of social order and economic development into which I was born."[5] White supremacy was resurgent in the wake of the Civil War, and multiracial democracy in America seemed ever more remote. In light of this, the question of whether history was really set on an ascending course spurred Black thinkers and their allies at the turn of the twentieth century to develop new theories of history, progress, and disappointment capable of making sense of their regressive times.

This chapter will trace engagements with questions of history and progress in the work of three African American writers around the turn of the twentieth century—Du Bois, Ella Sheppard, and Charles W. Chesnutt—each of whom worked at the intersection of writing and music to theorize history and Black disappointment in the aftermath of Reconstruction. In their work, zones of overlap between writing and music prove to be key locations for processing conflicts between ideas of progress and experiences of nonprogress. In different but related ways across Du Bois's nonfiction, Sheppard's musical arrangements, and Chesnutt's fiction, transcriptive practices register conflicting desires, temporalities, and theories of history, and they help people navigate a time of acute disappointment.

Belief in the inevitability of historical progress was widespread in the late nineteenth century, but over the twentieth century people have found such a belief increasingly difficult to sustain. In the most common accounts of this decline, the First World War appears as the defining moment when presumptions of progress began to run aground, but the trouble with progress, and its status as an object of profound and ongoing disappointment, constituted topics of discussion for African Americans long before the problems with progress were acknowledged more widely.[6]

During what historian Rayford Logan dubbed the nadir of American race relations—the period in US history running from the late 1870s through the early twentieth century, which saw the consolidation of Jim Crow, an epidemic of lynchings, and the undoing of Reconstruction-era reforms—African American writers explicitly addressed questions of temporality, working to understand, among other things, how to think about historical progress when conditions were reverting to a previous state, rather than advancing.[7] The novelist, musician, and magazine editor Pauline Hopkins discussed the matter as one of historical regression when she wrote in 1900, "Let us compare the happenings of one hundred—two hundred years ago, with those of today. The difference between then and now, if any there be, is so slight as to be scarcely worth mentioning. The atrocity of the acts committed one hundred years ago are duplicated today, when slavery is supposed no longer to exist."[8] Hopkins's critique repeatedly emphasizes time, the unstable quantity of years ("one hundred—two hundred") that have passed "between then and now," in order to decry the untoward "duplicat[ion]" of the past in the present. Her statement implicitly contrasts post-Reconstruction regression with the idea that motion through history might be expected to bring improvement, that the present is not supposed to be a copy of the past. Similarly, the editor Francis J. Garrison (son of abolitionist William Lloyd Garrison), after reading Chesnutt's 1901 novel *The Marrow of Tradition*, wrote in a letter to Chesnutt that current conditions for African Americans resembled not even those of one or two centuries ago, as Hopkins had suggested, but something much older: "The frequent burnings at the stake, which were scarcely known in slavery days, indicate still more how little we have advanced from the dark middle ages."[9] These complaints register a disappointment in the failure of juridical emancipation to secure real freedom, but their language also reveals them to be at heart expressions of disappointment in historical progress.

Some of the most far-reaching articulations of this disappointment took place through transcriptive practices at the intersection of sound and writing. In *The Souls of Black Folk,* where Du Bois takes a sustained look at history and disappointment, his discussion begins with, ends with, and draws its overall structure from instances of writing sound and writing about sound, and he participates in a longer history—which I'll briefly reconstruct in these pages—of published transcriptions of African American song, and of the accompanying texts that seek to frame and contextualize those transcriptions. Sheppard, a founding member of the Fisk Jubilee Singers, was also one of that chorus's first transcribers; her transcriptions of spirituals were published in one of the books from which Du Bois drew the musical epigraphs for *Souls.* In Sheppard's choral arrangements, she highlighted the impossibility of making a transcription that accords precisely with performance practice, embedding incommensurable elements in her written music. And the fiction writer Chesnutt—whose early success as a writer of dialect stories, alongside his day job as a sonically attuned legal stenographer (he was a devoted proponent of a stenographic system known as phonography, in which stenographic symbols correspond to spoken sounds rather than written letters), attests to the central importance in his career of transcriptive practices—instituted a temporal irregularity at the heart of his novel *The Marrow of Tradition* that I'll argue is best understood as a transcription of a musical figure.[10]

In different ways and across different forms of writing, the three main figures of this chapter suggest that to navigate a time rife with violence, injustice, and disappointments of history and progress, it's important to understand what it means to live amid a discordant mix of temporalities. Further, their work offers clear indications that transcriptive practices, which convene unsettled encounters between writing and sound, provide especially useful means of thinking through the disappointments of history and progress at the turn of the twentieth century. Through a range of transcriptive practices, people negotiated conflicts over which political desires to record and preserve, and how best to do so, when the irregular and nonprogressive movements of history rendered those desires untimely.[11]

Singing True: Du Bois, Sorrow Songs, and the Sound of Thwarted Progress

In *The Souls of Black Folk*, Du Bois pursues an explicitly dialectical inquiry into the problems of history in the post-Reconstruction era, arguing that setbacks and progress, past and future, are related to each other in intricate and interdependent ways. This theme runs throughout *Souls*, arguably his most disappointed book, which he late in his career described as "a cry at midnight thick within the veil, when none rightly knew the coming day."[12] His exploration of history and disappointment reaches its fullest expression in his treatment of the Sorrow Songs, which he calls "the music of an unhappy people, of the children of disappointment," while also identifying them as the key to historical motion.[13] His reflections on progress and on these songs—especially when considered alongside other treatments of African American song from around the same time, as I will do in this section—set out a philosophy of time and history in which old cultural forms can point toward the future more effectively than can new constructions, and in which transcriptive practices, by staging and mapping encounters between sound and writing, are especially able to register the clashes, resonances, and amplifications that come into play in the unruly overlap of multiple temporalities.

Among the prose pieces that are collected in *The Souls of Black Folk*, Du Bois addresses the question of progress most explicitly in the essay "Of the Meaning of Progress." Here he tells of his two summers spent teaching rural Black youths in Tennessee, and he narrates his return to the town years later to see how the community has fared.[14] He taught there as a hopeful undergrad, a faithful missionary of uplift and a scholar in search of transformative knowledge, but his faith in such optimistic endeavors has since been shaken, and the essay portrays its narrator struggling to access some grounds for hope amid changes that make straightforward faith in progress difficult.[15] The windowless, doorless hut where Du Bois once led his charges in spelling and songs has been dismantled, he finds, and replaced by "a jaunty board house . . . with three windows and a door that locked." The old uncomfortable, backless benches have been transposed to the new habitat unchanged, but "the blackboard had grown by about two feet." Faced with such quantifiable expansion—three windows, two added feet—Du Bois feels conflicted. Where his old schoolhouse once was, he writes, "stood Progress; and Progress, I understand, is necessarily ugly." As he sits nearby and looks "on the Old and the New I felt glad, very glad, and yet—"[16] The paragraph cuts off here, midsentence; the next begins, "After two long drinks I started on." In each instance of doubling here ("Progress; and Progress"; "glad, very glad"; "two long drinks"), the repetition undermines the original, suggesting that Du Bois has to try too hard to arrive at an optimistic analysis of what he sees. These excessive augmentations betray a reality that resists attempts at rational measurement.

Some of Du Bois's former pupils have found success as farmers, while others have been far less fortunate, and Josie, once an eager learner who "had about her a certain fineness, the shadow of an unconscious moral heroism," died young, apparently of overwork and a broken heart. To calculate from these several lives some overall gauge of the trajectory of a town, a race, or an educational project is no easy task. "How shall man measure Progress there where the dark-faced Josie lies? How many heartfuls of sorrow shall balance a bushel of wheat?"[17] Notwithstanding the clear impossibility of weighing mournful hearts, these are live questions for Du Bois, who was one of the first American sociologists to receive a thorough training in statistics and quantitative analysis, and who had just concluded work on *The Philadelphia Negro* when he wrote this essay on measuring progress.[18]

Throughout *Souls*, Du Bois calls for precise inquiry into the problem of the color line. But his "Progress" essay shows his faith in empirical study to be far from absolute. Du Bois has committed himself to the project of discerning meaning in people's lives through measurement and study. Yet interpreting sociological data is no simple task, as the essay's conclusion emphasizes: "And all this life and love and strife and failure,—is it the twilight of nightfall or the flush of some faint-dawning day?" He mulls over this question "sadly," abandoning the effort it had taken to profess gladness, as he returns to Nashville "in the Jim Crow car"—his own experience functioning as both data point and interpretive frame.[19]

This question about hope and progress returns at the end of Du Bois's book, when he focuses on the Sorrow Songs that have been resounding all along in the hybrid poetic-musical epigraphs to each chapter. In deciding to assign a paramount role in *Souls* to these songs, Du Bois was offering his own addition to what was by the turn of the twentieth century an established genre of publications about Black music: books that combined transcriptions of African American songs with written reflections on them by their collectors, conductors, and critics. In Du Bois's papers, a "Bibliography of the Negro Folk Song in America," dated ca. 1903, lists nineteen song collections published between 1855 and 1902, along with some dozen periodical articles.[20] Where these other books tend to issue their reflections in prefaces by white musical directors and ministers that precede and set the stage for the transcriptions, thus framing and selling them in advance—an updated, intermedial variation on the prefatory attestations of authenticity offered by white guarantors in advance of slave narratives—Du Bois not only reverses this order but does so repeatedly, emphatically, and on multiple levels, using transcriptions as prefaces to each of his essays and placing his reflection on the songs at the end rather than the beginning of his book.

In doing so, Du Bois is also joining a long-running series of contestations about transcribing African American song. The many nineteenth-century transcription collections set forth markedly conflicting ideas about the status of music sung by African Americans. In particular, these books' prefaces and interpretive essays frequently take up the question of how the transcriptions relate to the songs themselves. Where can the songs' true versions be said to exist? Are transcriptions capable of rendering these songs accurately, or are distortions and losses inevitable? Where loss does occur, what precisely is lost and how does it fall out? Some accounts say the songs are impossible to transcribe, while others describe them as being fully encapsulated in the transcriptions. In Chapter 2, I'll discuss in greater depth how this very disagreement makes transcription a particularly useful tool for thinking about disappointment, which itself entails instances of a political impulse traveling between forms and practices, with inevitable transformations or losses. For now, it is enough to let these texts prepare us to appreciate the way Du Bois's intervention interrupts and transcends two opposing discourses: one about Black songs as being marked by an irreducible difference from Western art music, and one about the songs as fungible commodities to be bought, sold, learned, and freely reperformed. On Du Bois's account, the Sorrow Songs expand the canon of Western culture to make space for themselves, while their commercial deployment obscures their true worth as meaningful human expression rooted in an experience of disappointment.

In *Slave Songs of the United States,* the 1867 volume that was among the first book-length collections of African American song transcriptions (and is the first listed item on Du Bois's bibliography), the editors write of a mismatch between Black voices and such instruments of cultural legibility as paper, movable type, white voices, and musical scales. "The best that we can do, however, with paper and types, or even with voices, will convey but a faint shadow of the original," the editors write. "The voices of the colored people have a peculiar quality that nothing can imitate; and the intonations and delicate variations of even one singer cannot be reproduced on paper."[21] In their resistance to being transcribed, the singers of these songs strike the editors as being other than human: "And what makes it all the harder to unravel a thread of melody out of this strange network is that, like birds, they seem not infrequently to strike sounds that cannot be precisely represented by the gamut."[22] Creating sounds that take the shape of a "strange network" rather than a linear scale, or gamut, the singers defy adequate encapsulation in writing, allowing only "a faint shadow" to be reproduced.

The editors' use of the word *gamut* builds a "strange network" of its own, connecting the transcriptive practices of *Slave Songs of the United States* with a literally foundational transcriptive practice: the invention of modern staff notation by the medieval monk Guido of Arezzo. Combining a Greek letter with a syllable from a Latin hymn, Guido named a low G written on the first line of a staff "gamma ut," nomenclature that was eventually shortened to "gamut." His notational system was built on a six-note hexachord system, though, rather than the contemporary octave scale; even the seemingly fixed system of notes to which the nineteenth-century editors of *Slave Songs* were accustomed, and to which they contrasted the purportedly unusual singing of formerly enslaved people, was itself a historically contingent creation.[23]

Despite the difficulties of transcribing strange networks of sounds from creaturely singers, the editors add, they have transcribed the songs the best they could manage, with the aim of addressing an extinction crisis: "These relics of a state of society which has passed away should be preserved while it is still possible," they write, since as live practices, the editors believe, the songs will disappear as the people who lived under slavery die out.[24] Yet even the transcriptions will not adequately preserve the songs, the editors lament. The songs are already escaping, even in the process of their being written down.

In the 1874 book *Hampton and Its Students*—which includes a collection of fifty transcriptions, many of which Du Bois drew on for the epigraphs in *Souls*—the question of faithfulness shifts in emphasis. Not concerned primarily with the question of whether the songs can be accurately preserved on paper, this book of transcriptions now occupies itself with whether the practices can be transplanted, in performance, from plantation to concert hall without changing them irreparably. In other words, could staged performances of these songs, such as those offered by the chorus of Hampton students, claim to offer a faithful facsimile of the experience of hearing enslaved people sing—which is apparently what listeners are hoping to find? Helen W. Ludlow, a teacher at the Hampton Institute, answers in the affirmative: "The peculiar strength of the Hampton Chorus is the faithful rendering of the original slave songs, and Mr. Fenner has been remarkably fortunate, while cultivating their voices to a degree capable of executing difficult German songs with a precision of harmony and expression that is delicious, in that he has succeeded in preserving to them in these old-time melodies that pathos and *wail* which those who have listened to the singing on the old plantations recognize as the 'real thing.'"[25] The Hampton Institute depended materially on income from performances of these songs by its students, so it is unsurprising that the songbook would endorse the concerts' authenticity as Ludlow does here. Yet the ensemble's musical director, Thomas Fenner, undermines this endorsement in the "Preface to Music" that he contributes to the volume. He writes of a contrast between the songs' natural habitat of group worship and the songs as performed on stage: "Half [the music's] effectiveness, in its home, depends upon accompaniments which can be carried away only in memory. The inspiration of numbers; the overpowering chorus, covering defects; the swaying of the body; the rhythmical stamping of the feet; and all the wild enthusiasm of the negro camp-meeting—these evidently can not be transported to the boards of a public performance."[26] Fenner here argues that the songs suffer from a diminution when removed from their original context. In his emphasis on physical presence and rhythmic physical movements, he bears out Brent Hayes Edwards's assertion that when direct transcription of socially situated Black sound presents difficulties, "vernacular musical form is transcribed through a figure of the black body."[27]

In the case of the spirituals, though, the exchange value of these songs was also beginning to rely on the notion of their being transcribable through, or at least for, white bodies as well. The attempt to render the songs salable commodities, exchangeable for money in the burgeoning sheet-music market, required the idea that Black bodies and voices in performance on a stage could be easily exchanged with white bodies and voices in a parlor. In 1872, Theodore F. Seward, introducing the first edition of the collection *Jubilee Songs: As Sung by the Jubilee Singers,* a book of songs performed by Fisk University's pioneering ensemble, chose not to sell readers on the singular plantation authenticity of a concert experience or camp meeting. He instead advertised the songs' suitability for being sung by anybody: "It is believed that the selection of melodies here presented will not only prove interesting as a study, but that they will, by their quaint forms, their inherent beauty, and their genuine pathos, bring a new element of pleasure into any social circle into which they may be introduced."[28] In publishing and selling these songbooks, the Fisk group was banking on the desires of audiences—particularly white audiences, who would less likely be familiar with the repertoire already—to sing these songs themselves, and Seward replaced the songs' previously lauded quality of archaic mournfulness with a new set of selling points: novelty, beauty, and pleasure.

Just as strikingly, Seward's preface takes extra care to disavow any inadequacy on the part of the transcriptions, and to promise singers that the transcriptions contained in the book—many of which he himself had written—will permit them to sing the songs to perfection:

> The public may feel assured that the music herein given is entirely correct. It was taken down from the singing of the band, during repeated interviews held for the purpose, and no line or phrase was introduced that did not receive full indorsement from the singers. Some of the phrases and turns in the melodies are so peculiar that the listener might not unreasonably suppose them to be incapable of exact representation by ordinary musical characters. It is found, however, that they all submit to the laws of musical language, and if they are sung or played exactly as written, all the characteristic effects will be reproduced.[29]

These songs, then, are not only beautiful, not only singable, but submissive and law-abiding as well, as formerly enslaved persons and their descendants were being urged at this time to be.[30] And an equally submissive, law-abiding readership, obediently performing the songs "exactly as written," are promised the reward of reproducing the "characteristic effects" that until recently had been regarded as inextricable from the Black people who originated them.

This approach was commercially effective: H. L. Mencken reported that by 1893, the Jubilee book's various editions had already sold 180,000 copies.[31] When the collection's second edition was published in 1884, it included Seward's original note, while adding a short second preface that doubled down on the suitability of the songs for social singing, and on their unsurpassed *value:* "The interest felt in the 'Jubilee Songs' has proved to be much more than a mere temporary curiosity. They afford such a novelty and variety in the singing of social circles and home entertainments, that the demand for them continues unabated from year to year. To meet the wants of the public for a more complete collection of these remarkable songs, 16 pages of choice melodies have been added to the original book, making 80 pages in all without increasing the price."[32]

In the decades following Emancipation, then, collections of songs sung by African Americans variously depict the songs as being practically untranscribable or yielding easily to notation; as being a historically grounded social practice, "relics of a state of society which has passed away," or being an evergreen commodity that can be bound and sold in books; as being ineffable, context-specific performances poignantly reminiscent of slavery's degradations, or being eligible for pleasing reproduction by anyone.

By 1903, when Du Bois set out to write about the Sorrow Songs, educated African Americans were by many accounts less than enthusiastic about this music of slavery. Despite the material gains the songs had enabled—such as Jubilee Hall, the staid redbrick edifice at Fisk constructed with $20,000 of the profits from the Jubilee Singers' world tour—many African Americans considered the songs an unseemly practice, a leftover from slavery best ignored. In his essay in the 1874 Hampton volume, Fenner wrote that "the freedmen have an unfortunate inclination to despise [this music], as a vestige of slavery."[33] John W. Work II, a graduate of Fisk who returned to work at the school in 1897, noticed a similar tendency. He wrote retrospectively in 1915 that "for many years it was impossible to induce the students of Fisk to sing these songs, even after that famous first company had sung this institution into new life. For years one would be as likely to hear Negro Folk Songs in St. Peter's at Rome as in

Fisk University." He then related a scene of conflict and refusal that likely dates from the early 1870s: Professor Adam K. Spence, Fisk's second principal, used to "rise in chapel service and attempt to 'start' one of these songs, requesting the students to 'join in,'" upon which the students "would 'join in' with a chorus of cold silence. They knew enough to comprehend slavery dialect and bad grammar, and they would have none of either."[34] As Work acknowledges, the students' refusal of the songs was itself an active musical undertaking, not a mere absence of song but a chilly performed silence.

The reluctance was not limited to Fisk. In 1882, the Hampton Folk-Lore Society's Alice Mabel Bacon remarked, "Any one who has had much to do with the educated negroes of the present day knows that by them the old stories and superstitions and customs of their own race are only too apt to be looked down upon as all bad, and to be forgotten as quickly as possible."[35] The same year, in an *Atlantic Monthly* article, Jonathan Baxter Harrison warned that "the old negro music will soon disappear. All the educated negro ministers discourage or forbid the use of it among their people, and the strange, wild songs, whether religious or not, are coming to be regarded as relics and badges of the old condition of slavery and heathenism, and the young men and women are ashamed to sing them."[36] White transcribers' work to preserve "the old negro music," then, was undertaken in light of a perceived danger that Black people might not do enough to steward their own heritage.

Yet Black communities and institutions were undertaking just such stewardship. The Jubilee Singers' career in the 1870s and 1880s represents one prominent effort. A few years later, when Work took up his post at Fisk, the songs' reputation on campus had been diminished, a situation he set about trying to change. He wrote an article in the *Fisk Herald* lamenting "the almost avowed contempt which even the intelligent among us have for these melodies." Work went on to analyze this persistent contempt at length:

> It may seem at first thought that the reason for this is, that the rising generations want to get away from every vestige of slavery; because most of our evils are due to our previous condition. They imagine no doubt, that such songs are below us, and it is pure condescension and a compromise of dignity to let the world know that we appreciate them. But, what the best critics have pronounced "excellent," and the world has approved and wept over, let *us* not despise.

> It is neither condescension nor a compromise of dignity to love such songs, which have done more to place us favorably before the world than all else we ever had. . . .
>
> There is, no doubt, in this music some power that appeals to the very souls of men. Some may be pleased to advance the argument that people enjoy these songs because they are minstrel-like. We *must* admit that this music is rough and unpolished, but its theme is most sublime, in this respect, even rivaling "The Messiah."[37]

The commercial success of the songs, it seems, cut both ways. On the one hand, it enabled schools serving Black students to raise money, build buildings, and gain critical acclaim. On the other hand, it made the songs suspect, aligning them with minstrelsy instead of the sacred.[38] Work argued that the songs should instead be valued on purely aesthetic grounds: their "sublim[ity]," their homology with Handel's polished choruses, and the judgment of "the best critics."

In the years leading up to Du Bois's momentous 1903 study of the Sorrow Songs in *The Souls of Black Folk,* then, we can discern two primary attitudes toward slavery-era songs espoused by African Americans around the end of Reconstruction: first, a disdain for the songs, an aversion to these remnants and reminders of an older condition that was continually reasserting itself in social and political relations; second, an affirmation of the songs' value *despite* this revenant quality, based on the enthusiasm with which "the world" (that is, white listeners in Europe and the northern United States) greeted them, and a plainly articulated determination to cultivate feelings and aesthetic judgments in harmony with existing arbiters of high culture.

For Du Bois, however, the songs' link to the past and to old bad feelings is an integral element in their importance to African Americans' present and future contributions to American culture and consequently to world history. He calls them not "Jubilee Songs," the then-common designation that emphasizes freedom and joy, but "Sorrow Songs," and he begins his chapter on the topic by describing them as rooted in the past, in lowered affect, in oddness and ghostliness: "They that walked in darkness sang songs in the olden days— Sorrow Songs—for they were weary at heart. And so before each thought that I have written in this book I have set a phrase, a haunting echo of these weird old songs in which the soul of the black slave spoke to men." Du Bois calls the songs "the music of an unhappy people, of the children of disappointment."

And unlike Work, who asks people to disregard the songs' link to the old days and to focus instead on their aesthetic excellence, Du Bois celebrates the songs for both qualities in the same breath: "bursts of wonderful melody . . . full of the voices of the past."[39]

At the end of the Sorrow Songs chapter, the most Hegelian moment of *Souls* arrives, where Du Bois argues that African Americans—the third-person singular "Negro" of early essays here transformed into a collective "we"—have brought to the shores of the New World "a gift of the Spirit" that has not "been merely passive. Actively we have woven ourselves with the very warp and woof of this nation."[40] G. W. F. Hegel famously held that Africa had played no active role in world history. Du Bois, who had studied Hegel in Germany, argues against this notion at several points in *Souls;* when he chose to describe African Americans' contribution to America as "a gift of the Spirit," he likely had Hegel on his mind.[41]

The Sorrow Songs chapter is also where Du Bois attempts, for one last time in this volume, to resolve the question about history and progress he had allowed to dangle unanswered in "Of the Meaning of Progress": Are things getting better? How might we judge? "Through all the sorrow of the Sorrow Songs," he writes, "there breathes a hope—a faith in the ultimate justice of things. The minor cadences of despair change often to triumph and calm confidence. Sometimes it is faith in life, sometimes a faith in death, sometimes assurance of boundless justice in some fair world beyond. But whichever it is, the meaning is always clear: that sometime, somewhere, men will judge men by their souls and not by their skins." This hope is still pitched, like the progress of the earlier essay, first as an interpretive frame—he is discussing a hope he hears the songs manifesting—and then, immediately after, as questions: "Is such a hope justified? Do the Sorrow Songs sing true?"[42]

The songs' mere survival does not automatically imply their message's ongoing validity. That must be evaluated through study and reflection, and Du Bois accordingly proceeds to discuss the long arc of global human history and the three great gifts—song, story, and Spirit—that he argues Africans brought to the New World.

> Actively we have woven ourselves with the very warp and woof of this nation,—we fought their battles, shared their sorrow, mingled our blood with theirs, and generation after generation have pleaded with a headstrong, careless people to despise not Justice, Mercy, and

Truth, lest the nation be smitten with a curse. Our song, our toil, our cheer, and warning have been given to this nation in blood-brotherhood. Are not these gifts worth the giving? Is not this work and striving? Would America have been America without her Negro people?

Even so is the hope that sang in the songs of my fathers well sung.[43]

The fact of active cultural work makes a song of hope "well sung": that is, the effort itself has value. But Du Bois's initial question—"Is such a hope justified?"—has not yet been answered.

He concludes, "If somewhere in this whirl and chaos of things there dwells Eternal Good, pitiful yet masterful, then anon in His good time America shall rend the Veil and the prisoned shall go free."[44] That is, of course, a sizable *if*, especially for the hardly devout Du Bois. And "anon in His good time" sounds uncomfortably like the permanently extendable "all deliberate speed" that would be employed in *Brown v. Board of Education* to defer justice indefinitely in the middle of the color line's century.

Thus, amid the rhetorical questions that close the essay and the book, the question of hope's truth or justification remains open. Yet the essay ends not with that conspicuously uncomforting deferral; it ends, instead, with a song. Slipping into a lyrical riff on the word *free,* Du Bois writes of a chorus he hears singing: "free as yonder fresh young voices welling up to me from the caverns of brick and mortar below—swelling with song, instinct with life, tremulous treble and darkening bass." His writing is practically music here, words rounding into the rhythm and cadence of song. What he cannot bring himself to fully hazard through rational thought, he leaves to music to invoke, first approximating it in text and finally ceding space to it entirely. After all of the wordless musical transcriptions that have punctuated this book, he inserts one final song, this one with lyrics. "My children, my little children, are singing to the sunshine," Du Bois writes, "and thus they sing:" At this point in his text, he reproduces a transcription that unites words and music (Figure 1.1), marking a change from the abstracted, formalized musical staves that introduced each chapter. In "Of the Sorrow Songs" as nowhere else in *Souls,* he offers a full song as lyrical content combined with harmonic form, providing a score that his readers, at least those familiar with Western musical notation, might be able to sing for themselves without referencing any other resource. (Elsewhere in the chapter he also transcribes words and music to a tune his grandfather's grandmother

1.1 "Let Us Cheer the Weary Traveller," in W. E. B. Du Bois, *The Souls of Black Folk: Essays and Sketches* (1903; Amherst: University of Massachusetts Press, 2018).

had sung, but this song, "Do bana coba," is written for only one voice, and as Cheryl Wall points out, the African lyrics, which scholars have been unable to translate, "cannot signify."[45]) "Let Us Cheer the Weary Traveller" is more complete than *Souls'* other transcriptions in several additional ways: it renders a full stanza, rather than a phrase or fragment of a phrase as the epigraphs do; it occupies two staves bracketed together, rather than a single treble staff; and it features four vocal parts (soprano, alto, tenor, and bass) instead of just one or two. Du Bois's argument from "Of Our Spiritual Strivings" that historical advance requires a multitude of ideals "not singly but together, not successively but together, each growing and aiding each," is embodied in this harmonically multivoiced transcription.[46]

The transcription echoes Du Bois's discussion of African American history in other ways as well. As I discussed in the introduction, his account of the years leading up to and following the Civil War highlights the transition from a singular desire for freedom ("In song and exhortation swelled one refrain—Liberty") to a splintering of that object, post-Emancipation, into multiple partial ideals whose historical variability calls the truth of the entire endeavor into question: "Physical freedom, political power, the training of brains and the training of hands,—all these in turn have waxed and waned, until even the last grows dim and overcast. Are they all wrong,—all false?"[47] Similarly, in the transcription of "Let Us Cheer the Weary Traveller," unanimity prevails through the first three phrases: the two treble and two bass voices are all singing the same melody one octave apart, with the double-stemmed notes emphasizing still further the condition of many voices singing in functional unison. This monophony gives way in the final phrase, though, to stately four-part harmony.

The four-part arrangement rests, until the final chord, on a steady G in the two lower voices that offers a lower-frequency persistence running beneath the changing higher voices: the G, which is a shared note between the C major chord of "-long the" and the G7 chord of "heavenly," provides audible stability as the alto and soprano move in harmonious parallel sixths. The addition of the lower voices in "Let Us Cheer" produces a rich, full harmony that has no equivalent among the other transcriptions in *Souls*. It evokes a choral profusion, the post-unison harmony of "not singly but together" that Du Bois called for in his opening essay.

One brief line of text follows this transcription—"And the traveller girds himself, and sets his face toward the Morning, and goes his way"—and the essay is complete.[48] Du Bois himself is the weary traveler here, and he hears choral song as uniquely capable of cheering him when history and criticism and sociology come up short. But even then, he does not go "along the heavenly way" as the song invites; he goes, instead, "*his* way," toward not heaven but the circadian renewal of life on earth.

As discussed earlier, while the hope of the Sorrow Songs, the faith in the ultimate justice of things, may or may not be empirically true, Du Bois states unequivocally that the fact of African Americans' active contributions to the formation of America makes the hope "well sung." The outcome is not assured, but the active endeavoring, the "work and striving" that is audible in Black music as well as elsewhere, constitutes for Du Bois sufficient justification for having hope. And although that hope may remain suspended or disappointed, by finding form in song it is able to be a productive force in the world.

In Du Bois's list of the forms this productivity takes—"our song, our toil, our cheer, and warning"—music, work, and hope are all proprietary, culturally specific emanations from a particular people and provenance. But the *warning* defies ownership. It alone is so broadly applicable that Du Bois departs from his anaphoric repetitions of *our* to emphasize this. His language, too, echoes Old Testament cadences so overtly—"generation after generation have pleaded with a headstrong, careless people to despise not Justice, Mercy, and Truth, lest the nation be smitten with a curse"—as to unmistakably cast African Americans in a prophetic role vis-à-vis America as a whole. The trouble with historical progress had presented itself to the Black world before the white. But the curse of failing to achieve justice, Du Bois warns, will fall on the entire nation. For the time being, though, it stood as the particular responsibility of those who had already been disappointed by history to find ways of understanding and communicating that disappointment. Transcriptive practices, as Du Bois understood, offered a powerful means of doing so. And Ella Sheppard put those practices to good use in her work with the Fisk Jubilee Singers.

Writing All the Time: Ella Sheppard's Transcriptions

Sheppard was among the Fisk Jubilee Singers' first transcribers, a central figure in the group's historic project of transforming a primarily oral and ecclesiastical musical tradition into a key genre of choral concert music. Sheppard was also the pianist and effectively the assistant director of the Jubilee Singers, but in this section I will focus on her work as a transcriber, work that was essential to the group's development. As a Black transcriber of Black song, Sheppard helpfully complicates any simple narrative of white arrangers uncontestedly imposing Western musical epistemologies on Black music, disciplining and domesticating it in the process. In Sheppard's transcriptions, she wields Western musical notation while writing in fissures through which the songs can exceed the regularizing force of that notation, thus both surviving by dint of the notational scheme and not being wholly constrained by it. Her deployment of rhythm, language, and fermatas calls attention to the temporal, sonic, and intermedial complexities involved in transcription, rather than glossing over them as the Jubilee songbooks' essays from the same era do. Her work foregrounds transcription's value as a tool for theorizing about historical motion, temporality, and disappointment.

As she looked back on the first Jubilee Singers tours, Sheppard wrote, "Those were the days of the Ku Klux Klan and the Civil Rights Bill," of racist terror and promised government remedy: an unsettled time, that is, marked by coexisting possibilities of progress and its opposite.[49] In the late 1870s, when the Fisk group set out on those early tours, the law Sheppard names had just been passed. Within a few short years, the Supreme Court would invalidate the law and gut the Fourteenth Amendment's equal protection clause, rendering the latter a handful of words on paper with no means of enforcement. A decade later, the Court would issue its landmark ruling in *Plessy v. Ferguson,* making "separate but equal" a matter of settled law, as it would still be when Sheppard penned her memoir for the *Fisk University News* in 1911. The KKK, its first iteration still extant but dwindling during those first tours, would be reborn in 1915, shortly after the memoir was published. It was unclear, even in retrospect, whether those early tours had taken place in the twilight of nightfall or the flush of some faint-dawning day.

When the Jubilee Singers first set out on tour to raise money for Fisk, they sang mainly classical and sentimental songs, only adding more spirituals to their programs after it became clear that these songs held the power to attract attention, audiences, and donations.[50] This change required serious work; it wasn't as if the group members already had a full complement of shared songs that they could simply start performing. "To recall and to learn of each other the slave songs demanded much mental labor," Sheppard wrote of this process, "and to prepare them for public singing required much rehearsing."[51] With her repeated use of "much," Sheppard pointedly foregrounds the intentional effort, the labor and art, that went into these performances. Listeners, critics, and even other arrangers at the time tended to erase this labor, implying instead that the songs simply emerged out of the biographical and genetic memories of enslavement and its hardships. But even as Sheppard emphasizes the work involved, she modestly downplays a crucial element of the work as well, declining to mention her own labor as a transcriber of the songs: accounts of the group indicate that she herself was the one who transcribed many of these songs as the singers taught them to one another.[52] Sheppard's work as a transcriber had by then been amply erased by others as well. In the Jubilee songbooks that were published during her tenure with the group, she receives no transcription credits, even though histories of the group reliably mention her work in that regard.

She did receive published credit for her transcriptions in one instance. The Cincinnati-based music company J. Church published several songs of the Fisk Jubilee Singers as stand-alone sheet-music editions in 1880, including three songs that credited Sheppard as the transcriber: "My Lord's Writing All the

Time," "I'm Going to Sing All the Way," and "Reign, Massa Jesus, Reign." Even these songs are reprinted in the Jubilee songbooks without her name attached: in the 1880 edition of *The Story of the Jubilee Singers; With Their Songs*, they are credited as having been published by Church, but without any mention of Sheppard. The multiple mediations and labors that are mapped in the stand-alone sheet music get simplified in book form to a merely commercial transaction. Yet the mediations Sheppard herself institutes are central to these transcriptions' interventions.

In contrast to the claims made in the Jubilee songbooks that the arrangements are both faithful to the original and easy to perform, Sheppard's transcription of "I'm Going to Sing All the Way" provides indications that it is not an entirely accurate record of a performance event and can't be accurately sung. Her transcription uses lyrical variation and copious fermatas to call attention to the very problem of transcribing, to force awareness of the hybridity and instability of the transcribed spiritual as a form, to explore the potentials of multiple temporalities, and to reflect on the halting and uncertain quality of historical motion in the wake of Reconstruction.

This transcription foregrounds its impossibilities and incommensurations right from the beginning. Although the cover gives the song's title as "I'm Going to Sing All the Way," the title on the first page of sheet music reads "O I'm Going to Sing All the Way." This added "O" lets us know that once we get beyond the music's cover page, its commercial come-on, an extra expressive element is going to enter the scene. And when the song begins, yet another vowel is added: the first line is written as "O I'm a going to sing." Similarly, the second part of that sung sentence is revealed as being not merely "all the way," as in the title, but "all *along* the way"—the line lengthened by a word that both doubles the preceding "all" and appends an acknowledgment of length. These three successive additions communicate clearly that this song's transcription is about something that takes longer than advertised, something whose temporality is stretched out and altered as it unfolds.

Sheppard is transcribing not only prolongation but unfulfillable promises about the future. The first measure of music records something impossible and demands something from its singers that is technically undoable: singers are asked to render the words "going to," three syllables in all, as two syllables gotten out in the space of two extremely brief sixteenth notes, with the word "going" assigned to a single syllable and a single note. "Going to sing" is repeated six times in the first two measures, always with this practically unsingable notation. In each instance, the words "going to" would clearly have to be sung as something

O I'M GOING TO SING ALL THE WAY.

AS SUNG BY THE JUBILEE SINGERS.

Transcribed by ———— * ———— Miss Ella Sheppard.

3383-3

1.2 First page of "O I'm Going to Sing All the Way," transcribed by Ella Sheppard (Cincinnati: John Church, 1880). Reproduction courtesy of the Lester S. Levy Collection of Sheet Music, Sheridan Libraries, Johns Hopkins University.

closer to "gonto." In order to transform this transcription back into a performance, singers would be obliged to depart somewhat from the written music, to release themselves from the score's contradictory demands for fidelity to a Black original, on the one hand, and adherence to rules of white written language, on the other. Sheppard's admittedly minor decision, to transcribe lyrics in such a way that they don't precisely line up with the notation, reveals transcription's status as not a mere practice of translation but an opaque material form that does work of its own, in this case registering the incommensurability of the demands imposed on the song by the value systems in which it is embedded. This detail also might land differently on the music's multiple possible consumers and performers: white amateur musicians propping up this score on their parlor piano in anticipation of a pleasant afternoon's diversion might find themselves flummoxed by the demand that they sing "going to" in two sixteenth notes. Some educated Black musicians might find themselves faced with a dilemma of their own, knowing full well that the transcription is a respectability-oriented sanitization of dialect and having to decide how to negotiate the competing expectations that collide in the concert spiritual.[53]

Theorizations of prolongation and temporal variety are visible throughout the song. The score's first page, for instance, is studded with plentiful fermatas. Notated as a dot with a curved line arcing over it, a fermata signifies an unmetered pause, an indefinite prolongation of the note or rest over which it appears. It may mark the place where a performer lets a note ring out into the air an extra moment; it may mark the spot where a conductor stills a whole symphony of strings. It is where motion meets stasis, where metered rhythm meets a temporary suspension of time.

Songs often end on fermatas, but "I'm Going to Sing Along the Way" begins with them: we're made to wait before we even get going. The piano's first note, an eighth note played by the right hand, is marked with a fermata. The left hand begins at the same time with an eighth rest; this silence, too, is prolonged indefinitely by a fermata. With this hitch in time, the song's supposed beginning doesn't guarantee motion right away, and some elements are suspended in silence. Further, the first measure is a pickup measure of only one and a half beats, beginning as it were just past the midpoint of a four-beat measure. While this is a common notational device, here it nevertheless accentuates the sense that song begins in a sort of suspended time.

After the double bar line, a notation that indicates a strong boundary between two sections of a piece of music (and that here arrives just past the midpoint of the four-beat measure, passing along the pay-it-forward nature of the opening pickup measure), the first sung note also takes a fermata—the treble voices are asked to prolong their opening "O"—which is matched in the piano's right hand. This fermata is on the very "O" that was absent on the sheet music's cover and was only revealed once the score was opened up. The expressive "O" is thus no insignificant pickup syllable. It could have been a throwaway, if time in this song were a straightforward matter; but through the addition of this fermata, we find that the expressive and unmarketable "O," the something extra that is omitted from the commercial framing but that the transcriber has slipped into the song's interior, gets elongated and emphasized from the very beginning of the transcription.

Meanwhile, the corresponding rests in the left hand and bass voices do not get fermatas the way the opening left-hand rest did. Once you're reading the piece for the fermatas, this inconsistency stands out dramatically. Something in those voices is refusing to let silence equal stillness. Rather than a mere absence, this may be a deliberate chorus of cold silence. It could be a wary, watchful practice of refusal that is unwilling to be readable as outside history, an insistence on abeyance as a genre of temporal motion. In any case, something on the lower frequencies is brewing.

About halfway through the verse, another fermata brings the momentum up short just as the choir, which has been singing "going to sing" in antiphonal alternation for two bars, has finally come together to sing in homophonic harmony and to switch from singing about *singing* to singing about forward motion: "all along the way."

1.3   Detail from "O I'm Going to Sing All the Way," transcribed by Ella Sheppard (Cincinnati: John Church, 1880). Reproduction courtesy of the Lester S. Levy Collection of Sheet Music, Sheridan Libraries, Johns Hopkins University.

What's unusual here is that an eighth-note fermata in the treble voices is juxtaposed to a quarter-note fermata—a rhythmic value twice as long—in the bass clef. The rhythmic asymmetry, which is reproduced in the two hands of the piano part as well, is not a common sight in written music in general or among Fisk transcriptions. Fermatas usually line up: if a fermata prolongs an eighth-note-long note or rest in one voice, the other voices will have fermatas of an identical length. This is how the other fermatas throughout the Jubilee songbooks of this era work. But Sheppard chooses something different here. In this transcription, the men stay in suspension of forward-moving metrical time while the women move on ahead. The only way to make this measure work is to momentarily discard meter altogether.

In so doing, the singers are likely to realize how easy it was to do, how seamlessly normal it actually feels. In other words, this may be somewhat unusual as a moment of notation, at least to a musically literate reader who's willing to risk pedantry for the sake of an argument, but it's far from unsingable. It's easy enough to understand that in performance, the men would simply prolong their sung word "way" until after the women had sung "O," thereby holding "way" for a fermata-prolonged quarter-note's worth of time, and then they'd take up the silence that the following rest calls for. This means that it's a case where something that wouldn't necessarily sound unusual, or even feel unusual to perform, becomes a visible aberration only through transcription. The Jubilee songbook promised that the transcriptions all submit to the laws of musical language, and here those laws are being not broken but slightly bent, just enough to possibly invite our attention, at the very point in the song that deals with moving forward "all along the way." Subtly, in a detailed transcriptive practice, Sheppard embeds an indication that forward motion can't be divorced from more complex temporalities.

Recall that a very similar line, "along the heavenly way," provides the crux of Du Bois's final move in *Souls*, where he leaves it to that line to imply what he has trouble stating outright in written language: that the Sorrow Songs' hope might not be entirely misplaced. Sheppard's transcription here, which begins with an expressive, excessive "O," both prolonged and ever vulnerable to disappearance, and manifests the halting, heterogeneous quality of a putatively linear-progressivist "along the way," conveys an uncertainty about whether it actually is possible to attain unproblematic forward motion, and whether that is even the right way to figure one's desire. The Jubilee paratexts frequently mentioned the performance of these songs as staging a dramatic contrast of the singers' "former state of slavery and degradation with the present prospects and hopes of their race."[54] But what if that supposed movement from degraded past to present hope weren't as tidy as people wanted to believe? What if you found yourself swirled in the backwash of history, in a moment when things were getting worse instead of better?

Another musical term for a fermata is a *hold*. And when understood as a temporary lifting of rhythmic procession, an indefinite extension of a particular duration, where the wake of a chord or even a silence both travels through and dangles in time, unmetered—and where an artist might improvise an unscored cadenza—this kind of hold calls to mind Hortense Spillers's insight about the holds of slaving ships, the captive human flesh "literally suspended in the oceanic," and the temporary dissolution of gender difference that occurred there.[55] It also resonates with Christina Sharpe's theorization of the hold in *In the Wake,* where, riffing on Édouard Glissant, she writes of it as a space that simultaneously dissolves and gives birth.[56]

Much contemporary criticism that attends closely to the interactions of multiple temporalities gives short shrift to the political potentials of linear time, associating it with political inefficacy or worse.[57] The fermata, especially when thought of as a hold, can offer possibilities for cutting through binary formulations of temporality that identify linear time as always oppressive and nonlinear time as always aligned with freedom, formulations that miss the ways multiple temporalities operate and coexist.

Sheppard's transcriptions acknowledge and map out a polyrhythmic reality. This is even more explicit at the lyrical level in another of her 1880 transcriptions, the song "My Lord's Writing All the Time." In this song's A section, a series of soloist's lines consistently elicit the choral response "My Lord's writing all the time." In the B section, the chorus sings together of an all-encompassing audiovisual surveillance that fuels a divine scriptomania: "He sees all you do, he hears all you say / My Lord's writing all the time." Godly writing, here, means writing as a means of doing justice—since the Lord's writing is presumably an act of note-taking toward future punishment or reward—and it is also a writing that encompasses *all* the time. The proclamation that "my Lord's writing all the time" designates, on the surface, merely a constant act of writing. But "all the time" could be not just writing's adverb but its direct object. Like Sheppard—who in this transcription writes a considerable variety of times, from steady quarter notes to halfway syncopated dotted eighth- and sixteenth-note patterns—the Lord could also be writing all the possible kinds of time: not just progress or regression or stasis, linear or nonlinear, but all of it. And all of it, especially taken in toto, is what is seen here as furnishing the materials for doing justice.

In Sheppard's transcriptions, she suggests that singing, writing, and performing can confront historical conditions and investigate temporal complexities at the shifting borders between music and language, sound and text. Du Bois could not, in the end, guarantee that "a faith in the ultimate justice of things" was itself justified. For Sheppard, carving out fissures in forms to allow sustained reflection on and production within multiple temporalities meant opening up space for collaborative practices of justice. In her transcriptions, she embedded an understanding that when confronting the evils endemic to a historical reality whose times don't all line up, people's most creative responses need not simply submit to laws, of musical language or anything else. It is people's persistent desires—wherever we can find the seams in which to let them take root—that will be the key to our own survivals, and even to the ongoing possibility of justice.

To Gain Time: Charles Chesnutt's *Marrow of Tradition*

Multiple temporalities play major roles in Chesnutt's 1901 novel *The Marrow of Tradition*. The novel features a wide range of timescales and tempos, including clock time and promptness; delay, retrogression, and looping; the slow, deliberate time of proper justice (in contrast to the quick reactivity of extralegal action); and the even slower *longue durée* of linear-progressive historical time and generational succession. In the end, it is a fermata-like suspension of forward motion that holds the key to the novel's insight about responding to such a profusion of temporalities.

The book's multistrand plot is built around two main narratives. In one story line, a Southern town hurtles toward a deadly riot—a fictionalization of a white supremacist coup d'état that took place in 1898 in Wilmington, North Carolina, during which a white mob killed between fourteen and sixty Black residents, ousted the town's interracial government, and reinstated all-white rule. In the novel's other main plot, the deceptions and longings underpinning a multigenerational family saga are revealed. Janet Miller, a Black woman, and Olivia Carteret, a white woman, are half sisters. Their father, the white patriarch Sam Merkell, has been dead for years, and Janet—now the wife of a prominent Black doctor, William Miller—has long yearned for recognition from Olivia. Olivia is married to a local newspaper editor, Major Carteret, who is one of the climactic race riot's three instigators. At the end of the novel, white mobs have destroyed Dr. Miller's hospital and killed the Millers' young son. Yet in the final scene, a grieving Janet Miller convinces her husband—who is, thanks to the mayhem, the only doctor left in town—to save the life of the Carterets' own sick child. (Alongside these two interlocking stories, there is also a comparatively lighthearted love triangle, in which a racist white man and a decent, upstanding white journalist vie for the affection of Major Carteret's half sister, Clara.)

As we've seen, African American writers of this era, as well as their sympathizers, often describe their time as being marked by a combination of regression and stasis. White supremacists in this era, for their part, often pressed their cause in a language of progress, evolution, and scientific modernity: popular books of the time such as John H. Van Evrie's *White Supremacy and Negro Subordination* (1868) asserted that "the negro" was immune to evolutionary progress, and that the "white race" held a monopoly over the future while the formerly enslaved, shorn of the allegedly civilizing and protective effects of the peculiar institution, were embarked on a backward slide into barbarism and, perhaps, eventual extinction.[58] Rather than concluding that linear time was a tool of white supremacy best resisted, though, many African American writers instead claimed it for their own, arguing that progress and evolution could be crucial means and temporalities of a still-elusive Black freedom—even when those concepts seemed to buckle under the pressure of being deployed in such a way.

Chesnutt, for instance, used evolutionary tropes to his own ends when grappling with the idea of progress. His 1900 essay "The Future American"—bearing, among its several subtitles, "What the Race Is Likely to Become in the Process of Time: A Perfect Type Supposably to Be Evolved"—straightforwardly proposed a program of progress via racial "amalgamation."[59] In *The Marrow of Tradition* and related texts, however, Chesnutt directly mocks evolution ideology and flips it on its head, meanwhile insisting on the fact of progress, not as an eventual triumph of race mixing but as a function of time itself. In *Marrow,* he writes that Dr. Miller "liked to believe that the race antagonism which hampered his progress and that of his people was a mere temporary thing, the outcome of former conditions, and bound to disappear in time."[60] Chesnutt seems to have agreed with his fictional character: in an essay Chesnutt published in conjunction with *Marrow*'s release, explaining his intentions in writing the novel, he insists that the new book is "not a study in pessimism, for it is the writer's belief that the forces of progress will in the end prevail, and that in time a remedy may be found for every social ill."[61]

Within this credo, however simply stated, lies something more complex: "in time a remedy may be found" suggests that one must look for such a remedy in time itself. Indeed, elsewhere in the essay he reiterates the novel's temporal focus. "The old order has passed away," he writes of the postslavery South, "but these opinions [that is, of white supremacy and Black inferiority], deeply implanted in the consciousness of two races, still persist, and *The Marrow of Tradition* seeks to show the efforts of the people of a later generation to adjust themselves in this traditional atmosphere to the altered conditions of a new era."[62]

Chesnutt's approach to temporality in *Marrow* begins by reversing and scrambling racist pseudoscience's progressivist schema: In the first half of the novel, white supremacists manipulate time and interfere with the proper unfolding of linear temporalities. Members of the Merkell and Carteret families conceal Sam Merkell's last will and testament in order to deprive Janet Miller of the inheritance her father intended to leave her; their warping of linear time and generational succession cheats the patriarch's Black daughter of the familial recognition she deserves. Major Carteret delays the republication of an antilynching editorial from the town's African American newspaper, waiting for the most strategic moment to deploy it for propaganda purposes rather than hewing to a standard of timely newsworthiness. And the "grandfather clause" that is instituted by the state legislature toward the end of the book revives slavery-era racial hierarchies by repeating and looping time, explicitly causing statuses from the past to hold true in the present.

While the forces of white supremacy in *Marrow* are consistently associated with belatedness, retrogression, and manipulation of linear time, Chesnutt's African American characters are paragons of punctuality and guardians of linear time. On more than one occasion, Chesnutt goes out of his way to announce a Black character's prompt arrival somewhere, and the white characters comment on how admirably on time the Black characters are, even to the point of personifying promptness: "Sandy is punctuality itself," the patrician old Mr. Delamere proclaims of his trusted servant.[63] And when another servant re-creates how Sam Merkell explained his decision to live with his Black housekeeper, the justification is based on her reliable, punctual orientation to time: "Fac' is, I could n' git 'long widout Julia. She 'd be'n runnin' dis house like clockwo'k befo' you come, an' I likes her ways" (6).

Yet this reversed binary is not as simple as it seems, as the novel is skeptical of the possibility that justice might be done via a restoration of linear time. When Olivia finally offers restitution, Janet rejects it as coming too late to do any good: "Now, when an honest man has given me a name of which I can be proud, you offer me the one of which you robbed me, and of which I can make no use" (328). And the precise timing and linear temporality that are faithfully provided by Black characters prove of immediate benefit only to white survival. The book begins with the urgent drama of a white child's premature birth, and it ends with Dr. Miller's decision to save this child's life at the last possible moment, as announced in the novel's closing line: "There's time enough, but none to spare" (329). By contrast, there is not "time enough" in the book, it would seem, for Miller and his family: his hospital is torched by a white mob and burned to the ground, and his only child is killed in the rampage. For Black life, linear time seems at first to offer few benefits.

Still, the book does not, on its face, suggest that the Black characters would have been better served by nonlinear temporalities. As just outlined, Black life suffers here from time that is not linear *enough*. The best chance Chesnutt can offer for Black survival is a longer, generational temporality that is no less linear for its failure to appear fruitfully within the frame of the novel itself. Only the slow progress of generations—the children the Millers will supposedly go on to have after the death of their firstborn, the maturing of what Chesnutt calls the "chip-on-the-shoulder stage" of proud Black servants, and the passing of this generational "phase" that must be measured in decades, not minutes— only this long, slow time, guided by patient principles of justice and mercy, holds any promise of victory for Black people in the twentieth century, if it even comes that soon (42).

In the *longue durée* of species life, then, whites may be due for their come-uppance, an irony that is heightened by the white characters' smug assumption that evolution favors them. Throughout the book, Chesnutt portrays and skewers the evolution / devolution ideology that was popular at the turn of the century as a justification for white rule. The narrator reports sardonically that in Southern discourse, "vital statistics were made to prove that [the Negro] had degenerated from an imaginary standard of physical excellence which had existed under the benign influence of slavery" (238). Carteret writes in his newspaper that North Carolina must work to "confine the negro to that inferior condition for which nature had evidently designed him" (79). And the town's prominent white citizens regale a visiting Northern delegation with talk of the "good old negro" of antebellum times and the unfortunate "degeneracy of his descendants" (115). Even the relatively openminded journalist Mr. Ellis, one of the least despicable white characters in the novel, falls for this line of thought: "No one could tell," he muses, while watching a dark-skinned dancer perform a cakewalk at the town's hotel, "at what moment the thin veneer of civilization might peel off and reveal the underlying savage" (119).

Here, too, Chesnutt is enacting a pointed reversal: the dancer Ellis is watching turns out to be the dissolute white heir Tom Delamere, in black-face. The "thin veneer of civilization" is thus a layer of burned cork—making Blackness, not whiteness, the civilized surface that those who lack it by birth must pretend to by artifice—and "the underlying savage" is revealed as nothing other than a core of white violence, since Tom, still in blackface, will soon cause an old woman's death. Here and elsewhere throughout *Marrow*, Chesnutt flips the terms of the evolutionary narrative so that it is the white race that finds itself on a decline toward barbarism at the dawn of the twentieth century.[64]

The temporal complexity of *Marrow* resides not just in its explicit discussions of timeliness and history but in narrative and metaphor as well. At a christening party held early in the book for Olivia's infant son, for instance, Tom Delamere shows up late but tries to deny that he has been the last to arrive, in a strange exchange that seems to go on for two beats too long.

> "You are the last one, Tom," [Clara] said reproachfully. "Mr. Ellis has been here half an hour." . . .
>
> "The rector is not here," answered Tom triumphantly. "You see I am not the last."
>
> "The rector," replied Clara, "was called out of town at six o'clock this evening, to visit a dying man, and so cannot be here. You are the last, Tom, and Mr. Ellis was the first." (17)

By contrast, Mr. Ellis, Tom's romantic rival, had been ready for the party an hour early and was obliged to kill half an hour reading magazines at his social club so as not to show up to the gathering awkwardly ahead of schedule.

Ellis's overeager temporal disposition is visible as well in the gift he brings the baby, a silver watch: "It was a little premature, he admitted, but the boy would grow to it" (22–23). For his part, Tom offers a napkin ring—an endless loop—and the elderly Aunt Polly brings an antique rattle, already so old that its once-white ivory has turned yellow (with the same inevitability, perhaps, that the town's racialized binary is tending toward "yellow" through what Chesnutt would have termed amalgamation), and whose handle will soon nearly choke the child to death. In contrast to the belated Tom, the too-early Ellis, and the stuck-in-the-past Polly, old Mr. Delamere's Black servant Sandy hits the perfect middle, departing so he can change his clothes and then returning "at the end of a quarter of an hour," precisely when he said he would come back (19). Thus by the end of the second chapter, *Marrow* has posited a scrupulous attention to linear clock time as the characteristic practice of Black characters, while the worst whites lag behind and lie about it, and the better sort kill time so as not to arrive too soon.

Yet even as adherence to linear time appears to constitute a practice of resistance to a regime of time-warping white supremacy, it at first excludes other possibilities for resistance. Much has been written of the train-car scene in which Miller is ordered, at the Virginia state line, to move to the Jim Crow car while his white Philadelphian mentor argues with the conductor in protest.[65] Less attention has been paid, though, to the temporal terms in which Miller declines to fight the requirement to move and tries to quiet his friend. "It is the law, and we are powerless to resist it. If we made any trouble, it would merely delay your journey and imperil a life at the other end" (55). Arguing and resisting, to Miller, are distasteful only in part because they are (he believes) ineffectual. Even more markedly, they are to be abjured because they would introduce delay, even life-threatening delay, into a rightfully linear process. What's more, the linear process is bound to produce results in its own good time: when the Northern doctor continues to object, Miller seeks to calm him down by telling him that parallel progress is inevitable, using terms that closely echo his credo of progress quoted earlier. "'Never mind, doctor,' interrupted Miller, soothingly, 'it's only for a little while. I'll reach my destination just as surely in the other car, and we can't help it, anyway. I'll see you again at Wellington'" (55–56).

The most effective practice of resistance in *Marrow* turns out to involve not only linear or nonlinear time but a combination of the two. Midway through the novel, as three Black characters race against the clock to stop a lynching, time undergoes an odd suspension that permits the three men to air their disagreements about the best way to proceed. This suspended hour, which Chesnutt scholars have never addressed, holds the key to the novel's multiple temporalities.

This hour appears in a key episode that begins one morning, when a mysterious death is discovered, and continues through the evening of the same day, when the proposed lynching of Mr. Delamere's punctual servant Sandy is canceled. Throughout this section, Chesnutt repeatedly makes us aware of what time it is: the coroner's jury arrives at the supposed murder scene at nine o'clock in the morning; Carteret and his coconspirators meet at "about ten o'clock" to discuss the crime; and then—this becomes particularly important—Dr. Miller wakes up at "about eleven o'clock," having slept late after a long night at the hospital (178, 180, 187). This timetable makes clear that both white supremacy and Black resistance inhabit a common time frame, that of linear clock time, which cannot be disregarded or escaped. Yet this timeline also establishes the framework within which a necessary rupture in time will become discernible.

Marrow's suspended hour erupts out of, and retrospectively proves to have made possible, a scene of disagreement. Upon waking at "about eleven o'clock," Miller engages in a lengthy conversation with the lawyer Watson and the laborer Josh Green about the murder and the planned lynching. The three men brainstorm and disagree about several possible ways to save Sandy's life. Miller and Watson then head out to find help in town, promising Josh, "We'll be back in half an hour" (192).

They keep this vow precisely: "In half an hour they had both returned" is the line that directly follows their promise, standing as a one-line paragraph all on its own (192). Cast in iambic pentameter, the line announcing their promptness hews strictly to a classical form of ordered and predictable timeliness, which stands in sharp contrast to the "state of anarchy" that reigns in the bloodthirsty town.

This single-line paragraph also signals that the clean progression of narrative time that has dominated the chapter so far, as well as the clear association between Black characters and promptness that has held sway throughout the novel, is about to get complicated. The novel form, a tool for containing multiple timescales, in Chesnutt's hands now goes beyond a mere reversal of temporal values to suggest something even more transformative.[66] As the poetic rhythm of this line calls our attention to language unfolding in time, word by word, the novel's encompassing framework of narrative time momentarily gives way, in content as well as form.

To recap: we have been told that Miller awakens at "about eleven," starts discussing the situation with Watson, is joined by Josh, and then heads out with Watson for half an hour to search for one righteous white man who might save Sandy. Following this, they debrief one another and decide to seek out the elderly Mr. Delamere—Sandy's employer and possibly his unacknowledged father as well. At a bare minimum, this chain of events would have occupied forty-five minutes, taking the characters, one would think, close to the noon hour. Yet once they have decided to contact Delamere, the doctor checks the time—"Miller looked at his watch" stands on its own as another one-line paragraph, nearly a line of trochaic tetrameter but stuttered with pauses. And then, estimating that it will take him an hour and a half to reach Delamere, Miller announces that "it is now eleven o'clock" (195).

That is, nearly an hour after eleven o'clock, it is still eleven o'clock.

How to account for this strange occurrence, this doubled or vanished eleventh hour?[67] Time in the book is not breaking down or coming unmoored generally; indeed, the timetable becomes more exact, not less, as events accelerate toward the sunset hour when Sandy is scheduled to be lynched. Yet here, in the middle of a precisely timed chain of events taking place strictly according to clock time, we encounter this strange hiccup. As the town of Wellington hurtles toward its regression into injustice and barbarism, time falls back an hour.[68]

The question of whether Chesnutt is a literary realist or a writer of a more blatantly allegorical bent has been subject to debate,[69] but a breach of continuity this drastic is extreme even for Chesnutt, who for all his romance-worthy characters and coincidences almost always leaves the laws of physics intact. Surviving page proofs show that he went through extensive edits for this chapter, yet he never touched its odd timeline.[70] The suspended hour appears in the book's first edition and was never emended for subsequent printings, even as author and publishers alike continued to examine the text for errors after the book's initial release in October 1901.[71] Although Chesnutt may not have consciously intended to insert a temporal suspension, it was nonetheless harmonious enough with his inner sense of what would be possible—or even necessary—in such a situation that it never *looked* wrong to him.

This is especially worth remarking on because things frequently did look wrong to Chesnutt. Throughout his life, errors continually leapt out to him from all sorts of texts, his own work and the work of others alike. He was not shy about writing letters to inform people of mistakes they had made in print, then saving carbon copies of his letters as well as the replies he received. Not only was he a legal stenographer by training and profession; he also had lived his life with an oddly spelled last name, and a lifetime of correcting people on this point had doubtless had an effect on him. "My name seems to give you a good deal of trouble," he would write with barely cloaked aggravation to the secretary of Wilberforce University in 1913, after the school had flubbed the spelling on his honorary degree and then rendered it a different wrong way in a letter apologizing for the mistake. "With presumably my letterhead in front of you you have spelled it wrong twice in your letter of March 31st. I know it is a very unusual spelling. There is no 't' in the middle but two 't's' are at the end."[72] Published reviews of his books, as well, frequently weighed in on the latest work of Mr. Chestnut or Mr. Chestnutt. Being saddled with an easily misspelled surname had likely sharpened Chesnutt's sensitivity to textual errors in general, a sensitivity to which his considerable success as a legal stenographer attests. He was not a man to be sloppy about details. Further, as a member of the Ohio bar who transcribed many of the state courts' proceedings, he surely had had plenty of practice attending closely to the timelines of consequential sets of events.

Thus, since the suspended hour never announced itself to him as an error, we must conclude that despite its mathematical impossibility, it seemed right to him in a way that went beyond mere oversight, and we are justified in asking what this odd hour makes manifest.

First, it is a diegetic instantiation of the life-saving delay Miller and Watson urgently seek.[73] Again and again in this section, the breakneck speed of mob violence is opposed to the necessary delay that alone may save Sandy's life: "He'll be lynched to-night . . . unless we can stave the thing off for a day or two," Miller tells Mr. Delamere, who in turn expresses certainty that once the townspeople have listened to him, they will "wait for the operation of the law." Carteret tells Delamere that "there is but one way to gain time" (and then outlines, true to fuzzy-numbered form, not one but two ways: find the real criminal, or find a white person who will swear to having seen Sandy elsewhere at the time of the old woman's death). Carteret further points out that "whatever is done . . . must be done quickly," because the mob is impatient. Justice and Black survival in this episode appear to depend on the triumph of the slow, deliberate time of law and order over the quick reactivity of extralegal organization—but also on the ability of Sandy's defenders to match the lynch mob's speed, and to "gain time" by adding an extra hour to this high-stakes day (199, 200, 214, 215).

Even more important, it is in this hour that Miller, Watson, and Josh debate whether to defend Sandy physically, by fighting in the streets, or administratively, either by appealing to local or federal officials or by seeking the support of white men from the town. Josh favors direct action: "My idee is ter hunt up de niggers an' git 'em ter stan' tergether an' gyard de jail" where Sandy is being held (188–189). Miller and Watson are against this plan; they believe they have no chance of winning a street fight. Miller wants to ask the sheriff to telegraph the governor, or perhaps alert the president, but Watson has already failed at the former, and the latter will take too long: "The whole negro population of the South might be slaughtered," Watson says, "before the necessary red tape could be spun out to inform the President that a state of anarchy prevailed" (192). Finally Miller and Watson venture out to ask their white acquaintances for help. Upon their empty-handed return, their disagreement with Josh continues until finally, Miller suddenly thinks to contact Mr. Delamere: "Why haven't we thought of him before?" (194). The disagreement over strategy, the debate between militant and conciliators, is necessary in order for the best path to be found: the men apparently have to exhaust all their instinctive ideas before re-membering that Delamere has not yet been consulted.

Yet in the race to save Sandy's life, the time to have this discussion feels im-possible to spare. "We are wasting valuable time," Watson says during their debate; "it's hardly worth while for us to discuss a subject we are all agreed upon" (191). This is a direct echo of the Jim Crow car scene, where argument was seen as not just useless but an unaffordable temporal luxury. Yet here its necessity can no longer be repressed or soothed away—the seeming inevita-bility of a speeding locomotive's course is no longer reassuring when a white mob's bloodlust is driving the train—so a means of affording dissent after all must be devised. To cite Chesnutt's own words, *in time* a remedy must be found. In order for the necessary disagreement to play out, a disruption in linear time has to be instituted.[74]

The debate, the acknowledgment that the members of the community are not, in fact, "all agreed," as Watson wrongly suggests, occurs in a suspension of linear time, during which time both is and is not unfolding. This scene defies linear temporality while still hewing to it: even as a doubled or stalled eleven o'clock troubles clock time, it is still located within that framework; indeed, it could not be registered in the absence of clock time. Nobody ever loses track of time here, but time briefly jumps its own track, or stops in it. Thus we could say that rather than being negated or overturned, linear time here is put on hold.

Chesnutt institutes an unfixed time of suspension like that which a fermata, or hold, calls for in Western musical notation, as we already saw in Ella Sheppard's transcriptions. If, as Christina Sharpe proposes, the hold offers conceptual resources for a project of "inhabiting *and* rupturing" the episteme of Atlantic slavery's long afterlives, then this fermata in Chesnutt—where linear time is both inhabited and ruptured—invites an understanding of a hold, an in-between suspension, that might birth not only slavery's homogenizing dehumanization (as Spillers and Sharpe emphasize) but something more along the lines of what is evoked in an epigraph Sharpe draws from Glissant's *Poetics of Relation:* "The belly of this boat dissolves you, precipitates you into a nonworld from which you cry out. This boat is a womb, a womb abyss. It generates the clamor of your protests; it also produces all coming unanimity."[75] Here, what the hold births is clamor and cry, dissent and protest, multiplicity that does not undermine a social totality but constitutes it. This sort of hold gives rise to a social totality that can find time for disagreement and difference, even where there had seemed to be no time to lose.

It's important to be clear that the hold in *Marrow* does not show that his characters' previous attachment to linear time was misguided, or that nonlinear time is inherently liberatory. This eruption of nonlinear time within linearity is indispensable in order for the characters to have the disagreement that allows them to save Sandy's life, but *The Marrow of Tradition* does not finally endorse nonstandard time as an intrinsically utopian resource that is necessarily suited to the goals of the disadvantaged. Instead it suggests, almost despite itself, that the relation between progress and delay—that is, between linear and nonlinear temporalities—may be far less oppositional than the novel supposed at the outset, and that transcriptions of the junctures where multiple temporalities come into contact can make space for the sorts of disagreements and contestations that must be not only tolerated but cultivated if change is to be possible.

Marrow's suspended hour can help us think beyond the binary of oppressive linear temporalities versus liberatory nonlinear ones that structures so much recent thought on politics and time, especially in literary and cultural studies. Even criticism that attends closely to the interactions of multiple temporal structures commonly gives short shrift to the political potentials of linear temporalities, associating them with political inefficacy or even ontological dissolution. In writing about Langston Hughes and Harlem nightlife, for example, Shane Vogel sets up a stark binary of temporalities, "the reified clock of rationalized time" versus "musical sets and the flows of musical time," discounting the possibility of more multivalent interactions.[76] And Bruce Barnhart, in his consideration of jazz's influence on African American modernist novels, argues that art that too closely reproduces a society's dominant temporalities is incapable of challenging "the exclusionary machinations of this society."[77]

Similarly, Michelle Wright sees "linear progress narrative[s]" as excluding "women, children, LGBTTQ Blacks, and Blacks outside the United States or the Caribbean" from discussions of Blackness.[78] In her book *Physics of Black-*

ness, Wright argues that linear narrative forms make Blackness impossible to think of at all: "Forcing nonprogressive narratives into linear narrative frameworks," she writes, "will cause a qualitative collapse of Blackness" and possibly create "an either/or Blackness according to which one must choose one interpretation over the other to reposition Blackness in that linear spacetime."[79] Even in its admirable commitment to avoiding either-or logic, this argument remains enclosed in it. It leaves the two halves of the linear/nonlinear schema locked in an opposition that can be speculatively circumnavigated but never transformed, let alone transcended.

Sharpe's concept of "the wake" suggests a more generative approach to this temporal antinomy. Building on the notion of Atlantic slavery's long aftermath, she investigates the idea of the wake as "the track left on the water's surface by a ship . . . a region of disturbed flow," as "a watch or vigil held beside the body of someone who has died," and as wakefulness, as heightened consciousness.[80] For Sharpe, the wake is stubbornly persistent, a manifestation of a too-long *longue durée,* and yet continually in motion; it operates simultaneously as condition and as practice. If it were true that "forcing nonprogressive narratives into linear narrative frameworks [produces] a qualitative collapse of Blackness," as Wright claims, then it would be impossible to think of the Middle Passage and its wake as constitutive spaces of historical and ongoing Blackness. Yet Sharpe nevertheless does so with great power and insight, proposing wake work as "a mode of inhabiting *and* rupturing this episteme with our known lived and un/imaginable lives."[81] Chesnutt's suspended hour inhabits *and* ruptures the paradigm of linear temporality that functions so ambivalently in the lives of *Marrow*'s Black characters.

According to an older view of Chesnutt, the sort articulated by Amiri Baraka and SallyAnn Ferguson, this equivocation might seem evidence of Chesnutt's accommodationism.[82] But such a reading would hold up only if we insisted on a stable binary of temporalities mappable onto racial politics, a schema that the cultural and political history of the nadir asks us to resist. Alternatively, and more persuasively, we might be tempted to view Chesnutt's temporal hold as aligned with Lloyd Pratt's contention that much early African American life writing can be seen as trying, unsuccessfully, to repress "temporal variety" and shoehorn multiple temporalities into linear narrative form.[83] And to the extent that *Marrow*'s inhabiting of the novel form weds very old generic conventions, such as the love triangle and the disowned poor relation, with the extremely timely content of the 1898 coup on which the novel's climactic events are based, all while continually attempting to secure for the Black characters the blessings of historical progress, Pratt's encouragement to see temporal variety within linear narrative form is a helpful one.

But *Marrow* goes further, and the repression of multiple temporalities in this novel is even less complete than it is in the works Pratt analyzes, since the multiplicity is present not just on the formal level but also in the novel's manifest content and even in the language itself. *Marrow* arrives, in the end, at the realization that multiple temporalities are variably at work in the cruel politics of the nadir, and that they can be used by multiple actors for multiple purposes. Indeed, when the riot gets under way, the white supremacists who were so at home in looping and delay prove themselves perfectly capable of being prompt, a change so dramatic that it seems almost supernatural: "At three o'clock sharp the streets were filled, as if by magic, with armed white men" (274).

Just as white supremacy makes itself at home in many temporal frames, Chesnutt finally allows resistance to inhabit multiple temporalities as well: the determined punctuality of the book's early pages is eventually joined by the swift extralegal reactivity of Josh Green's self-defense militia, Josh's own suicidal drive to avenge his mother's death, the slow unfolding of generational succession ("You are young . . . and may yet have many children," Olivia tells Janet, who does not dispute the claim [326]), the refusal of that very succession (when Janet disowns her suddenly contrite sister and rejects the tardily offered inheritance), and the concerted delay that Miller implements in the final scenes, when a white child's survival depends on Miller's prompt aid, and Miller withholds his help until the child's parents—the Carterets—are humbled and defeated, their fiercely guarded privilege proved worthless, at least for a moment.

Chesnutt's importance as a theorist of nadir temporalities has been remarked on in relation to his Conjure Tales, with their comment on plantation nostalgia and the persistence of slavery.[84] Yet here *Marrow* shows itself to be an equally pivotal text in taking stock of the author's complex understanding of time and chronology—which is to say, narrative. In the face of the nadir's negations of progress, *Marrow*—rather than suggesting that linear time was a dead end and nonlinear time holds the key to something better—demonstrates that the most unhelpful thing of all may be the misguided attempt to map a clear value binary onto different temporalities.

This is a lesson that those of us who, faced with alarming political and ecological futures, with ongoing and escalating disappointments, might find ourselves attracted by the radical allure of nonlinear temporalities would do well to take seriously, and it is a lesson that gives the novel's closing line an entirely new resonance. In light of Chesnutt's complex understanding of time and narrative, "There's time enough, but none to spare" is readable as a clear endorsement of tuning in to the potentials of a wide range of temporalities. We can ill afford to rule out any of them ahead of time.

CHAPTER 2

TRANSCRIBING LOSSES

The Popular Front and Its Afterlives

" Of the Sorrow Songs" is frequently discussed as the last section of W. E. B. Du Bois's *The Souls of Black Folk,* but *Souls* doesn't actually end with that essay. There is one final paragraph after the Sorrow Songs essay, titled, appropriately enough, "The After-Thought." It begins with an intriguing appeal: "Hear my cry, O God the Reader." Describing his writing as a cry, a sound that God might attend to not just as a listener but also as a reader, Du Bois casts his own utterance, in this paragraph and retrospectively in *Souls* overall, as a transcriptive encounter between sound and writing. He combines them as a way to reshape a world that is itself in need of synthesis, as he emphasizes elsewhere in the book. This paragraph is a prayer that the ideas in the book might bear real fruit in the world, that from its pages might sprout "vigor of thought and thoughtful deed to reap the harvest wonderful."[1]

Du Bois's closing address echoes the beginning of Psalm 61 (a psalm that opens, "Hear my cry, O God; attend unto my prayer," and whose heading highlights its own transcriptive status by noting that it is meant to be accompanied by the music of stringed instruments) and cycles back to the poem in *Souls'* opening epigraph, lines by Arthur Symons in which the cry of the ocean and the cry of the speaker's heart echo each other:

> And the heart shall be weary and wonder and cry like the sea,
> All life long crying without avail,
> As the water all night long is crying to me.[2]

Over the course of Du Bois's book, this oceanic cry of the heart takes the form of the book itself, and by the end it presents as not only audible but actionable— at least potentially—through transcriptive practices heeded by a God who is understood to be not only a listener, as hailed by the Psalmist, and not only a writer, as in Ella Sheppard's transcription of "My Lord's Writing All the Time," but a reader as well. If God might hear the cry of the author, and "the ears of a guilty people [might] tingle with truth," Du Bois writes, then "these crooked marks on a fragile leaf"—that is, the book itself—may "be not indeed / THE END." The words "THE END" do double duty here at the close of the "After-Thought," both completing the sentence and, positioned as they are on their own line of text, serving as the structural marker of the book's conclusion.

A two-word paratext that fuses syntactically with text, an end that both is and is not the end while linking back to the beginning, a formless cry that asks to be actualized in the world through a transcendent attentiveness that is simultaneously a listening and a reading: the conclusion of *The Souls of Black Folk* gestures to the ways Du Bois's transcriptive practices throughout the book—practices that aspire to approach or approximate sound in writing while simultaneously lending sound some of writing's durability—generate productive instabilities in writing that can archive disappointment, maintain an open stance toward possible futures, and potentially reshape the world if encountered attentively through a hybrid listening-reading practice. Du Bois's "After-Thought" additionally directs our attention to the practices through which human sounds that are neither music nor speech—cries, for example—are registered in writing. Taking cues from Du Bois, the present chapter will explore how transcriptions of what I'll call paramusical soundings have worked to convey political disappointment. It will tune in to the audible signals people create that travel alongside music (or, less often, speech), that hitch a ride like sonic burrs on more definite forms, and that pose productive problems for direct transcription as written language or notated music.[3]

This chapter attends, in reading and listening, to the Popular Front period of the mid-1930s onward, and it discusses that period's paramusical soundings and the transcriptive practices they engender. In this historical archive, it locates traces of transformations in American leftists' desires for imminent revolution and a multiracial revolutionary working class. To investigate what happened when the Communist Party's ideology pivoted away from the direct pursuit of those two objects, I will discuss two figures who aren't usually discussed together, the writer Tillie Olsen and the singer-guitarist Huddie Ledbetter (also known by his stage name, Lead Belly), listening to the sounds of disappointment that resonate at the edges of transcription in Olsen's fiction and Ledbetter's music. Where unruly sounds cause trouble for and in transcription, we can find records of feelings that manage to endure despite, and even because of, the problems they create for writing.

The Hybrid Sounds of Tillie Olsen

In a key scene near the end of Olsen's story "Tell Me a Riddle," an elderly woman who has been brought home to die begins to emit disquieting noises: "Sound bubbled in her throat," Olsen writes, also mentioning "whimpers, gurglings," and a "swarm of sounds."[4] The "sounds" in the swarm include the noises of a body near death, as Olsen makes clear, but they emerge amid and travel in conjunction with fragments of political language and song that register outdated utopian expectation. Earlier in the story, the woman, Eva, had argued with her husband, David, over whether they should move to a retirement community run by his fraternal organization: David craves the collective life such a place would provide, while Eva, after her lifetime of care work, craves solitude. This conflict has inspired readings of the story attuned to the affective labor demanded of women within the nuclear family.[5] Yet the sounds in the story recast its struggle over community and solitude, highlighting Olsen's interest in not just private and personal conflicts but public and collective ones.[6] Eva's paramusical soundings play an important role in conveying her disappointed political desires and in making them audible to others.

As Eva lies dying, she voices bits of political slogans, speeches, and songs, interrupted by noises that Olsen does not transcribe onomatopoetically but rather refers to indicatively:

> *Even in reality* (swallow) *life's lack of it*
> *78,000 in one minute* (whisper of a scream)

Eva laments human atrocities—"78,000" refers to one estimate of the number of people killed instantly in the bombing of Hiroshima—and arrives at a broken quotation from a speech Victor Hugo gave to a workers' congress in 1879:

> *No man one   except through others*
> *Strong   with the not yet   in the now*
> *Dogma dead   war dead   one country*

In Hugo's speech, he had predicted that "in the twentieth century war will be dead, the scaffold will be dead, animosity will be dead, royalty will be dead, and dogmas will be dead; but Man will live. For all there will be but one country—that country the whole earth; for all there will be but one hope—that hope the whole heaven."[7] Eva's discontinuities and omissions, though, turn Hugo's hopeful prognostications into what sounds more like a list of casualties: "*Dogma dead   war dead.*"

Olsen tells us that David "tried not to listen" to Eva, "but trapped with her the long nights in that little room, the sounds worked themselves into his consciousness, with their punctuation of death swallows, whimpers, gurglings." As "punctuation," the untranscribed bodily sounds provide a syntactic architecture for the sonic whole: the elements that we might imagine to be the least formally grounded actually shape and determine the form. They also ensure that the content is not ignored, since it is precisely Eva's conjunction of speech and noise that frustrates David's attempts to shut out her words.

Eva voices political desire, and a belief that the utopian horizon may be already present—"*Strong   with the not yet   in the now*"—while "a melody, ghost-thin, hovered on her lips." It is her nonlinguistic and nonmusical noises, though, that most effectively turn her language and song into what the story describes as sounds: a sonic mixture in which it is precisely those parts that cannot be adequately transcribed that allow the meaningful whole to be fully heard.

As the ghostly melody wends through Eva's words, her singing first sparks resentment from her husband, who feels excluded. David imagines "that for seventy years she had hidden a tape recorder, infinitely microscopic, within her, that it had coiled infinite mile on mile, trapping every song, every melody, every word read, heard, and spoken—and that maliciously she was playing back what said nothing of him." His paranoid metaphor of auditory surveillance and tape editing is based on his memory of Eva listening to a phonograph record, lifting the needle when he entered the room. Yet the song she sings has been preserved most meaningfully as something at once less concrete and more alive than a record or a tape.

Following Eva's scrambled Hugo quotation, we learn what song is haunting her deathbed. She sings the whole first verse of a song based on a utopian 1880 poem by John Addington Symonds, described in the story as "a song of their youth of belief":

> *These things shall be, a loftier race*
> *than e'er the world hath known shall rise*
> *with flame of freedom in their souls*
> *and light of knowledge in their eyes.*

Following the first verse, Eva then sings most of the song's second and finally trails off with a fragment of the fourth and final verse, interrupted by the noise—again, more pointed to than properly transcribed—of her unruly body: "*And every life* (long strangling cough) *shall be a song.*"

Eva dies a few pages later, so we'd be forgiven for thinking that her broken song represents an ongoing desire for transformation—indeed, an expectation of it—that is undermined, even canceled out, by the demise of the person voicing it. A reader might take her death as the death of political desire itself.

But the story gives us clear indication that this desire survives beyond Eva's own life. The lyrics of her song's last line are difficult to take seriously as an actual prediction of the future. But here the line is interrupted by a "long strangling cough"—an ongoing spasm of sound produced amid and by constriction. This sound changes the line from an invalid expectation into a complex experience of ongoing desire in spite of its nonfulfillment. Eva's disappointment actively shapes her speech and song; it makes her words unignorable.

David's first reaction to his wife's ongoing desire is sarcasm: "In the twentieth century, hah!" he scoffs, dismissing the Hugo quote and throwing down cards in a bitter game of solitaire. But Eva's music-noise amalgam cuts through his defenses. Just after "*And every life* (long strangling cough) *shall be a song*," Olsen writes,

> Without warning, the bereavement and betrayal he had sheltered—
> compounded through the years—hidden even from himself—
> revealed itself,
> > uncoiled,
> > released,
> > *sprung*

To convey the effect Eva's sounds have on David, Olsen uses literary form that turns the page into a sonic score of sorts. Eva's performances are typeset with line breaks, italics, and unusual indentations, but this is the first place in the story where anything else is laid out the same way. Eva's disappointed desires are summoning forth her husband's repressed grief, and Olsen represents this on the page by allowing the choppy, unfluid, emphatic cadence of Eva's utterances to reshape David's discourse.

As Eva's sounds affect her husband, he begins to mourn for their shared "youth of belief," their past collective aspirations to make the twentieth century a time of peace. "Lost, how much I lost," he whispers, in tears. "'Aaah, children,' he said out loud, 'how we believed, how we belonged.'" The sound of this song-noise hybrid pushes him to acknowledge loss and to imagine explaining it to his children. Eva's paramusical soundings, which Olsen transcribes using a combination of descriptive words and typographic elements, allow her ongoing desire to extend beyond the boundaries of her lifetime.

The story asks what it means to go on orienting one's life according to a transformation that has not arrived, and how such a seemingly dead-end commitment could have a future. Olsen's investment in these questions was far from impersonal. When she began publishing in the early 1930s, she was also active in Left politics, and she quickly became a rising star of the Communist-affiliated proletarian literature movement. The revolutionary horizon seemed tantalizingly close back then; in a biographical note she sent to *Partisan Review*'s Philip Rahv in 1934, she wrote—as a young mother—that she was raising a "future citizeness for Soviet America."[8] She sold a proposed proletarian novel to Random House but was never able to complete it.[9] The outline she drew up shows that the final section was to be set after the revolution, but she never managed to write it: the transformation she desired was apparently impossible for her to render properly in narrative. She abandoned the novel, writing in a postcard to her editor, "I have decided not to publish this book. It's too lousy. I guess there isn't anything more to say."[10] She wrote little for nearly two decades.

By the time she returned to fiction writing in the late 1950s, with the McCarthy era in full swing, the Soviet America she once expected would have looked very far away. "Tell Me a Riddle" was among the first stories Olsen completed after beginning to write again—one of her first opportunities to reckon imaginatively with what it had been like to go on yearning for a new postcapitalist world that was no longer on its way. She spoke of the story as being based on conflicts between her own mother and father, who had been politically active in Russia before moving to the United States. Yet in the long afterlife of 1930s US Communism, David's incredulous question—"Still you believed?"—likely resounded for Olsen herself. How could one hold to a belief in a transformation whose time had passed, or keep alive a desire for a revolutionary horizon no longer visible?

"*Still* you believed?" suggests an error: to believe in something that has already failed to occur is to be mistaken. But in "Tell Me a Riddle," the past tense in which David frames that belief contrasts with Eva's continued attachment to the future tense, which the story commits to as well: "These things shall be," the first line of Eva's song, also serves as the story's unattributed epigraph. Her desire for a different world is disappointed and persistent at once, and it finds ongoing form in the chorus formed by an old song, the noises of a dying body, and the heartfelt lament of its living listener. Eva's remembered song, punctuated by nonverbal noises that register both disappointment and the persistent mediating presence of her body, highlights the important work of paramusical soundings—and of Olsen's transcriptive practices approximating them—in conveying disappointed desires across history.

Disappointments of the Popular Front

When Tillie Olsen joined the Young Communist League in the early 1930s, it was a heady time for Communism in the United States. Since 1928, the Communist Party, in the United States and elsewhere, had been guided by a party line stating that worldwide revolution was right around the corner, and that the working class must be properly organized in order to lead it. This was called Third Period ideology: the idea that global capitalism had entered its third and final historical phase. It spurred the revolutionary certitude that allowed Olsen to write in her *Partisan Review* bio, without any apparent irony (though not without a certain élan), the line about rearing a "future citizeness for Soviet America." Many Americans looked at the apparent success of the Soviet Union, contrasted it with the privations of the Great Depression at home, and concluded that the future clearly belonged to Communism. The party's membership in the United States more than tripled between 1930 and 1934.[11]

In the mid-1930s, the Communist party line changed dramatically. As Adolf Hitler and Benito Mussolini built power across Europe and threatened the stability of the Soviet Union, the Communist International decided to abandon the Third Period ideology, adopting instead the United or Popular Front approach: a strategy of building broad coalitions to combat the worldwide rise of fascism. The Popular Front's implementation in the United States was codified at a June 1936 gathering where the party resolved to work in coalition with labor unions and the Democratic Party. Third Period cadres had looked forward to a Soviet state stretching from sea to shining sea, but Popular Front–era Communists now reprinted the text of the Declaration of Independence in the *Daily Worker*'s Fourth of July issue, driving home its new slogan that Communism was twentieth-century Americanism.[12] In the wake of the rebranding, white-collar workers and professionals streamed into the party.

Cultural and political historians have long argued that this shift to the Popular Front was a good move for Left politics and a good move for political art.[13] The Third Period's political line had indeed been divisive in many ways, such as the stance of demonizing liberals and socialists as "social fascists," which prohibited pragmatic coalition building. Popular Front culture was in many ways more inclusive, appealing to broad audiences and spreading leftish ideals in accessible formats.

Yet this change also entailed significant losses and spurred real disappointments that are rarely discussed. For one thing, it came with a drastic change in the party's approach to race and racism. In the first decades of the twentieth century, the white Left in the United States had by and large treated race as solely an epiphenomenon of class, which led to organizing strategies that denied the significance of racism and held little appeal for African Americans. This changed in 1928, when the Communist International adopted a line known as the Black Belt thesis, coauthored by African American Communist Harry Haywood. The Black Belt thesis framed US racism as a variant of imperialism whereby the American nation was subjugating a distinct nation of Black people within its borders, especially in the majority-Black areas of the American South. "Self-determination for the Black Belt!" ran the slogan, which was debated, pro and con, in the pages of the NAACP's *Crisis* magazine in May 1935. The Black Belt thesis itself was not universally embraced by Black activists, even Communist-adjacent ones. But by most accounts, the Communist Party in the Third Period era really did consider battling racism—the common phrase for it was "white chauvinism"—to be a key party priority, with the party devoting significant resources to organizing African Americans and to educating white party members on how to combat their own racism.[14] While setting itself in direct opposition to more middle-class Black community institutions such as churches and the NAACP, the Communist Party organized high-profile campaigns against lynchings and Jim Crow, and it coordinated the legal defense for the Black teenagers falsely accused of sexual assault in the Scottsboro case. On occasion, party members who showed signs of white chauvinism were critiqued and corrected; the party put at least two men on trial for it, one in Harlem and one in Milwaukee.[15] The Milwaukee trial, in 1933, drew the favorable attention of the Black newspaper the *Chicago Defender,* which asked, "Is there any other political, religious, or civic organization in the country that would go to such lengths to prove itself not unfriendly to us?"[16]

The Popular Front era's new openness to coalition building led to a watering down of the party's antiracist priorities. The intense self-criticism around white chauvinism petered out, and the Black Belt slogan was all but abandoned.[17] After 1935, the Communist Party in Alabama, embracing the new big-tent approach, on several occasions made common cause with groups that enforced segregation, and it endorsed an elected official whose Klan affiliations drew protest from Black people.[18] Many Black members quit the state party.

The ideological shift brought other disappointments as well. The task of organizing workers to lead the revolution and create authentically working-class revolutionary culture was no longer as important as attracting a wide range of people to the party. Richard Wright's memoir "I Tried to Be a Communist" records his experience of this change. When the Popular Front began, he had been working at the party's behest for the John Reed Clubs, organizations that encouraged young workers with little or no literary training to express themselves in writing. Now he was summarily told that the John Reed Clubs were being dissolved and replaced with the American Writers Congress, a group aimed at organizing famous writers to sign on to a broadly progressive, but not necessarily revolutionary, agenda. Wright recounts, "I asked what was to become of the young writers whom the Communist Party had implored to join the clubs and who were ineligible for the new group, and there was no answer. 'This thing is cold!' I exclaimed to myself. 'To effect a swift change in policy, the Communist Party was dumping one organization, then organizing a new scheme with entirely new people!'"[19] The speedy reorientation had effects beyond the merely organizational. In a July 1937 essay published in the *Saturday Review of Literature*, the critic Alan Calmer wrote that the Popular Front, by doing away with the doctrinal certitude that had made Third Period Communism a reassuring scaffold for creative work, was proving disastrous for writers: "It was a relief to see the old 'leftist' excesses routed, but these excessive emphases were wiped out so thoroughly that there remained no (Marxian) emphasis at all. . . . The collapse in the demand for his work from the dwindling leftwing literary press, together with his own confused dissatisfaction over the earlier agitational forms of expression, topped off by the fear that the contradiction between political tactics and art was insoluble at least in the present era, sent him staggering. Largely for this reason, there has been an alarming mortality of youthful talents."[20] For Calmer, then, the Popular Front represented not an enabling period of creative permissiveness but a newly debilitating absence of faith in the possibilities of left-wing literature. According to Calmer, this was the case not just for him but for many others as well, and this quite likely included the members of the John Reed Clubs, who, as Wright recognized, were being abruptly abandoned by the party.

This was the political backdrop of Olsen's decision to abandon her proletarian novel. The rise of the Popular Front entailed the loss, at least for some artists whose careers were not already fully established, of a reassuring and artistically enabling conception of the importance of properly revolutionary art: a sense, that is, that they could make anything that might matter to the world.

Communists and fellow travelers also lost the expectation of imminent revolution, a once-common note in party-related messaging that faded out in the mid-1930s, and they lost the clear focus on a politicized working class that was to bring it about. The Third Period's emphasis on "workers" was replaced in many places with "the people" or "Americans": the Workers Music League, for instance, was dissolved and replaced with a new organization, the American Music League. If leftists had once been motivated by the seeming proximity of a revolutionary horizon, a new day breaking any moment thanks to a propitious lineup of global conditions and stark contradictions and bold action by workers, the outlook after the middle of the decade was far murkier.

The Popular Front focus on "the people" and "America" dovetailed with related trends in US culture around the same time, including a nationalistic drive to identify uniquely American cultural traditions and a nostalgic yearning to connect with the nation's preindustrial past in the face of modernist innovation.[21] One of the manifestations of this focus within the left, beginning in the mid-1930s, was an increasing interest in folk culture and folk music. The left-wing folk music revival wouldn't be in full swing for a few more years—a "Grapes of Wrath Evening" in March 1940, at which Woody Guthrie and Pete Seeger performed alongside Huddie Ledbetter, is often cited as its beginning—but the change was already under way by 1935. In that year, the anthology *Proletarian Literature in the United States* published folk-style protest lyrics alongside the more traditional genres of fiction, poetry, and literary journalism. A growing interest in folk music also helped reshape the leftist Workers Music League, where modernist composers including Charles Seeger had striven to impress Arnold Schoenberg protégé Hanns Eisler and to pen the next revolutionary anthem to rival the "Internationale." When the group was dissolved in 1936, then relaunched as the American Music League, its new mission statement proclaimed a determination "to collect, study, and popularize American folk music and its traditions"—a project that Charles Seeger's son Pete would soon take on.[22]

This was the context within which Ledbetter, an African American guitarist and singer, became a headlining figure in New York City's left-wing cultural scene in the mid-1930s. It also helped set the stage for an intriguing detail Ledbetter added to his singing after the end of Third Period ideology, a paramusical gesture that I will argue makes audible some of these undersung disappointments of the Popular Front.

Take This Hammer: Lead Belly and Transcribing
the Sounds of Labor

On June 22, 1937, Huddie Ledbetter recorded the worksong "Julie Ann Johnson" for the Library of Congress.[23] He had recorded the song several times before, but he performed it differently this time. Having begun his musical career playing in Texas and Louisiana and then continued to hone his craft during several prison sentences, he had spent some time after his release collaborating with the folklorist John Lomax, who had met him on a song-collecting trip to Louisiana's Angola Prison. Ledbetter's vast repertoire, finger-picking prowess, and clarion baritone made him a hit among the folklorists in Lomax's academic networks. By the time Ledbetter made the 1937 recording of "Julie Ann Johnson," though, he had broken with Lomax and had settled into a career playing music for audiences connected with leftist circles in New York City.

On the 1937 recording, Ledbetter prefaces "Julie Ann Johnson" with a brief explanation that nods to the folklorists' love of taxonomy and authenticity. "An axe-cutting song," he announces. "When the boss is down yonder in Texas, presently you have double-headed axes. And it's about fifteen or twenty men on the log. And when I'll give the word 'Julie Ann Johnson,' well, all the axes fall together. Not one axe, but every axe got to fall right on the log at the same time."[24] Formally, Ledbetter is showing how conversant he is with the sort of authoritative categorization his previous academic audiences would have appreciated—"an axe-cutting song"—while his narrative content offers a vision of solidarity, attunement, and collective rhythm that would have been especially attractive to his Popular Front–era leftist audiences in New York: "Not one axe, but every axe got to fall right on the log at the same time."

A moment later, we hear an indication that there's something else at work that neither the folklore field nor the activist milieu can entirely account for in narrative. A cappella, Ledbetter sings out the words "Julie Ann Johnson" on a descending and rising third, and then, in the pause before the next line, he expels a bit of air from his lungs, making a sound that isn't present on his previous recordings of the song. It's decidedly audible but not quite vocalized, something like a *huh*. His singing voice grows quieter as this verse goes on, suggesting that Ledbetter has turned his head away from the mic lest his exhalation overwhelm the equipment. The three *huh*s in this verse become progressively less forceful, a bit breathier, as if in this way, too, he is experimenting with a new element rather than repeating something well practiced.

The verse is over, and before starting the next, he again describes the rhythmic cooperation between workers. "When I holler 'Julie Ann Johnson,' the other fellows answer. Every time the axes fall between them, they've got the rhythm going right on." He presents himself as a song leader in the field, acting as not just an explicator of manual labor but an orchestrator of it. In the next verse, he issues one hoarse and raspy *heh*, then one barely there exhalation, and then one pause with no audible breath at all; he's still exploring how it sounds, perhaps wondering how his listeners will respond. The recording fades out on the third verse.

Within a few years, this sound would become a central, deliberate, voiced element of the song. In a 1940 recording he made for a commercial release with the Golden Gate Quartet, multiple singers, perhaps all five of them, rasp out a decisively vocalized *hah*, rhythmically accented, which grows louder, more sustained, and ever closer to speech as the song continues, accelerates, and picks up layers of harmonies.

It's impossible to say for certain why Ledbetter added this sound to his singing when he did, what prompted him to amplify it as time went along, or what made the sound such an iconic gesture that another song featuring the same sound, "Take This Hammer," became one of his signature tunes, perhaps second only to "Good Night, Irene." But we do know that Ledbetter and his leftist audiences in this period would likely have been feeling keenly the immense ideological and cultural changes that were under way on the Communist left. For a listenership that was being told to forget about Black workers (and possibly felt reluctant to do so) and get on board with folk music instead, Ledbetter offered his audiences a politically acceptable way to keep alive the dream of a revolutionary Black working class. And adding a paramusical, not-quite-transcribable sound of labor to his performances proved a particularly powerful way for him to do it.

An agile performer with an extensive mental catalog of songs and an acute ability to read a crowd, Ledbetter adjusted his performances throughout his career to changing demands, remaking himself at times as a bluesman, a political commentator, even a popular children's musician. One incident from the annals of the proto–folk revival speaks to his ability to switch modes on the fly. In the mid-1930s, Ledbetter played two nights at Camp Unity, a racially integrated summer resort in upstate New York, where the composer Earl Robinson worked booking musicians. The first night, Ledbetter scandalized his audiences with songs of rough-and-tumble working-class African American life. These songs jarred with the respectability-based racial politics of the audience, and Robinson let Ledbetter know it.

> A lot of left-wingers, especially black people, were upset with this man from the South—they called him Uncle Tom—because he would pass the hat after he sang, and do a little buck and wing, and they were trying to get out of that image . . . of Negro people being second class. The first night . . . he sang songs about prostitutes and yeller-gals and gun-toting-razor-slashing, black "niggers" and stuff like that, and this was anathema, this was terrible for these people in this camp who were striving so hard for equality. And so, "What kind of person is this to bring here? What kind of good does he do for equality or anything else?"[25]

"The camp," Robinson recalled in another account, "was in an uproar."[26]

His second night, Ledbetter added other songs to his set list, explicit protest songs he'd written recently that trod more predictable terrain for his audience: his class-conscious anti–Jim Crow song "Bourgeois Blues" and his song about the Scottsboro case. This performance calmed the uproar, and Ledbetter's position in the left-wing cultural sphere was safe. Similarly, his decision to introduce the *hah* could well have grown out of an astute realization that his audiences were missing something—a sense of a proximate revolution, brought about by a strong, militant Black working class—that he could evoke for them sonically.

Another reason for his shift could be related to his breaking ties with John Lomax—who for all his fascination with folk culture was still an old-school Texan with distinctly traditional ideas about race—and linking up with John's young, radical, New York–based son Alan. John Lomax had trained at Harvard in the then-nascent field of folklore studies, at a moment when the field's adherents were eager to distinguish it from the similarly young field of theater studies. Academic folklorists took a wary view of theatricality, which they associated with femininity and inauthenticity. Accordingly, John Lomax discouraged Ledbetter from overtly theatrical performative displays. Outbursts of breath, mimetic of hard labor, would not likely have been welcomed.[27]

Alan Lomax's ideas about performance, ethnography, race, and transcription, on the other hand, were deeply influenced by his working relationship with Zora Neale Hurston, who did not share the elder Lomax's purist attitude toward folklore. Alan became a fan of Hurston's after reading her anthropological account "Hoodoo in America," published in the *Journal of American Folklore* in 1931. In the summer of 1935, he invited her along on a folklore-collecting trip to Georgia and Florida. Alan was eager to learn from Hurston, and Hurston hoped to hold his work to a high standard of precision and depth; as she wrote in a letter to his father that summer, "I carefully insisted that he see further than the surface of things. There has been too much loose talk and conclusions arrived at without sufficient proof. So I tried to make him do and see clearly so that no one can come after him and refute him."[28] The connection between the two folklorists recently led Jessica Teague to conclude that "Alan Lomax's model for transcribing the voice came from Zora Neale Hurston."[29] Teague makes this assertion with reference to Lomax's later work transcribing oral histories with Jelly Roll Morton for the 1950 book *Mister Jelly Roll,* but Lomax's work with Hurston may well have led him to encourage Ledbetter to amplify his paramusical soundings as well.

It's helpful, then, to think about this intriguing addition to Ledbetter's music as taking form in conversation with the interests of his collaborators and the desires of his changing audiences—desires that by 1937 were becoming decidedly disappointed, in ways that had no means of easy expression. At this key moment in the history of the American Left, during a time when Ledbetter sang frequently for gatherings of Communists and fellow travelers, he began punctuating his renditions of worksongs with percussive exhalations of breath that represented manual labor and its power—the repressed voice of the Black worker. The very month that Calmer was writing his piece about Popular Front disappointment for the *Saturday Review,* Ledbetter was stepping up to a microphone for the Library of Congress and softly, experimentally, adding sounds of labor to his recorded music.

I'm calling the *hah* a sound of labor in part because it's never entirely clear whether Ledbetter intends the sound to approximate a tool employed in manual labor, a sharp expulsion of a worker's breath, or a deliberately ambiguous amalgam of these that is more about the moment of impact and exertion than about the precise object causing the sound. In a 1940s radio recording of "Take This Hammer" for an audience of children, Ledbetter spotlights the question of who says *hah* and he leaves the results inconclusive. Calling "Take This Hammer" his "theme worksong," he tells the children, "There's something a little funny about that song, different from all the other type of worksongs. Every time the hammer said *hah*—the men—the hammer falls."[30] Here Ledbetter seems to conflate the hammer and the men, as if distinguishing them is irrelevant, or as if the confusion of the worker with the work is itself the point. Outside the prison, the sound of breath archives the sound of the tool with which it would have originally sounded in unison. Because the sound of breath can't easily be heard by an audience until the sound of the tool, which had drowned it out, is gone, the sound of breath simultaneously proves the tool's absence and makes that absence speak, an ambivalent sonic memorial at the represented site of manual labor. Breath isn't just about work, though; it's also about life itself. Within a context of anti-Blackness, as Ashon Crawley points out, to perform and draw attention to one's breath "from within the zone of blackness . . . is to offer a critical performative intervention into the western juridical apparatus of violent control, repression, and yes, premature death."[31]

The sound also posed a difficulty for transcription, standing as a sort of countertranscriptive practice in Ledbetter's music. All folk songs, practically by definition, present some difficulties for the transcriber, and transcription is sometimes understood to have a carceral and murderous relationship to songs: John Lomax once wrote, "Worse than thieves are ballad collectors, for when they capture and imprison in cold type a folk song, at the same time they kill it."[32] But work sounds, unpitched, created by tools and breath, inhabiting the border between music and noise, are especially resistant to transcription, potentially enabling a song to escape incarceration and death.

The history of transcribed American folk song is full of disagreement over how to transcribe paramusical soundings generated by manual labor. In the 1899 book *Old Plantation Hymns*, William Eleazar Barton notated the sound of steel on rock with a D-sharp, as if the tool and stone were themselves members of a multivoiced chorus, sounding first a dissonant major seventh, then a more stable major third (Figure 2.1).[33] In the accompanying text, Barton writes, "A single musical phrase of a succession of a half dozen notes caught on a visit to such a place sticks in one's mind forever. Even as I write I seem to be in a tunnel of this description and to hear the sharp metallic stroke and the syncopated chant." Here, as we saw with Olsen's "Tell Me a Riddle," the paramusical sounding of the *Chink! Chink!* causes an otherwise unremarkable musical phrase to "stick in one's mind forever." Barton was primarily a church leader and writer, not a musicologist. Yet in notating a work sound on an approximated pitch, Barton was in step with the guidelines for

2.1 "Railroad Song," in William Eleazar Barton, *Old Plantation Hymns* (Boston: Lamson, Wolffe, 1899).

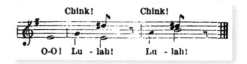

transcribing percussion that the French composer Hector Berlioz had set out in his widely used 1844 book *A Treatise upon Modern Instrumentation and Orchestration,* where unpitched percussion instruments are given approximate pitch values—the side drum is assigned a low D, the tambourine a higher A—and notated with ordinary notes.[34]

The Berlioz text was still au courant in the early twentieth century—a New York–based publisher brought out a new edition in 1904—but Natalie Curtis Burlin's 1918 Hampton songbook broke with his practice, using innovative notations to signify exhalations. Rather than assigning a pitch to the sounds, she transcribed them as headless note stems. And by combining a comma with a parenthetical exclamation at the end of a line of lyrics, she produced an unfinished syntax, a punctuational purgatory in which the *huh!*'s ambiguous status, neither fully part of the song's lyrics nor entirely external to them, unsettles the song's syntactic structure (Figure 2.2).

Burlin did not use this strategy exclusively. Offering just the lyrics in the course of an essay discussing hammering songs, Burlin underlines not only the "huh!" but other sung syllables as well, so that the breath is left with no distinctive notation at all (Figure 2.3). Here, too, a certain conflation of the hammer and the breath can be seen as upending the very possibility of musical transcription.

Within the Lomaxes' 1934 book *American Ballads and Folk Songs,* several songs include the sound of tools falling or breath being expelled, and a range of notations are used. Sometimes such a sound is written as a note bearing the same pitch as the note preceding it—to which it is sometimes joined with a tie and sometimes not—and bearing a duration much longer than such an exhalation was likely to have lasted. In Figure 2.4, for example, a "violent exhalation of breath" is supposed to continue for a full two beats, an effect that, in addition to being very different from anything audible on the Lomaxes' recordings of such sounds, would be almost physically impossible to produce. In other places within this same book, such sounds are transcribed as headless note stems, as in the Burlin scores; sometimes they show up as mere accent marks over words; and in some cases, the Lomaxes decline to transcribe the sound on a staff at all but merely write an underlined "huh!"

In 1934, Alan Calmer—not yet disappointed by the Popular Front—reviewed the Lomaxes' *American Ballads and Folk Songs* in the Communist literary magazine *New Masses.* His review criticized the book for not including enough songs that voiced overt, explicit protest against racism or bosses, along the lines of the "Negro Songs of Protest" Lawrence Gellert had been publishing in *New*

148

2.2 "Hammerin' Song: Choral Harmonies," in Natalie Curtis Burlin, *Negro Folk-Songs: The Hampton Series, Books I–IV, Complete* (Mineola, NY: Dover, 2001). Originally published in 1918–1919 by G. Schirmer, New York.

Ain't no ham-mer—huh!
In dis moun-tain—huh!
        Ring like mine—huh!
        Ring like mine—huh!

Capt'n tol'-me—huh!
Heard ma ham-mer—huh!
        Forty-nine mile—huh!
        Forty-nine mile—huh!

*Hammer falls here, while the men expel their breath with a sharp ejaculation.

2.3 "Hammerin' Song," in Natalie Curtis Burlin, *Negro Folk-Songs: The Hampton Series, Books I–IV, Complete* (Mineola, NY: Dover, 2001). Originally published in 1918–1919 by G. Schirmer, New York.

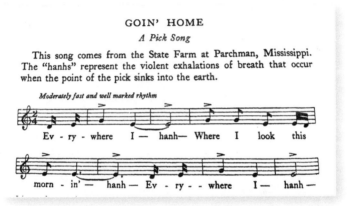

GOIN' HOME

A Pick Song

This song comes from the State Farm at Parchman, Mississippi. The "hanhs" represent the violent exhalations of breath that occur when the point of the pick sinks into the earth.

Moderately fast and well marked rhythm

Ev - ry - where   I — hanh— Where I look this

morn - in' — hanh — Ev - ry - - where   I — hanh —

2.4 "Goin' Home," in John Lomax and Alan Lomax, *American Ballads and Folk Songs* (Mineola, NY: Dover, 1994). Originally published in 1934 by Macmillan, New York.

Masses.[35] But Calmer also remarked on the tool and exhalation sounds as a particularly noteworthy part of the book, writing approvingly that when the book transcribes axe blows and audible exhalations, it demonstrates how the "songs are rough, homespun workers' products" with melodies that are "born out of the rhythms of their labor."[36] Calmer's review supports my assertion that people who experienced a loss in the shift from the Third Period to the Popular Front may well have been particularly interested in the way labor itself shaped music through the inclusion of sounds of tools and breath. In 1934, this interest could still be expressed plainly in songbooks and in the pages of *New Masses*. But its eligibility for such explicit acknowledgment was about to change.

As we have seen, such sounds had been regular features of transcriptions of worksongs since at least 1899. The Lomaxes' 1934 volume was doing nothing unusual by including them. Yet something changed between 1934 and 1936, between *American Ballads and Folk Songs* and the Lomaxes' next book. Their next book was *Negro Folk Songs as Sung by Lead Belly*, and it transcribed no such sounds at all.

Of course, we have no recorded evidence that Ledbetter had begun introducing those sounds into his performances by the time the Lomaxes and ethnomusicologist George Herzog were transcribing the singer's early recordings for the book. But it is striking that starting in 1936 and throughout the second half of the 1930s, almost none of the major published collections of African American or leftist songs transcribe work sounds. The sounds are occasionally mentioned in the explanatory texts that accompany the transcriptions, but in the Lomaxes' 1936 *Lead Belly* book, in Gellert's *Negro Songs of Protest* collection of the same year, and in the 1937 Communist songbook *Songs of the People*, which includes many folk songs ascribed to African American sources, these sounds have completely disappeared from the musical transcriptions themselves. The only book from this period where I have found work sounds transcribed is by an African American arranger, J. Rosamond Johnson's *Rolling Along in Song* of 1937. In this transcription (see Figure 2.5), Johnson uses an *x* on a note stem, while the parentheses around the "Huh" serve several possible purposes: giving the "Huh" a unique notation that clearly distinguishes it from sung syllables, potentially marking the "Huh" as approximating rather than directly indexing its sonic referent, and perhaps, too, notating the occlusion under which such sounds were operating, especially in musical notation, by 1937.

During the first four decades of the twentieth century, in the work of white transcribers and in explicitly left-wing publications, work sounds went from being difficult to notate yet interesting enough to merit the effort, to vanishing from transcription altogether. At the same time that the figure of the worker and the worker's body became both unspeakable and ungrievable on the Communist left, the sound of the body at work—and specifically of the Black body at work—was being erased from white people's transcriptions of African American worksongs.

But what if Ledbetter's audiences—Black as well as white—hadn't relinquished an attachment to the idea of the worker, or of the redemptive power of a militant Black worker in particular, even if such attachment was no longer easily writable? As a sensitive performer keenly attuned to the desires of his

He's A-Choppin' in de New Groun'

178

audiences, Ledbetter would have had a clear understanding that these desires had not faded when their presence on paper did. And he knew, as well, that what can't be easily written can still find sonic form.

The worksong that would become Ledbetter's most well known was a representation both of labor and of its refusal. Ledbetter first recorded "Take This Hammer" for a 1940 album consisting entirely of prison songs; according to John Szwed, Alan Lomax taught Ledbetter the song specifically for this album.[37] It became a staple of his repertoire for the remainder of his too-brief career, and shortly after his death it became a signature song for the folksinger Odetta. The lyrics are as follows:

> Take this hammer *(hah!)* and carry it to the captain *(hah!)*
> Take this hammer *(hah!)* and carry it to the captain *(hah!)*
> Take this hammer *(hah!)* and carry it to the captain *(hah!)*
> Tell him I'm gone, tell him I'm gone
>
> If he asks you *(hah!)* was I runnin' *(hah!)*
> Tell him I was flyin', tell him I was flyin'
>
> If he asks you *(hah!)* was I laughin' *(hah!)*
> Tell him I was cryin', tell him I was cryin'
>
> They wanna feed me *(hah!)* cornbread and molasses *(hah!)*
> But I got my pride, well I got my pride

By registering a laborer's fantasy of walking off the job, "Take This Hammer" gives form to the departure of the worker, and of the militant Black worker in particular, from leftist discourse, suggesting a possibly liberatory dimension of that departure. The figure of the revolutionary worker may have been welcome for leftists who were missing the certainty and optimism of the Third Period. But for people whom that figure cast in a romanticized and taxing role, it also fed fantasies of refusal and flight.

"Take this hammer," Ledbetter sang, "and carry it to the captain." The hammer, a staple of the worksong genre, represents, directly, work itself; it represents via synecdoche the militant worker; it represents via symbolism half of the Communist insignia; and, sung in the voice of a Black Southerner, it represents the political power some Communists had understood that African Americans could bring to a political movement that truly and reliably prioritized their interests—a movement that, it increasingly appeared (even if Communists were slow to realize it), would have to be led by African Americans themselves.

The hammer in the song becomes inoperative, out of service, but still materially persistent, with undimmed powers of expression—still able, in its inoperative state, to *tell* somebody something. But in the same gesture it also passes out of the hands of the worker and into the hands of the captain—just as the dream of a world-historical proletariat was being relinquished, under the Popular Front, to a chain of command altered and defined by the new exigencies of wartime. With the hammer's sound stilled, all that's left is the breath: *hah!*

Now that the Left was less focused on workers' power and antiracism, listeners' desires regarding these political objects could no longer be adequately invoked through narratives like the short texts with which Ledbetter had formerly prefaced his songs, and they could no longer be approximated in most published transcriptions. Difficult to account for in text, these political desires found voice instead in a sound that had never been encapsulated by any of its transcriptions and that was therefore well positioned to survive attempts to erase it. At least some of Ledbetter's listeners still longed to be on the side of radical workers and Black self-determination, and Ledbetter found this way to give sonic form to their untimely desires through the paramusical sounding of labored breath.

One important question remains. What attitude accompanies Ledbetter's performance here? If his leftist audiences longed for a symbol of their lost object, a heroic Black worker to lead them all to revolution, and if Ledbetter performed for them as that worker between the lines (as Hortense Spillers would say) of his worksong, we need not assume that he gave it to them straight.[38] Like the song's speaker, who boldly walks off the job or at least fantasizes openly about it, Ledbetter might not have been showing up for his own job without protest.

His performance could well be a version of what Sonnet Retman, building on Henry Louis Gates Jr.'s work, has theorized as "signifying ethnography," a use of "repetition and reversal" to "implicat[e] the ethnographer and the reader"—or, in this case, the listener—"in the activity of searching for 'the authentic.'"[39] After all, Ledbetter did end up choosing, as what he would later call his "theme worksong," a song about refusing to work, about the pain and indignity of the work site. Against his listeners' idealization of labor, Ledbetter posed a protest and a quitting.

This, then, is not just a sound of disappointment. It is also a sound of a multiracial collaboration in which political desire is voiced across divides in a way that makes critique possible, rather than shutting it down in a premature act of self-congratulation that effective solidarity has already been achieved. Here we find an acknowledgment and performance of a collective political desire, combined with an act of signifying that communicates, at least to a careful listener, a critique of the way such desire puts some people in a compromised, marginal, or overly symbolized role. It's a sound not of solidarity, exactly, but of the desire for it, and of its possible conditions.

Decades later, the civil rights folksinger Odetta, who would sing "Take This Hammer" with a guttural roar for much of her career, talked about her love of the worksongs. She said they were connected with "the anger, the venom, the hatred of myself and everybody else and everything else. I could get my rocks off within those worksongs and things, without having to say, 'I hate you and I hate me, and'—well, you can't even do that now, you know."[40]

If Odetta heard that in the songs, and in the noises that hitched a ride with them—heard their ability to convey untimely and even impossible feelings, to say the otherwise unsayable—surely some of Ledbetter's disappointed audiences heard it too.

"O Yes" and White Tears

But what of those who could scarcely bear to listen? Tillie Olsen's short story "O Yes," written in 1956 and far less well known than "Tell Me a Riddle," offers up scenes of failed solidarity, and of possible listening across racialized difference that collapses into agonizing overidentification; it grants a clearer sense of both the possibilities and the limitations that come into play when paramusical soundings seek an adequate hearing across difference.

"O Yes" is one of the three short stories that accompany the longer "Tell Me a Riddle" in Olsen's classic 1961 fiction collection, which is also titled *Tell Me a Riddle*. This story focuses on a friendship between two girls that is becoming strained as the girls enter middle school, and on the reactions of the girls' respective mothers to the changes in that relationship.

In the story's first scene, which occupies half of its twenty-two pages, Carol (who is white and, it is strongly implied, of Jewish heritage) attends her childhood friend Parialee's baptism at a Black storefront church.[41] The emotional singing, the preacher's dramatic sermon, and the ecstatic experience of another schoolmate in attendance overwhelm Carol to the point where she faints and has to be carried out of the building. In the second half of the story, a pop song on the radio reminds Carol of the service, and she cries about the end of her friendship with Parialee and about the racism she sees at school, finally lamenting, "Oh why is it like it is and why do I have to care?"[42] She says she feels like the racist acts are happening to her too. If this all sounds like a cringeworthy white-tears elegy for interracial solidarity, I'd like to argue that this quality is precisely what makes the story worth reading. It's intellectually as well as politically important to account for failures of solidarity and to be curious about what apparently well-meaning white people make of their fantasies when a perceived possibility of interracial cooperation seems to fade.

In the church service, Carol is discomfited from the start. She is disturbed first by seeing a boy from her math class singing in the choir, by her worry that he now might try to talk to her at school where other kids could see, and by her difficulty in reading his facial expression ("sullen or troubled, though it is hard to tell").[43] She then becomes troubled by her inability to analyze the polyrhythmic song she hears. Within the African American church service, where, as Spillers details, "reading" occurs through the ear and hinges on hearing what is audible between the lines of scripture, Carol finds herself functionally illiterate.[44] "If it were a record," Olsen writes, "she would play it over and over, Carol thought, to untwine the intertwined voices, to search how the many rhythms rock apart and yet are one glad rhythm."[45] Carol fantasizes about being able to tame and analyze the multiple rhythms through repetition, to gain mastery over a heterogeneous solidarity by disaggregating it, "untwin[ing] the intertwined voices," and to remain, herself, safely outside the collectivity this music registers and performs.

Her wish to play the song on a recorded loop recalls the part in "Tell Me a Riddle" where David bitterly imagines Eva as harboring an internal tape recorder, "trapping every song, every melody, every word read, heard, and spoken."[46] In both cases, sound recording appears as an act of surveillance and control. Carol wishes to objectify the music she hears, to make an artifact and its study replace a living practice. A little later in the story, as the preacher's and congregants' sounds further alarm her, she longs to make a record that could downsize the proceedings and edit out the noisiest parts: "If she could make what was happening (*what* was happening?) into a record small and round to listen to far and far as if into a seashell—the stamp and rills and spirals all tiny (but never any screaming)."[47]

However much Olsen may indeed intend some critique of Carol's aspirational sound editing, she also sees herself as aligned with it. In 1988, Olsen told an interviewer that "O Yes" was the story where "I was able to reap for the first time [my] years and years of noting down the consummate way that black language was used. I had so many. Usually it was on phrases that I would put in my, either my three-by-six cards or the loose leaf little notebook, what I could jot down." Later in the interview, she refers to this miniaturizing activity as "noting," and she ends by saying, "I had, for years, in a sense, trained my tape-recorder ear."[48] "O Yes," then, is itself a transcription project, driven by a listener's fantasy of her ear as a powerful recording device capable of collecting the sounds of other cultures.

To distract herself from the singing and the preaching, Carol sinks into a reminiscence of the grade school she and Parialee, whose nickname is Parry, had attended. That school's name, Mann Elementary, evokes both the lineage of democratic public education, with its reference (we learn later in the story) to the nineteenth-century reformer Horace Mann, and the idea of universal humanity. The sonic memories Carol brings up to defend herself against the seemingly noisy difference of the church service are marked by playful reciprocity, symmetrical games where difference seems irrelevant and reversible: "Parry, do pepper. Carol, do pepper. Parry's bettern Carol, Carol's bettern Parry."[49]

"O Yes" was written two years after *Brown v. Board of Education,* mere months after the Montgomery bus boycott and the killing of Emmett Till. As a *Brown v. Board*–era story about two girls at an integrated school who nevertheless inhabit two increasingly different educational and social realities, "O Yes" implicitly questions the effectiveness of juridical reforms in dismantling systems of injustice that persist in the practices and attitudes of teachers and administrators. As a story from the early days of the civil rights era, a moment when the resilience and vulnerability of Black children were concertedly on display, "O Yes" aims to reckon, albeit clumsily, with the role of right-feeling white children (and their parents) in such a moment. "O Yes" also dates from the same year that Nikita Khrushchev delivered a famous speech decrying the late Joseph Stalin's failures as a leader, including revelations that shook the revolutionary faith of Communist sympathizers in the United States as elsewhere. In light of this and of Olsen's Communist affiliations, we can additionally read "O Yes" as another elegy for revolutionary certitude, and specifically for the sorts of interracial solidarity whose outlook had changed since the shift to the Popular Front.

The white characters in this story show no awareness of the nascent civil rights movement as an opportunity for a new solidarity. Any purchase on collective conceptions, other than some vague all-encompassing humanity, is inaccessible to them, reduced to an object of interracial envy. This makes the project of transcription that appears here an anxious and possessive one. The story can only move forward through paramusical soundings that throw that project off course.

The first few pages of "O Yes" are heavily punctuated by italicized quotations from real and invented spirituals. But soon this music, amenable to lyrical transcription in orderly couplets, gives way to paramusical soundings that the story can't contain. The turning point comes when Carol hears the first "scream":

Did someone scream?
It seemed someone screamed—[50]

This scream, which Ashon Crawley teaches us (unless we already knew) to understand as a whoop, a deliberate element of some African diasporic religious practice, is not transcribed in the story; it is only registered through the incredulous perception of the main character, who is not even certain what she's heard.[51] The story's soundtrack shifts at this point from spirituals to a sermon, and after the congregants begin to respond to the sermon—"the ushers brought a little woman out into the aisle, screaming and shaking"—Olsen turns over the story to the preacher and congregation for more than a full page, abandoning the controlling containment of quotation marks and allowing the antiphonal sermon to remake the story's form, much as Eva's fragmented utterances reshaped "Tell Me a Riddle."

> *Yes*
>
> When it seems you can't go on any longer, he's there. You can, he says, you can.
>
> *Yes*
>
> And the burden you been carrying—ohhhhh that burden—not for always will it be. No, not for always.
>
> *Stay with me, Lord*[52]

Just as Eva's sounds broke through to David in "Tell Me a Riddle," here the sounds of the congregants, the "powerful throbbing voices. Calling and answering to each other," allow the preacher's message of persistence amid difficulty, and of eventual redemption, to move Carol deeply. But she can't handle its intensity. Overwhelmed by the sounds and movements, by the sight of another girl from school convulsing in the tender hands of the ushers, by the sound of that girl's "torn, tearing cry," Carol is "drowned in the sluice of the slow singing and the sway."[53] She faints and has to be carried from the church.

At the end of "O Yes"—after intervening sections that focus on the experiences of Parialee's mother, Carol's mother, and finally Parialee herself—we find ourselves back with Carol and her hysterical listening. Upon hearing a song on the radio that reminds her of the spirituals from church, she literally rips the knob off the radio and "runs down the stairs, shrieking and shrieking," not in an embrace of breath and sound but in an attempt to cut them off: "Rocking and strangling the cries." She asks, belatedly, for an explanation of the sounds that have been haunting her: "Mother, why did they sing and scream like that? . . . I hear it all the time."[54]

Carol's mother, Helen, searches for a way to help Carol understand what she heard in church, and she knows several workable explanations, but she rejects them all. First she thinks of explaining that emotion is "*a characteristic of the religion of all oppressed peoples, yes your very own great-grandparents.*" She thinks of saying, "*The special history of the Negro people—history?—just you try living what must be lived every day—*"[55] Helen knows several possible analyses that would help locate Carol's confusion amid history, politics, and the specifics of her own heritage, but she seems to believe that it would be bad mothering to educate or contextualize. Instead she envelops Carol in a maternal embrace conducted in silence:

> And said nothing.
> And said nothing.
> And soothed and held.[56]

Why does Helen decide that mothering should involve only wordless comforting, even when explanation is precisely what the child requests? As the story's final moment will reveal, Helen's own overwhelming sense of lack prevents her from helping her daughter learn to understand and listen to difference. The mother's failure to understand her own loss leads her to bequeath a legacy of hysterical fragility and mournful passivity to the next generation.

Carol is particularly afflicted by her identification with Vicky, the girl who was held up by kind ushers that day in church. Vicky has been getting in trouble in school and may be expelled: "'But I remember how she was in church and whenever I see her now I have to wonder. And hear . . . like I'm her, Mother, like I'm her.' Clinging and trembling. 'Oh why do I have to feel it's happening to me too?'" Acknowledging at once racism at school and her own seemingly unchosen sympathy that breaks upon her in waves of sound, she concludes, "Oh why is it like it is and why do I have to care?" Helen's response is nonverbal: "Caressing, quieting."[57]

Carol's pain here has a long history. A sense of a wound as being shared, "a bodily experience of anguish caused by identification with the pain of another," is a classical trope in the history of sentiment and sympathy, especially when experienced by white women about women of color.[58] Such sentiment was intentionally mobilized by Black as well as white writers during slavery, but its pitfalls are easily apparent: an identification with another's pain easily tips into a fetishization of that pain.[59] And sympathy with an other can, in the course of its sentimental operations, risk collapsing the other into the sympathizing subject, or extending the subject's sympathy only insofar as the other is like the self.[60]

Helen does not speak aloud for the rest of the story. Instead she sinks into an inner monologue, casting Carol's sympathetic suffering as a sacrament of that oceanic, undifferentiated humankind that the evanescent Mann Elementary has already revealed as an expiring dream: "*It is a long baptism into the seas of humankind, my daughter,*" Helen thinks. "*Better immersion than to live untouched. . . . But how will you sustain?*" Helen "shelter[s] her daughter close, mourning the illusion of the embrace." This mourning initially seems to apply to the illusion that a mother's arms can protect from the pain of the world, but another meaning is suggested by the story's final sentence: "While in her, her own need leapt and plunged for the place of strength that was not—where one could scream or sorrow while all knew and accepted, and gloved and loving hands waited to support and understand."[61] This sentence, especially read in light of the very similar and more explicitly political sense of mourning in "Tell Me a Riddle," points toward what Helen herself is lacking: she longs to be part of a collective that can embrace and support her, but she is not. Perhaps she once felt that belonging; perhaps that is the embrace she is mourning; perhaps she now wonders whether she ever really had it, or whether it was an illusion all along. Whatever the case, it is gone now. And this lack drives her to offer a deliberately apolitical embrace, to seek solace in making that meager and uncompensatory offering.

In contrast to the collective maternal we saw in the church ushers' care, Helen's version of motherhood privatizes collective functions and transcribes political disappointments into interpersonal ones: the pain of a lost solidarity is experienced as a single broken friendship, and the injustice of racism is reduced to the tears of a sensitive white girl who is being taught that taking on another's pain as her own makes her a better person, and one ever more vulnerable to pain, with no escape in sight.

Helen's own desire is for communal and communing support, whether this is to be found in a church, a movement, a party, or mother love. But she articulates this desire through the symbol of the gloved hands, which both centers the particularity of the Black church and evacuates that particularity. When hands are gloved, after all, it can be difficult to discern their color. And an affinity that longs for difference to be irrelevant, or that awaits the magical saving power of the other, is a solidarity that has failed before it has begun.

This, then, is what a counterproductive reckoning with lost solidarity looks and sounds like. It looks like a drastic privatization of relation: paring down care and concern to asymmetrical one-on-one relationships of either bloodline-dependent mothering or projective identification, or both. It sounds like an attempt to disaggregate and analyze collectivity instead of participating and supporting, until the only means of alliance is a shared collapse. It looks like attempting to re-create the *feeling* of support and solidarity in whatever scaled-down and unscalable form, stripped of all its historical and political content. It sounds like the old, dogged fantasy that white tears are a sign of virtue. Above all, it sounds like a clear indication that how we transcribe past losses has long-lasting implications for how we address crises in the present.

CHAPTER 3

"I STAND MUTE"

Civil Rights Cacophony and Quiet

In the summer of 1966, a television news program about a civil rights march highlighted a brewing conflict within the civil rights movement. The hourlong CBS special *The March in Mississippi* described the conflict as a "struggle to see whose philosophy would guide" the monthlong march—"the moderates or the militants."[1] The footage chosen to illustrate this struggle reveals it as a disagreement specifically about which collective desires to embrace in the face of disappointment, and a disagreement that plays out through contests over a movement's soundscape.

First we see Martin Luther King Jr. in his shirtsleeves out in the countryside, asking a dozen or so people a familiar question: "What do you want?"

For years now, there has been only one answer to give, and everyone gives it in unison. "Freedom!"

"When do you want it?" he asks jovially.

"Now!" they reply. Everybody in the scene seems to be quoting themselves, as if they have been asked to perform the chant for the camera.

"*How much* do you want?" A new twist, seemingly rehearsed beforehand: as if the old chant might not be quite enough anymore, as if some clarification might be needed.

"All of it!" They all laugh.

The film cuts to Stokely Carmichael, the then newly elected chairman of the Student Nonviolent Coordinating Committee (SNCC). He, too, is outdoors; it is night, his face illuminated against the dark that surrounds him. "From now on," he exhorts his audience, "when they ask you what you want, you know what to tell 'em. What do you want?"

"Black power!" This new answer has an entirely different rhythm from the old. Its three syllables, all bearing equal stress in the collective reply, do not mimic or invite a measured series of footsteps as the neatly trochaic "Freedom" had. This response dreams of a different sort of action.

As the clip continues, Carmichael rewrites the movement catechism still further by following up not with another well-known question but with a deliberate reiteration of this newly voiced collective desire. "We want black power," he affirms.

The crowd repeats, with more fire: *"Black power!"*[2]

Throughout this book, we've been tracking how political desire persists and changes in times of disappointment, and how disappointment gives rise to aesthetic and cultural practices, most notably sonic and transcriptive ones, that unsettle existing structures and make new solidarities possible. This chapter will trace the sonic practices that emerged during the James Meredith March Against Fear, a monthlong civil rights march in the summer of 1966, when disagreement about collective desires produced a distinctively disappointed soundscape, one whose cacophony and quiet were resistant to transcription.

The civil rights movement had ample cause for disappointment in the summer of 1966. Recent legal victories at the Supreme Court and in Congress had had little effect on the political disempowerment, economic marginalization, and vulnerability to racist violence affecting Black people in the United States. *Brown v. Board of Education* had imposed no concrete timeline for remedy, allowing many school districts to go on operating segregated schools indefinitely. Even after the Voting Rights Act passed, registering Black voters in the South could still mean risking one's life. Indeed, the toll of the mid-1960s backlash was devastating: four young girls in the Sixteenth Street Baptist Church bombing in Birmingham; four civil rights workers in Philadelphia, Mississippi; several activists involved with the 1965 marches in Selma. Taken as a whole, a decade's worth of civil rights victories seemed to have amounted to more violence, more dehumanization, more reactionary resistance to change.

Martin Luther King Jr. accurately diagnosed a shadow of disappointment resting upon the movement that summer. "We have been the victims of so many broken promises and deferred dreams," he told a rally at Chicago's Soldier Field in July. "I understand our legitimate discontent. I understand our nagging frustrations. We are the victims of a crisis of disappointment."[3] And disappointment was indeed endemic; yet activists were not its passive victims. Prompted by it, people were discussing whether it made sense to continue working with the same template of strategy, tactics, and desires that had brought some legislative change but frustratingly little substantive alteration in the lived experiences of African Americans. This was the context within which a fragile coalition of civil rights groups set out in June 1966 to traverse the state of Mississippi by foot, following the intended path of an idiosyncratic man whose plans to make the trek alone had been derailed by violence. The sonic archive of the James Meredith March Against Fear demonstrates that in times of disappointment and disagreement, the most important records can arise from sonic practices that, resisting transcription, register as cacophony and quiet.

The March Against Fear

In June 1966, the civil rights activist James Meredith, who had made headlines several years earlier by enrolling at the all-white University of Mississippi, announced he would walk across his home state—alone, or with whoever might care to join him—to encourage Black Mississippians not to be afraid. He called his planned journey a "march against fear." Midway through his second day of walking, he was ambushed by a man with a shotgun on the side of the road who put between sixty and seventy pellets of heavy-gauge birdshot in Meredith's head, neck, shoulders, back, and chest, sending the wounded marcher to the hospital and forcing him to suspend his trek.[4]

As Meredith recovered in a Memphis hospital, civil rights leaders pulled together to pick up where he had left off. But the coalition that had come together to helm the March on Washington three years earlier proved challenging to reassemble now. SNCC, the Southern Christian Leadership Conference, and the Congress of Racial Equality managed to reach a working agreement, but the NAACP and the Urban League backed out over disputes about how much to criticize President Lyndon Johnson.

Even among SNCC, the Southern Christian Leadership Conference, and the Congress of Racial Equality, differences remained. They disagreed early on about how to handle the Deacons for Defense and Justice, a Louisiana group whose members carried guns and preached armed self-defense instead of passive resistance in the face of violence. The group had volunteered to do security for the march, and at SNCC's insistence the coalition accepted their offer. To many observers and later scholars, the decision to include the Deacons "signified a shift in the civil rights movement, which had been popularly projected as a 'nonviolent movement.'"[5] Indeed, the March Against Fear has gone down in history as a major turning point in the civil rights movement, which was then in the midst of a multiyear transition between its classical phase, which is usually dated 1954–1965, and the Black Power era, which would be in full swing by 1968.[6] Narratives of the march often highlight tension between King, who personifies the nonviolent philosophy undergirding the classical phase, and SNCC chair Stokely Carmichael, whose brasher style and reluctance to abjure self-defense made him an early icon of Black Power. (Carmichael, looking back years later, would seek to downplay the scope of disagreement between himself and King in 1966: "There was no debate on nonviolence, that was clear. The debate was on self-defense."[7])

Under Carmichael's leadership, SNCC was increasingly questioning the value of the classical civil rights strategy of submitting to brutality in public as a spiritual and public-relations tactic.[8] In light of this, the group had initially been ambivalent about joining the March Against Fear; there had been so many marches recently, many of them drawing violence from white mobs and law enforcement, and SNCC wondered whether holding more marches was the smartest strategy. Carmichael recalls that he and his colleagues were "tired . . . of these wretched pointless marches, appealing to whom? Accomplishing what?" To Carmichael, Meredith's march had been "a bad idea" from the start: "What exactly was a 'march against fear' anyway?" Yet he finally decided that Meredith's "ill-conceived, almost stillborn infant" of a march might present an opportunity for SNCC anyway: that "maybe, just perhaps the idea's very weakness—its vague, ill-defined, amorphous quality—could be its greatest value. What if we could give it some serious political meaning?"[9] In an unfixed space marked by exhaustion, vagueness, and futility, Carmichael saw an opportunity to make new meaning and convey new ideas.

At a press conference King and Carmichael held toward the beginning of the restarted march, King reflected on its urgent emotion and temporality. "I think the national outrage is so great, and there is such an upsurge and—and such a spontaneous response, that it will be possible to do it, although we don't have time for mobilization as we've had in other instances. And I think the spontaneity, the—the outpourings of the moment will make it possible for us to mobilize forces within a matter of hours that we haven't been able to mobilize before."[10] In this striking statement, King audibly hesitates before his acknowledgments of urgency and spontaneity, as if trying to slow down the necessary haste with which everything has been arranged. He seems to be working to think through what "the spontaneity, the—the outpourings of the moment" will mean for this march.

This is the last formal comment in the press conference. The two civil rights leaders begin standing up to leave. A journalist calls out, "Dr. King," but Carmichael holds up his hand while rising, as if to stop the questioning. Once he has stood up, the camera, with its fixed angle, no longer captures his head or face. "No more questions," says an off-screen voice that sounds a great deal like Carmichael's. "No more questions, gentlemen." The pressing forward, then, is primarily Carmichael's doing, but King goes along easily: "We've got to *march* now," the elder leader agrees.[11] Despite his seeming concerns about the haste, King is ready to march.

Disagreement among the different groups at the march's head developed as the marchers made their way toward Mississippi's state capital, and soon this disagreement took sonic form. King writes about the march in his 1967 book *Where Do We Go from Here: Chaos or Community?*, where he begins his discussion of intramovement disagreement by narrating it as a struggle over sound and quiet. His opening anecdote takes place toward the beginning of the trek, where dissent becomes audible during a pause in the action:

> Once during the afternoon we stopped to sing "We Shall Overcome."
> The voices rang out with all the traditional fervor, the glad thunder
> and gentle strength that had always characterized the singing of this
> noble song. But when we came to the stanza which speaks of "black
> and white together," the voices of a few of the marchers were muted.
> I asked them later why they refused to sing that verse. The retort was:
>
> "This is a new day, we don't sing those words any more. In fact,
> the whole song should be discarded. Not 'We Shall Overcome,' but
> 'We Shall Overrun.'"
>
> As I listened to all these comments, the words fell on my ears like
> strange music from a foreign land. My hearing was not attuned to
> the sound of such bitterness.[12]

Here, a conflict about how to proceed in a moment of suspension plays out as disagreement over a song. King describes the refusal to sing as nevertheless linked to sound—"strange music," "the sound of such bitterness"—and describes his sense of bewilderment as a matter of hearing: in his telling, he is so innocent regarding bitterness and resentment that his ears are not calibrated to perceive it properly.

By using this anecdote to introduce disagreement over nonviolence and interracial coalition, King casts that disagreement as a contest over what sort of sound the movement should embrace as its soundtrack: a noble song or strange music, glad thunder or the synesthetic sound of bitterness. The alternative song suggested is only a theoretical one: I have found no record of anybody ever actually singing "We Shall Overrun." The question of what sounds to generate instead, though, remains unresolved. Just as a basic working agreement within the movement was giving way to disagreement about terminology and tactics, and an apparently clear hierarchy was being complicated by an influx of other intellectuals, organizers, and grassroots activists, the soundscape of civil rights was likewise switching over, as this chapter will discuss, from a canon of songs based on spirituals and old labor songs to a cacophony of clashing chants, the quiet of hypothetical and unsingable songs, and the ambient noise of grass-roots action.

A few months later, a venerated movement musician would use music as a synecdoche for the disappointments of the classical civil rights strategy. In an essay for the folk music magazine *Sing Out!*, Julius Lester—who had served as a SNCC song leader and had written several articles about freedom songs for the folk-music magazine *Broadside*—wrote with bitter irony about the experience of singing freedom songs while enduring brutality in public: "You simply put your body in the struggle . . . [and] red-necks and po' white trash from four counties and some from across the state line were waiting with guns, tire chains, baseball bats, rocks, sticks, clubs and bottles, waiting as you turned the corner singing about This Little Light of Mine and how you were going to let it shine as that cop's billy club went upside your head shine shine shining as you fell to the pavement with someone's knee crashing into your stomach and someone's foot into your back until a cop dragged you away." The musical metaphor is a key moment in Lester's essay, which is titled "The Angry Children of Malcolm X" and chiefly addresses the waning appeal of nonviolence within the movement. His decision to connect singing and passive resistance points to the long-standing link between the nonviolent strategy and the songs that frequently accompanied it, while also highlighting sound as a key arena for political disagreement amid disappointment to play out. Like King, Lester cast the shift within the movement in musical terms, but unlike King, he celebrated that shift, scorning the movement's great anthems as being out of step with changing times: "Now it is over. The days of singing freedom songs and the days of combating bullets and billy clubs with Love. We Shall Overcome (and we have overcome our blindness) sounds old, out-dated and can enter the pantheon of the greats along with the IWW songs and the union songs."[13]

Years earlier, when he was feeling more optimistic about music, Lester had written in a civil rights songbook, "A song is to be sung. If it remains on the page, it is the same as a new automobile that is bought, placed in the garage and kept there."[14] Now he was proposing that the most widely sung song of the movement should be converted from performative event to archival object. Yet he surely knew that the Industrial Workers of the World and union songs had hardly been confined to the garage: they had been revived, cast into service again, as civil rights songs. A line Lester had previously praised for its reference to an explicitly racialized "us," "Us black folks haven't got a chance unless we organize," came from a slight redo of the mineworkers' song "Which Side Are You On?" And "We Shall Overcome" didn't need to enter anew any hall of fame to join the union songs; it had been there since the South Carolina tobacco workers' strike of 1945, when the old hymn "I'll Overcome" was first reworked into a political anthem by Black women on the picket line. These women taught it to Zilphia Horton, an organizer at the Highlander Folk School, which is where Pete Seeger heard it and started singing it, and where it eventually caught on with civil rights activists.[15]

Why was "We Shall Overcome" a target for marchers in Mississippi seeking to express their disappointment in nonviolence? Perhaps it was the tempo of this slow, stately theme, this song that even Congress of Racial Equality founding father James Farmer likened once to a funeral dirge, its languid descents suited possibly to a march but all wrong for anything quicker or more nimble.[16] The lyrics, too, flowed thick with patience: We *shall* overcome . . . *someday*.[17] As Julius Fleming has recently detailed, Black patience is "a large-scale racial project that coerces performances of patience among black people as a way to invigorate and reinforce anti-blackness and white supremacy."[18] Many were now questioning this demand to perform patience in the face of ongoing violence.

Lester, like the dissenter in King's book, proposed replacing the anthem with a song that was not quite a song. In his epitaph for "We Shall Overcome" in *Sing Out!*, he wrote,

> Now they sing
>> Too much love,
>> Too much love,
>> Nothing kills a nigger like
>> Too much love.[19]

Unlike "We Shall Overcome," a song whose embrace of a multiracial choir is written into the words, Lester's song was almost literally unsingable by white liberals. Not just the racial slur, though that would have been enough, but the biting sarcasm of the words, too, made it a shibboleth that repelled any possibility of interracial singing. This notional song expressed a bitter disappointment in the old objects and tactics, a sense of having been betrayed, disrespected, even killed, by the love-based approach of the movement's classical phase—indeed, by that emotion itself. Although "Too Much Love" was chanted and sung occasionally for some time after 1966, it seems to have never caught on.[20]

The most important vocalizations of the March Against Fear were not sung words but chanted ones. During the march, the conflict over the sound of the movement ratcheted up at a rally in Greenwood, Mississippi. The whole day had been tense: Carmichael was arrested earlier in the day when police challenged the marchers' right to put up a tent. When he was finally released from jail, he went straight to the rally. There, as he passed his SNCC colleague Willie Ricks, Ricks told him it was time to bring SNCC's Black Power slogan, which the group had been talking about for years, to the stage. "The people are ready," Ricks told Carmichael. "Drop it now."[21]

Carmichael took the stage and issued a historic call, framing it specifically as a reaction to disappointment in the old chanted desire. "We been saying

3.1   Stokely Carmichael (second from right) at the rally in Greenwood, Mississippi, where he publicly introduced the slogan "Black Power" during the March Against Fear, 1966. Photo by Bob Fitch. Bob Fitch Photography Archive, Department of Special Collections, Stanford University.

freedom for six years and we ain't got nothin'," he said. "What we gonna start saying now is Black Power!"[22]

When King recounts this speech in *Where Do We Go from Here,* he leaves out the part about the six-year failure of calls for freedom, emphasizing instead the cacophony that came next: "Willie Ricks, the fiery orator of SNCC, leaped to the platform and shouted, 'What do you want?' The crowd roared, 'Black Power.' Again and again Ricks cried, 'What do you want?' and the response 'Black Power' grew louder and louder, until it had reached fever pitch."[23] King here telegraphs a pronounced discomfort with the roaring crowd and its excessive, high-volume repetitions ("again and again," "louder and louder"). He declines to transcribe each repetition, as if reluctant to amplify the intensity by reproducing it in writing.

A more direct attempt at transcription takes place in an account of the same moment by SNCC activist Cleveland Sellers:

> The crowd was right with him. They picked up his thoughts immediately.
>
> "BLACK POWER!" they roared in unison.
>
> Willie Ricks, who is as good at orchestrating the emotions of a crowd as anyone I have ever seen, sprang into action. Jumping to the platform with Stokely, he yelled to the crowd, "What do you want?"
>
> "BLACK POWER!"
>
> "What do you want?"
>
> "BLACK POWER!"
>
> "What do you want?"
>
> "BLACK POWER!! BLACK POWER!!! BLACK POWER!!!!"[24]

By reproducing multiple repetitions, using capital letters, and amassing exclamation points, Sellers works to represent on the page the waves of rhythm, volume, and excitement that made the moment in Greenwood so electrifying.

By contrast, King continues his transcriptive demurrals. He relates how the newly introduced slogan becomes grounds for a pitched sonic battle between factions in the march, but he still declines to transcribe that battle itself: "For a day or two there was fierce competition between those who were wedded to the Black Power slogan and those wedded to Freedom Now. Speakers on each side sought desperately to get the crowds to chant their slogan the loudest."[25]

A newspaper article that reported from the march corroborates King's account of a sonic contest, while using capital letters and exclamation points to more directly represent the competition:

> "What do you want?" somebody shouts.
> "FREEDOM!" has always been the answer, but on the march "BLACK POWER!" is beginning to drown out "FREEDOM!"[26]

Even this transcription, though, does not fully convey what is audible in archival footage. The civil rights documentary *Eyes on the Prize* includes a scene where, in response to the chanted question "What do you want?," some marchers seem to respond "black power," others "freedom," and others perhaps something else, difficult to decipher out of the ragged chorus.[27] Years of disciplined unanimity of declared political desire have, as Carmichael pointed out, not brought victory. Staking out a question about desire as a place to audibly register disagreement was a key practice of disappointment on the march, and the resulting cacophony was practically impossible to transcribe precisely.

A combination of this clash of chants and the challenges to "We Shall Overcome" can be heard in footage of the march's rally in Canton, Mississippi.[28] As a knot of demonstrators, who have just been teargassed by state troopers, are staggering toward a safer gathering spot, one person—sardonically, it seems—yells "Freedom." Another person retorts, "Black power." Perhaps trying to avoid an all-out clash of slogans and desires, several people at this point attempt to unite the crowd with "We Shall Overcome." But the singers sound tired and embattled, and when the verse ends, instead of somebody calling out the first line of another well-worn verse, a man's voice breaks into the music, throwing it off. "Whitey got to go!" he yells.

The singers do not continue their song. The man repeats: "Whitey got to go!" Because this line's meter perfectly matches that of the song's other lines, it's possible that the man was attempting to line out a new verse: *Whitey got to go, someday.* But "We Shall Overcome" proved in that moment unable to incorporate the new line or the feeling it expressed, while appearing equally unable to continue in the face of it. Out of the classical civil rights era's seemingly unanimous declarations of collective wants, a dissenting soundtrack had taken shape.

This eruption of discordant desires into the soundscape constituted not just a disagreement over how to approach a future freedom but a means of enacting that freedom, however partially, in the present. Still, while voicing disagreement might feel like a form of freedom to those enacting it, it doesn't necessarily play well to everybody watching at home. King seemed to recognize this; he writes of being deeply concerned by the noise, both aural and affective, that the clashing chants entailed. Toward the end of the march, he called an emergency meeting in a Yazoo City parish house, at which he proposed a compromise: they would use neither chant for the rest of the march. The other organizers assented.

And so, with the new and old signature chants equally stilled, and with "We Shall Overcome" muted, the alliance marched down the dusty highway without the accompaniment of its classic soundtrack. A reporter from the *Baltimore Afro-American* wrote of a meditative hush on the route: "Sometimes the group would break out in song. But mostly they trudged along quietly in the sweltering sun, as if each were seeking the relief of emotions through the relentless beat of a firm tread."[29]

When James Meredith resumed his own trek, just before the march's conclusion, he worked to amplify the quiet that had grown along its route. He banned all singing from his section of the march, and when the movement veteran Rev. James Orange started chanting "Freedom," Meredith pointed his walking stick at him and commanded, "Shut up, shut up."[30]

Meredith never publicly explained why he silenced songs and chants. But a contemporaneous news interview with Carmichael offers insight into the power of quiet at a political moment when sound, meaning, and strategy were all in flux. During the march, a reporter said to Carmichael, "Mr. Meredith, in whose name this march is being made, stood mute when asked if he would resort to violence. Where do you stand?"

Carmichael replied tersely: "I stand mute."[31]

Carmichael's answer repeats, and by repeating calls attention to, the reporter's implication that muteness in the face of a demand to repudiate violence amounts to a political position, a place one might stand. In response, the SNCC leader could have pressed his lips together and shaken his head, performing silence directly. Instead he spoke these three words, speech about not speaking. The reporter's question translated Meredith's literal silence, his muteness, into language and stance; Carmichael's repetition of the reporter's words tilts that language toward noise, as repetition often does. His answer announces and heralds silence while also breaking it: it's impossible to say "I stand mute" without telling an untruth. It's an infelicitous speech act that deftly rejects the terms of debate being offered. If freedom songs had been a way for the classical civil rights movement to audibly manifest a nonthreatening attitude, Carmichael here demonstrates how powerful it can be to simply refuse to reassure—a refusal performed here in a noisy quiet.

Despite these refusals and sonic enjoinments, the March Against Fear was not a deliberately silent protest along the lines of, for instance, the NAACP's 1917 Silent Protest Parade in New York City. In the 1917 demonstration, which was planned in the wake of race riots in Saint Louis and organized to decry lynchings and other killings of African Americans, thousands of marchers arranged themselves according to age and gender, with children marching at the front of the formation, then women, and men at the back. The New York march's rigorously stage-managed setup—children and women dressed in white, men in suits of more somber shades, a sparse row of drummers setting the rhythm, a printed exhortation to potential marchers that "YOU MUST BE IN LINE"— contrasts with the pluralist, improvisatory mood of both Meredith's march and the coalition that formed to carry it on.[32]

Unlike the 1917 march, whose highly disciplined mass hush arose from premeditated strategy, the March Against Fear's numerous instances of quiet— that is, of refusal to speak or sing, or refusal to appear sonically intelligible— were largely ad hoc and emergent. The march stands as a striking example of quiet's deployment in the course of the midcentury African American freedom struggle. Kevin Quashie's concept of quiet as an underrecognized aspect of Black experience is useful here.[33] His concept focuses on quiet not primarily as a sonic quality but rather as a sensibility or experience of interiority and intimacy, but there's nevertheless a reflectiveness at the heart of Quashie's idea of quiet that fits well with this scene of marchers walking calmly, temporarily relieved of the responsibility to present any particular public image, free to tap into their own feelings. "I got the strong impression that being out there on the road with us, and with his people, was almost like a holiday for Dr. King," Carmichael wrote, "[a]s if he were out of a straitjacket. . . . And that out here, marching, talking, sleeping in the tent, he was relishing that freedom."[34]

Although eruptions of quiet, whether in 1917 or 1966, are not always precisely silent, they participate in silence's "multifarious and polysemic" qualities, the way its particular meaning in any instance is dependent on the circumstances where it appears.[35] They also demonstrate the capacity of quiet—arising from its openness to interpretation, its resistance to being assigned any one political function—to stage collectivity and coalition where speech or song have difficulty doing so.[36] In the summer of 1966, a refusal to traffic in easily transcribed sound allowed disagreement and coalition to bloom together, quietly.

Similarly, King and Carmichael, holding different views about Black Power, both agreed to allow the phrase's ultimate meaning to remain unspecified. In the CBS news special on the march, a reporter asks King whether he and Carmichael "have the same things in mind" when they use the phrase Black Power. King responds, "I'm not sure about that. I can only give my position and I think he would have to give his."[37] Just as strikingly, by September 1966 SNCC was to announce that it would no longer attempt to define the phrase for the media—recognizing that the phrase's very status as the site of a possible cacophony or quiet, and thus of a coalition that depended on not saying too much or not being precisely transcribable, was part of its potency.

In going quiet, this march of dissenters through the Mississippi countryside foregrounded the political communication produced by its mobile assembly of bodies, rather than by the vocalized assertions—whether spoken or sung—that are often presumed to be the political point, indeed the proof of the political character, of such assemblies. The March Against Fear, in other words, bears out Judith Butler's contention that "it matters that bodies assemble, and that the political meanings enacted by demonstrations are not only those that are enacted by discourse, whether written or vocalized." Butler is writing here of the communicative power of assembled bodies over and above whatever message those who gather might issue in other form: "The gathering signifies in excess of what is said, and that mode of signification is a concerted bodily enactment, a plural form of performativity."[38]

There is also more at work in such a gathering, though, than just bodies together and the words they might speak. Bodies, after all, rarely assemble in space without being attended by some sound, even if it does not register as a clearly vocalized or easily transcribed collective utterance. In a march, for instance, there will usually be the sound of feet—the *Afro-American* reporter wrote of "the relentless beat of a firm tread," individual and collective, with its direct line to "the relief of emotions."[39] A rural march's soundscape may also include the Dopplered roar of a passing truck, the sibilance of roadside insects, or casual conversation among the marchers: "There we'd be trudging along, mile after mile, discussing every blessed thing under the sun," Carmichael fondly recalled.[40] In addition, a march carries the possibility of a discordant chant breaking out, one people have never heard before, one the crowd has not yet learned to proclaim in tidy unison—and may never choose to.

In Carmichael's account of the march, he recalls thinking that the march's initial lack of a clear program could make it a useful stage for "some serious

3.2 *Left to right:* Willie Ricks, Bernard Lee, Martin Luther King Jr., Stokely Carmichael, Andy Young, Hosea Williams, and other marchers on the March Against Fear, 1966. Photo by Bob Fitch. Bob Fitch Photography Archive, Department of Special Collections, Stanford University.

political meaning."[41] Indeed, the vagueness of Meredith's original idea for the march, the haste with which other leaders took it up after he was shot, its unfolding in a movement interregnum during which the classical practices no longer felt sufficient but the Black Power period hadn't fully taken hold, and the commitment to do nothing for a period of weeks but walk down the side of the road, day after day, for 150 miles: all of this together did produce the march as a moment of simultaneous suspension and movement, akin to the fermatas I discussed in Chapter 1, which held open space and time for disagreement and coalition, and within which meaningful collective practices of cacophony and quiet could take shape.

Dramatize the Evils: Nonviolence and Performance

The conflicts over sound that took place during the March Against Fear are conflicts over performance as well, not just because they concern whether to sing or chant but because the longtime strategy of nonviolent direct action in the civil rights movement was explicitly conceived as one of dramatization. "I think," King said on *Meet the Press* in 1960, as lunch counter sit-ins in the South were making headlines nationwide, "sometimes it is necessary to dramatize an issue because many people are not aware of what's happening. And I think the sit-ins serve to dramatize the indignities and the injustices which Negro people are facing all over the nation."[42] Throughout his career, King repeatedly brought up the notion of nonviolence's power to "dramatize" injustices. In "Letter from Birmingham Jail," for instance, he wrote, "Nonviolent direct action seeks to create such a crisis and foster such a tension that a community which has constantly refused to negotiate is forced to confront the issue. It seeks so to dramatize the issue that it can no longer be ignored."[43]

As time went by, the word *dramatize* took on several meanings in the movement. Often it was used as in the foregoing quotations, to refer to staging a particular conflict or scene that would enact and display routine racism for a broader-than-usual audience. The word was used in other ways as well, though, especially in speeches to large groups of people. Near the beginning of King's "I Have a Dream" speech, he cast dramatization as a response to the disappointments of Emancipation and to a condition that drew added indignity from its dogged temporal persistence: "But one hundred years later, the Negro is still not free. One hundred years later, the life of the Negro is still sadly crippled by the manacles of segregation and the chains of discrimination. One hundred years later, the Negro lives on a lonely island of poverty in the midst of a vast ocean of material prosperity. One hundred years later, the Negro is still languished in the corners of American society and finds himself an exile in his own land. And so we've come here today to dramatize a shameful condition."[44]

The marchers in Washington, DC, were not technically displaying segregation or poverty in a dramatic manner as a sit-in or tent city would have done; nor, as they gathered at the center of the nation's political life, were they dramatizing being relegated to the corners of American society. King is here using the word *dramatize* in the looser, and rarer, sense of "to present or draw attention to in a dramatic way."[45] He would again use the word in that sense in a speech in the summer of 1966, shortly after the end of the March Against Fear. In this address to over fifty thousand people at Soldier Field in Chicago, which amounted to a profession of continued faith in nonviolence alongside an acknowledgment that people were feeling impatient with the slow pace of change, King would pronounce, "I am still convinced that there is nothing more powerful to dramatize and expose a social evil than the tramp, tramp, tramp of marching feet."[46]

We will return shortly to that sound of marching feet. For now, though, we can note that the two main meanings of *dramatize*—the one specifically referring to rendering an injustice literally available for spectatorship, the other more generally referring to the creation of a dramatic situation such as a mass rally or march—both rely on a shared notion of drama. The strategy of nonviolence acknowledged the fact that white supremacist violence, whether perpetrated by institutions or by individuals, frequently had a performative dimension, and the strategy aimed to make these performances of brutality available for audiences that its perpetrators had not intended. It was meant to serve as a means of reframing anti-Black violence, rebroadcasting it, and redeploying its performative and spectacular nature.

For King, the philosophy of nonviolence had never been grounded in a promise that nonviolence would mimetically call forth the same on the part of the opponent or bring about a change of heart in the angry white person coming face-to-face with a demonstrator. Indeed, movement strategist Bayard Rustin had written frankly that the strategy would at first demand of its practitioners "terrible sacrifice and long suffering."[47] The primary objective was to force an open confrontation—to stage, in other words, a display of racist violence and Black patience—which would put the brutality of the white power structure on display for a broad audience.

This emphasis on staging was not a new innovation. White supremacist violence had long had a performance-based aspect, with an intended audience wider than just the people who were the direct targets of the violence.[48] The reverberations of lynchings and similar acts were always meant to spread, to show white spectators that white power had been asserted again, and to impress on Black people the dangers that awaited them if they stepped out of line. And when activists wanted to combat the power of these performances, they enlarged the audience still further, in the hope that spectatorship by previously unintended observers would spur outrage and change. Frederick Douglass took his primal scene of witnessing the whipping of his aunt Hester and he rebroadcast it for the readers of his autobiographies; hundreds of writers of slave narratives, abolitionist speeches, and antilynching pamphlets performed similar operations. Saidiya Hartman has drawn our attention to the forms of constriction and subjection in which these reperformances inevitably participate, yet the tactic's many iterations and the faith in the power of enlarging an audience also constitute important elements in the history of antiracist practice.[49]

Similarly, civil rights workers in the 1950s and 1960s devised a strategy of boycotts, sit-ins, and nonviolent civil disobedience that was intended to redraw the parameters of performances of racist violence, to expand the audience to include spectators across the United States, and to present that audience with a striking contrast between brutal white violence and peaceful Black resistance. Just as networks of printing and distribution in the antebellum United States aided the dissemination of slave narratives and abolitionist pamphlets, the rise of nationally televised news broadcasts in the middle of the twentieth century undoubtedly conditioned the utility of staging dramatized confrontations with racist power structures in the South in the 1950s and 1960s.

"The nonviolent strategy," King wrote in *Ebony* in October 1966, a few months after the March Against Fear's conclusion, "has been to dramatize the evils of our society in such a way that pressure is brought to bear against those evils by the forces of good will in the community and change is produced."[50] Here the verb tense King uses for *dramatize,* the present perfect progressive "has been" that wavers between present and past, reflects a decided uncertainty about nonviolence's future as a strategy and even its immediate prospects. The popularity of the "Black Power" slogan, the spread of urban rebellions throughout Northern cities in the mid-1960s, and the ongoing realities of racism all suggested that the classical phase of the civil rights movement had come to an end, and that something else, something as yet not completely defined, was on its way.

In the *Ebony* article, King's account of nonviolence is full of passive verb forms and amorphous actors. "Pressure is brought to bear" by impersonal "forces of good will in the community," and "change is produced," almost as if on its own. This process of change depends on the existence of something that can be called "the community"—not *a* community or some specific regional or racial grouping, but an interrelated collection of people who are implicitly the audience for the dramatization. The constitution of such a community through spectatorship is a grounding element of the strategy of nonviolence. "The aftermath of nonviolence is the creation of the beloved community," he said in 1957.[51] Nonviolence is a performance intended for an audience of its own making.

This points toward one more level of significance for the muted voices of the marchers in Mississippi. I've already discussed how collective singing had worked, during the movement's classical phase, as a sonic manifestation of political desires that had been disciplined into at least functional unanimity. The sonic archive of the March Against Fear has revealed how the cacophony and quiet that emerged post–"We Shall Overcome" registered a plurality of political desires that exceeded and resisted any attempt to encapsulate them in a collectively sung anthem. The recognition of the dual subject-object role of "the community" in the strategy of nonviolence also beckons us to focus on the particular line that the singers rejected. The line "Black and white together" constituted a particular "we" for the affirmation that "we shall overcome." It defined an interracial community whose existence as a community was an essential element of the nonviolent strategy as King described it. Thus when some civil rights workers, including Carmichael and other SNCC activists, began questioning the philosophical and tactical wisdom of hewing to a strategy that depended on unreliable involvement from white liberals and had not yet brought meaningful change, this lyric in particular inspired some activists to refuse to perform as that disappointing community, and to seek instead other sonic means of catalyzing other coalitions.

James Meredith's original plans for his march had not included any deliberate strategy for building coalitions. He had made no specific day-by-day itinerary for his march; he had reached out to no churches or community organizations in advance to line up places to stay. "There are a million Negroes in Mississippi," he told reporters. "I think they'll take care of me."[52] He planned no rallies along the way, opting instead for improvised roadside encounters. The coalition that came together on short notice to continue his march was improvised too, and this coalition was faced with the task of continuing a march whose initial plan, such as it was, had not been of its own making.[53] Both King and Carmichael saw potential in this improvisatory quality, with Carmichael seeing an opportunity to inject "serious political meaning" into the march and King emphasizing its "spontaneity" as an asset that would help the movement "mobilize forces within a matter of hours that we haven't been able to mobilize before."[54]

This quality helped make it possible for the chant of "Black Power"—a chant that deliberately had no set definition—to emerge as the major news story about the march while it was going on. There had been no time to focus-group the march's messaging and to get everybody on board. Still, all the time in the world might not have been enough to produce a unified message at that moment. Listening closely now, we can hear the march's message as being precisely about multiplicity and disagreement amid disappointment. The overlapping chants of "Freedom" and "Black Power" voice a heterogeneous set of political desires that could amplify ad hoc roadside conversations in Mississippi; that could hear the mid-1960s uprisings in Watts and Harlem as particularly political noisemaking; that could express the disappointment of communities frustrated that the change they'd seen coming had not yet arrived.

The March Against Fear's story is about the noise of disagreement, but it is also about how to hear the persistence of coalition amid these differences. At the beginning of the march, Carmichael needed to convince members of SNCC's Central Committee to support SNCC's participation, despite the group's skepticism toward nonviolent mass marches.[55] He obtained the committee's approval, and he brought its ongoing ambivalence to the march: "I'm tired of marching, see?" he said in a speech in Senatobia, Mississippi, early in the route.[56] Performing an exhaustion with marching, a performance he would repeat in the pages of the *New York Review of Books* that fall, still he marched.[57] And when his SNCC comrades criticized King, the younger leader made a strong case for maintaining the coalition: "The greatest mistake we could make is to drive Martin Luther King Jr. out. . . . Whatever we do, we must keep Martin in."[58]

King, for his part, attempted to find harmony between the movement's history and its proliferating disappointments. Two weeks after the march's conclusion, he spoke in Chicago, as part of his new effort to encourage activism in the North. Here his call for continuity took place through a sonic metaphor—and this is where we return to those marching feet. "I am still convinced that there is nothing more powerful to dramatize and expose a social evil," he said, "than the tramp, tramp, tramp of marching feet."[59] In the place of the older and more passive tactics of "dramatizing" social evils, which required submitting songfully to white supremacist violence, here he emphasized the audible action of marching. He also seemed to acknowledge that in this new age of "fierce urgency," the sound that mattered most was not so much the ordered cadences of freedom songs as it was the less predictable array of sounds that attend bodies gathering and moving in space.

Even as King appeared to be embracing a shift from political song to action-generated sound, though, he was at the same time quoting a well-known political song. "Tramp! Tramp! Tramp!" is both the title and the refrain of a once wildly popular Civil War song about Union army prisoners of war who dream of being rescued: the chorus begins, "Tramp, tramp, tramp, the boys are marching / Cheer up, comrades, they will come."[60] Thus, even as King appeared to celebrate the new ascendance of action-generated sound, he also worked to connect it to the legacy of American political singing.[61]

King may have been underestimating people's new disappointment in old songs. Yet his choice of a song to quote poignantly underscored the very trouble with the old. The prisoners of war singing "Tramp! Tramp! Tramp!" do not actually hear the sound of their comrades coming to free them. The verses make clear that the prisoners are singing the sound *themselves*—to encourage each other through sadness, as if singing could substitute for the real thing or might even call forth its real-world counterpart, a sympathetic vibration in the form of actual human feet. The song's tempo could easily be the pace of marching feet, and the chorus's repetitions of "tramp," each bracketed with percussive consonants, create a powerful onomatopoetic effect that "left, right, left" or "one, two, three" would never have approached.

In the final verse, the warm glow of expectation nearly compensates for the prisoners' entrenched captivity:

> So within the prison cell we are waiting for the day
> That shall come to open wide the iron door.
> And the hollow eye grows bright, and the poor heart almost gay,
> As we think of seeing home and friends once more.

The song concludes on that note of hopeful expectation. The song's narrator knows that the enemy has been defeated in battle ("They were beaten back dismayed / And we heard the cry of vict'ry o'er and o'er") and thus feels confident that freedom is inevitable: since sound delivered news of the win, even as some on the winning side were inexplicably carted off to captivity, sound is trusted to deliver tidings of liberation as well. Yet the song does not depict the actual arrival of the liberating forces. It is a song about people who have supposedly achieved victory but who nonetheless remain imprisoned. All that remains to them of success is the sound of its tantalizing cry.

In this light, "Tramp, tramp, tramp" is revealed to be an inadequate transcription of a political sound that is stranded in the realm of discourse rather than action, sung by people who, despite having supposedly gained the victory they sought, can do no more than sing about it.[62] There can be some comfort to singing a song of hope when hope seems gone, as the popularity and long afterlife of "Tramp! Tramp! Tramp!" attest. But by the summer of 1966, much of King's traditional audience was past the point of finding relief from disappointment in a song.

In introducing the "Black Power" chant at the rally in Greenville, Stokely Carmichael referred to a disappointed multiyear desire: "We been saying freedom for six years and we ain't got nothin'." Over the long interval of the

March Against Fear, disappointed desires made themselves heard in song and speech, cacophony and quiet: an old chant clashing with a new and deliberately undefined one; an old song erupting within a speech that claimed to be done with songs; an audible declaration of muteness that itself spoke volumes; the tramp, tramp, tramp of a firm tread. The cacophony and quiet that anchored this march's soundscape allowed the elaboration of a strategic coalition that was able to survive in the face of disagreement and disappointment.

CHAPTER 4

SENSES OF SOLIDARITY

Voice, Vision, and Feminism in Crisis

Pat Parker inhaled sharply through her nose, then let the air out through her mouth. Her mic was live, the recording equipment sensitive: her breaths, along with the low electrical hum in the resonant room, were being caught on tape. In Medusa's Revenge, a lesbian theater space on Bleecker Street in New York's East Village, Parker's audience stood hushed and expectant. Now she breathed in again and launched into her poem, with percussive consonants exploding into comets of sound: "Don't let the fascists speak." With the next line, her voice smoothed and softened: "We want to hear what they have to say."[1]

It was a Tuesday night in November 1978: Election Day. By the next morning, three new Senate seats and fifteen House seats would have flipped Republican, which was a modest swing for a midterm election under a Democratic president but would later be seen as setting the stage for a broader political shift to the right. The audience didn't know this as they assembled at Medusa's Revenge that night, but many of them would have been well aware that a conservative movement in the United States was growing more powerful and that a mounting backlash against feminism showed no signs of abating. As attendees at an explicitly feminist concert—the final night of the Varied Voices of Black Women concert tour, which the lesbian-feminist music label Olivia Records had organized to showcase its Black artists—they would have known that the feminist movement was struggling to determine the best way forward in the face of increasing opposition.

The Varied Voices of Black Women tour is mostly remembered today, when it is remembered at all, for the fact that the Combahee River Collective helped the multiracial booking coalition Roadwork organize the tour's Boston concert.[2] But the tour is also worth remembering for the way its performances, especially Parker's, registered the complex dynamics that attended the feminist idea of voice at a key moment of feminist disappointment.

The figure of voice had been a mainstay of second-wave feminist thought since the 1960s. Early on, *voice* was commonly invoked to refer to women's individual and collective self-knowledge and self-expression, with the term's appearance in the titles of numerous second-wave publications attesting to its importance. In the late 1970s, however, as an initial period of expansion and success for the movement gave way to a time marked by widespread disappointment within and about feminism, feminists came to reassess the idea of voice as it had operated in the movement, newly sizing up the shortcomings of its most common figural deployments and endeavoring to understand voice as a robustly sonic medium, operating at the intersection of discursivity and embodiment, whose workings could most productively be understood in interaction with the visual realm.

The early second-wave conception of voice presumed a continuity between subjectivity and expression, and a seamlessness between sound and writing: feminists hoped that *women's voices,* whether spoken or written, would render women present in arenas from which they had previously been excluded.[3] This conception of voice at first had little room for an understanding of writing and sound as distinct modalities.[4] Yet transcriptive encounters between sound and writing, as well as considerations of the relationship between sound and image, eventually helped rearticulate this conception of voice in useful ways as feminists sought to navigate multiple forms of disappointment. This chapter will focus on poems, essays, and transcriptive practices from the late 1970s and early 1980s, including those of Parker, Audre Lorde, Adrienne Rich, and Hortense Spillers, to argue that the changing idea of voice became a key site for productive contestations within feminism during a time of intense disappointment. Faced with disappointment, feminists worked toward a more sonically precise idea of voice while also turning attention to vision, a pair of moves that enabled the development of a newly multimedia conception of feminist voice.

"Speak Let Them Speak": Listening to the Varied Voices of Black Women Tour

It is unsurprising that when the multiracial women's music label Olivia Records set out to plan a tour of Black performers, it chose voice as the guiding concept.[5] By the time the Varied Voices of Black Women tour traversed the Northeast in autumn 1978, "voice" had been a central figure in feminist thought and rhetoric for over a decade. Feminist newsletters, bookstores, and anthologies frequently included the word *voice* in their names, and feminist rhetoric and practice focused on encouraging and amplifying the voices of previously "silent" or unheard women. The Chicago-based newsletter *Voice of the Women's Liberation Movement* was among the first movement publications when it launched in 1968, and others quickly followed: *Notes on Women's Liberation: We Speak in Many Voices* (Detroit, 1970); *Woman's Voice* (Boston, 1970); the *Feminist Voice* (Chicago, 1971); *Women's Voices* (Buffalo, 1972). Around the same time, a feminist bookstore called the Woman's Voice opened in Denver. Anthologies of women's and feminist writing embraced the figure as well: the year 1970 saw the publication of *Voices of the New Feminism* as well as *Voices from Women's Liberation*. The literary anthology *American Voices, American Women* followed in 1973. (Carol Gilligan's classic psychology text *In a Different Voice* is a late outlier, appearing in 1982.)

As I will discuss at greater length later in this chapter, the idea of "women's voices" during this period evoked both the possibility of full and equal participation in a realm of rational discourse *and* the raw material of embodied experience that might alter the terms of such inclusion. On the most common second-wave account, for a woman to seize language was precisely to fuse the

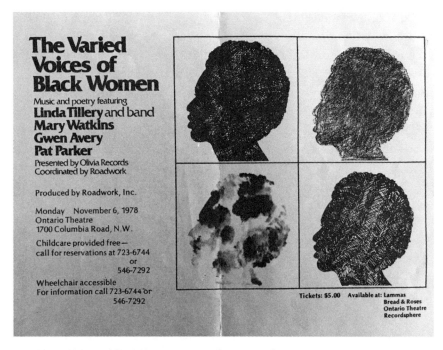

4.1 Varied Voices of Black Women concert flyer, 1978. Courtesy of Roadwork.

experiential and the discursive in order to allow women, as political actors, to show up and hold space across sonic and written formats.

Parker's poem "Don't Let the Fascists Speak," which is about a battle over free speech at San Francisco State College, demonstrates that by the late 1970s, some feminists, including women of color, were turning their attention to the insufficiencies of voice as a figure for political change, feminist or otherwise. Parker's poem is a particularly intriguing response to political ideas about voice and speech given its existence as an intermedial lyric object, available to us both as the version published in her 1978 poetry collection *Movement in Black* and as audio recordings.[6] The poem's multiple iterations register a set of transcriptive practices between performance and the page, and it offers a rich record of the role of such practices in processing feminist disappointment in voice at the end of the 1970s.[7]

Parker's performances of the poem are framed by the lyric genre, with its convention of a speaker's voice conveying personal experience, and her 1978 performance at Medusa's Revenge is additionally framed by the tour's rubric of "Varied Voices": her appearance onstage was being promoted to audiences as an instance of voice. Parker did not directly challenge these framings; indeed, she made the personal-experience framing explicit in her spoken introduction at the New York concert, when she told her audience that "this poem comes out of experience," dealing with an incident in which two neo-Nazis were invited to speak to a class at San Francisco State College.

Given this set of implicit promises that the poem would offer access to its poet-speaker's individual experience via voice, then, it's striking that the poem's prologue is a dialogue between two other voices, neither of which belongs to the poem's eventual speaker. The dialogue opens with a pair of lines that address speaking and hearing explicitly: "Don't let the fascists speak. / We want to hear what they have to say." In Parker's live performance, she adopts a different vocal delivery for each interlocutor, reading the anti-Nazi demonstrator's lines in an urgent, emphatic tone, all pushed air and plosives, while giving the free-speech absolutist's lines a disingenuously calm delivery. After the opening two lines, the dialogue returns to the poem's first speaker for the line "Keep them out of the classroom." In Parker's performance, the words "Keep them out," bookended with hard stops, soften into a pleading lilt for "of the classroom," communicating a dream of the classroom as a utopian space where all might agree that fascist propaganda is unwelcome.[8] In the prologue's final line, the idea of an ostensibly rational, neutral marketplace of ideas arrives swathed in Parker's ironically dulcet tones: "Everybody is entitled to freedom of speech."

Her slowed delivery is magnanimous and sarcastic at once. When the poem is seen on the page, this dialogue may be easily passed over, but in Parker's live performance, the distinctive sounds of multiple voices help complicate the presumption of a speaker's self-disclosure via lyric, setting up the poem to investigate the workings of voice more closely.

The prologue's first line, which doubles as the poem's title, marks the poem as being not so much an exercise of political voice, or even a statement in its favor, as it is a statement *against* it: an argument that the solution to repulsive speech might be not more speech, as the classical liberal stance would have it, but less. Throughout the poem, Parker engages with a free-speech fundamentalism that has a long tenure in US liberalism. The purportedly universal ideal

4.2 Pat Parker, Washington, DC, 1978. Photograph © J.E.B. (Joan E. Biren).
Used with permission.

of freely speaking and hearing is uttered in the poem by Nazi apologists, a re-membered grade school teacher, and floating bits of civics-class language that circulate freely through the poem. The ideal is first articulated in the last line of the poem's prologue—"Everybody is entitled to freedom of speech," insists the nameless student—whereupon it is met not with a direct retort but with an abrupt shift in register from the rhetorical to the poetic and intertextual. The next lines, where the poem properly begins, are:

> I am a child of America
> a step child
>   raised in the back room
> yet taught
>   taught how to act
> in her front room.

With these lines, the poem undergoes a marked transition into a recognizably lyric mode, recentering the poem from the contested ideal of rational speech to a subject whose lyric voice announces a slant kinship with America as such. The paired tracing of national genealogy ("a child of America") and domestic geography ("raised in the back room") also evokes the "darker brother" who sings America in Langston Hughes's "I, Too" (1926), that classic poem whose speaker holds forth from the kitchen while training an eye on the formal dining table. Parker's assertion that behavior is an "act" that must be repeat-edly "taught," rather than a matter of authentic expression, also sets the stage for the poem's consideration of vocal performance.

The prologue's claim about universal freedom of speech swiftly migrates from an attributed quotation—which was at first clearly citational thanks to italics and quotation marks on paper and to Parker's deliberate use of different tim-bres in performance—into the poem's own address, as in this passage where the speaker, appearing overwhelmed by the protesters' voices, eventually ren-ders their claims in her own typographic and sonic voice:

> the voices of students
> screaming
> insults   threats
> *"Let the Nazis speak"*
> *"Let the Nazis speak"*
> Everyone is entitled
>   to speak

This poem stages and transcribes a rough polyphony, in which shouts and bits of ideology migrate with seeming freedom between citational address and the speaker's own voice and back again.

> look to a Black teacher
> *the bill of rights*
> > *guarantees*
> *us all the right*
> > my mind
> remembers   chants
> article I   article I
> & my innards churn
> they remember.

The declaration of universally guaranteed free speech, which the poem's narrator initially absorbed as "a greasy-legged / Black child / in a Black school / in the Black part of town," is presented in italics, indicating the teacher's voice, but the narrator is an active participant in the lesson as well. The concept spurs movement both in her intellect and in her viscera:

> my mind
> remembers ...
> & my innards churn
> they remember.

This pairing of a remembering mind and churning innards occurs three times in the poem. Twice the innards "conjure images," where the images that churn up—of a Black Panther being arrested for making a speech, of Nazi death camps, of "faces in a college / classroom" to which Nazis have been invited to speak—challenge the supposed neutrality of the right to free speech and dramatize the San Francisco State students' disconnection from the concrete, historical consequences of the speech they are so eager to hear.

> conjure images
> of jews in camps –
> of homosexuals in camps –
> of socialists in camps –
> *"Let the Nazis speak"*

"Let the Nazis speak"
    faces in a college
      classroom
"You're being fascist too."
"We want to hear what
they have to say"

The conjured images, here, bring in a reality that the support of speech as such elides, a reality that must be faced if the stakes of the poem's conflict are to be adequately assessed. Yet the consideration of these images is repeatedly interrupted by intemperate speech whose own nondeliberative quality is telegraphed by repetition and hyperbole (*"You're being fascist too"*), speech that obscures archival traces of genocide and replaces those images with the banal sight of "faces in a college / classroom." The word "classroom" occupies its own line, well indented from the margin, mirroring the poem's ongoing, continually frustrated wish for a pedagogical space set apart from ordinary life, for a classroom where unworkable ideals might be not ingested and parroted ("article I article I") but examined and critiqued. Yet this classroom is not actually a privileged space for rational discourse; it is hemmed in and infiltrated by emphatic voices calling recklessly for more speech, speech that brings the students further away from reckoning with history and its casualties.

One way to state the poem's defining tension, then, is to say that it stages an opposition between an overinvestment in speech and a recognition that some truths can be better accessed via images. This maps, if loosely, onto the other opposition I have already noted, the one between the remembering mind and the churning innards. In this schema, language and speech are the territory of the mind, while the innards remember and conjure images.

On the third appearance of the mind / innards opposition, toward the poem's conclusion, this contradiction is ostensibly resolved through an unlikely recourse to US constitutional law. Amid a volta signifying epiphany, the speaker brings mind and innards together by recalling the Supreme Court's decision about shouting "fire" in a crowded theater.

    my mind remembers
    & now I know
    what my innards
        say
    illegal to cause

> people
>
> to panic
>
> to run
>
> to hurt

The doctrine against panic-causing speech resolves the poem's mind / body division, allowing the speaker's innards to finally speak for themselves. The image of "innards" is a recurrent one in Parker's poetry, variously signifying family, lineage, interiority, and intuition.[9] Directly counterposed to the mind as it is here, "innards" evoke an ineluctably physical dimension of existence: its prelinguistic, preinterpretive churn points to involuntary processing that takes place out of sight, only dimly audible even at close range. This churning is useful, though, as a blunt indicator that *something* is up. If Parker's innards and their invisible tumult offer a way of knowing, it is knowledge that awaits further interpretation before it can be put to use.

An accumulation of images and memories at last enables the innards to produce a sort of speech, allowing the poem's narrator to reframe the principle at stake as one of personal safety:

> there is no contradiction
>
> what the Nazis say
>
> will cause
>
> people
>
> to hurt
>
> ME.

"Don't Let the Fascists Speak" resolves its contradictions by simultaneously foregrounding the narrator's own body and returning to the realm of constitutional law that framed the poem's dilemma in the first place. Memories of civics class sharpened the poem's initial problem: How is it defensible to proscribe certain types of discourse in a society that allegedly enshrines a universal right to free speech? If images of clear exceptions to this supposed principle, and of its worst-case consequences, deepened the problem without resolving it, this is partly due to the noisy quality of the opposition's speech. Just when the poem seems on the verge of identifying the impossibility of a truly neutral right to free speech, the counterprotesters' clamor becomes so loud and excessive that it derails the poem's own imagistic line of reasoning.

> *speak let them speak*
>
> *speak let them speak*

120

The only way to silence them, to get the last word, is to apply the same First Amendment jurisprudence on which the noisy rabble bases its own racket. Yet the poem is not entirely right about the legal principle where it seems to find relief. And its legal error makes the poem a document not only of the counter-protesters' disingenuous investment in speech as such but also of an ongoing desire for inclusion in a set of democratic ideals that have already disappointed even at the moment when they seem to offer resolution.

The legal decision to which Parker refers, which determined that some speech could be curtailed if it was the equivalent of "falsely shouting fire in a theatre and causing a panic," dates from the 1919 Supreme Court case *Schenck v. United States*.[10] The poem presents this as a valid precedent, but in fact the decision was partially overturned in the 1969 case *Brandenburg v. Ohio*, a decade before the poem's composition. The later case construed illegal incitement much more narrowly, limiting it to cases where "such advocacy is directed to inciting or producing imminent lawless action"—no longer mere panic or running, contra the poem's claim—"and is likely to incite or produce such action."[11] Parker, who was born in 1944, would have been learning her grade school constitutional law lessons during the half century that passed between the decision in *Schenck* and its partial vacation in *Brandenburg*. The solution she arrives at by the poem's end is already outdated, a relic of midcentury liberal optimism that by the 1970s is enjoying untimely and unwarranted trust.[12]

"Don't Let the Fascists Speak" does not indicate any awareness that its expressed faith in *Schenck*-era limitations on harmful speech is already past its time, but it does directly depict the liberal free-speech ideal as disappointing, and it suggests that a turn to images might be a useful reaction to that disappointment. To that end, the poem articulates a coalitional constituency delineated not by a single identity audible as voice (or even voices, as the Varied Voices of Black Women tour seemed to promise) but rather by a shared inhabitation of an image-world, a visual archive of oppression and confinement—

> conjure image
> of that same Black man
> going to jail
> . . .
> conjure images
> of jews in camps –
> of homosexuals in camps –
> of socialists in camps –

This constituency comes together through visual juxtaposition and through collective action *against* voice:

> Blacks jews some whites
> seize the bullhorn

The act of seizing the bullhorn might be mistaken for an investment in voice or speech were it not for the fact that these activists proceed to say nothing for the rest of the poem. The next lines, "*We don't want to hear/your socialist rhetoric,*" are the pro-Nazi demonstrators' words, but we hear no such rhetoric. Perhaps the pro-Nazi demonstrators mistakenly expect their opponents to counter speech with more speech (which they hypocritically seek to shut down). Instead, the coalition that seizes the bullhorn has apparently done so to turn it off. Voice here is not a disembodied exercise of rational discourse. It's a sonic, physical act subject to mediation and re-mediation: through a bullhorn, through printed lines on a page, through a recitation at a concert that is amplified for the audience and recorded for future listeners.

"Don't Let the Fascists Speak" illustrates, again, an observation made in Chapter 3: that superimposed voices, when not orating in unison, can quickly generate a cacophony, one well suited to communicating refusal and dissent but less adept at articulating specific alternatives or paths forward. Parker's use of superimposed images, though, also indicates that *visual* superimposition can offer the opportunity for what Nicholas Mirzoeff and Nicole Fleetwood have each theorized as countervisuality and as vision-based practices capable of undermining visual regimes of power.[13]

Despite its lyric form and first-person narration, then, "Don't Let the Fascists Speak" confronts the shortcomings of voice and speech as political instruments and looks instead to the political possibilities of images, investigating superimposition as a practice of forging solidarity across a range of subject positions. What matters most here is not individual acts of voiced self-disclosure but the ability to picture a coalition.[14]

Across its multiple iterations as historical performance, archived audio, and printed text, "Don't Let the Fascists Speak" also foregrounds the problem of mediation as a key factor in the construction and disappointments of feminist voice. Parker's reading of "Don't Let the Fascists Speak" at Medusa's Revenge was taped, for later broadcast, by an African American radio producer named Donna Allegra, the host of WBAI's *The Lesbian Show*, and the very process of archiving that audio introduced additional distortion. When the recording aired one month later, it was accompanied by an expression of disappointment in the sound: "This concert was recorded live at Medusa's Revenge on November 7, 1978. It was recorded in spite of massive equipment problems and subsequently is not up to our usual standards. We're presenting it anyway, in the hopes that you will be touched by the talent and energy generated by the performers. You have just heard Gwen Avery. The next voice you hear will be Pat Parker's."[15]

This disclaimer hints at the trouble mediation posed for the dream that varied voices might easily render Black women present in feminist milieus. In light of this trouble, Allegra registers a hope for touch instead, and a hope that the voice of a poet, in particular, could connect with listeners despite any noise generated by "massive equipment problems." The performed disappointment of this apology, its affective hyperbole, is striking. Allegra's ambiguous wording, sharp and impersonal at once, doesn't tell us whether this is self-castigation or blame-casting. It doesn't tell us *whose* equipment failed, and it doesn't clarify whether the fault lay with the audio engineer in charge of running live sound at the venue, or the radio producer futilely trying to capture the electricity of a feminist concert in a downtown cabaret space on a Tuesday night in November, or something else entirely, something out of everybody's control.

And when we consider that the disclaimer was recorded after the concert, and thus after the rightward lurch effected by that day's midterm elections had become evident, it's possible to hear in this disclaimer a concern that feminism itself was, in the closing weeks of 1978, faced with massive equipment problems of its own. Could talent, energy, and voice hold feminism together if the basic tools of the movement were failing? What if voice was one of the faulty pieces of equipment that wasn't working as expected?

The disclaimer's presence in the archive asks us to be curious about how the Varied Voices of Black Women tour actually *sounded*. The recording of the show that made its way from WBAI to the Pacifica Radio Archives to the Internet Archive sounds like nothing more catastrophic than a recording made with one or two microphones in a performance venue not optimized for live recording. When Mary Watkins and her band launch into their fusion song "Witches' Revenge," the keyboards come across more clearly than the guitars. The drums and cymbals don't sound terrific, but the cowbell cuts right through everything, as cowbells are wont to do, and it's obvious what a brilliant drummer Linda Tillery is. Overall, what the recording registers best are the exclamations and laughter from the audience, the hoots and hollers from the women in attendance, who are all having what sounds like a marvelous evening out.

But what was the sonic experience of the audience members who came out to hear the Varied Voices of Black Women? As it turns out, this question spurred a remarkable degree of controversy at the tour's Boston dates, revealing how conversations about and perceptions of sound itself, as opposed to simple notions of voice, registered disagreement and disappointment within feminism.

When the Varied Voices tour, with the help of the Combahee River Collective, put on two well-attended shows at Boston University's Morse Auditorium, the local feminist newspaper *Sojourner* sent its jazz critic, a white writer named Cathy Lee, to review the performances. Lee was unimpressed. During the first concert, she reported, sonic troubles ruined the evening: "The sound ranged from muddy to inaudible depending upon location in the hall. Microphones on stage failed almost as often as they worked."[16] In her view, these equipment problems encompassed more than just microphones or mixing boards; they served, rather, as indicators of much larger problems with feminism and with efforts to build multiracial alliances. "On Friday," she wrote, "technical problems plus bad vibes led many women to feel abused and cheated—feelings that are not likely to lead to working coalitions against oppression by race and gender."

Abuse, cheating: in Lee's account, ostensible sound trouble bleeds into an overarching vibrational malaise that escalates, with astonishing swiftness, into an intimate relationship gone horribly wrong. Lee blames the Black women and their allies behind the show for these issues, noting resentfully that it had been particularly difficult for her to hear the music well because "the best seats were taken by members of the Production Collective or their friends"—a group that included many members of the Combahee River Collective.[17] Lee thus implies that the sonic travails fell mainly on white women while an in-crowd of women of color and their closest allies hoarded all the sonic goodness in the room. For Lee, the feelings of abuse that such sonic failure provokes jeopardize possible "working coalitions against oppression by race and gender"—that is, bad sound, or the perception of it, endangers the very possibility of multiracial feminism.

Lee writes that although the concert featured many songs and poems celebrating love between women of different backgrounds, these overt embraces of diversity were undermined by audience members' feelings, which, although unvoiced, were sensed in a diffuse way, at least by Lee herself: "Other feelings emanated from some of the women in the hall, unspoken but intense feelings of distrust or outright hatred for those different from the women of the hour, Black Lesbians."[18] These intense but inaudible emanations seem to be a sort of subsonic vibration—the aforementioned bad vibes, not heard by the ear but sensed by unspecified means. Yet this complaint is clearly linked to the complaints about the concert's sound; like sound, the unpleasant feelings simply emanate, intensely, from their supposed source. Problems with sound easily bleed into problems with feelings.

Unsurprisingly, Lee's review drew an outpouring of criticism: the subsequent issue of *Sojourner* devoted two full pages to letters rebutting her review. Confronting Lee's diagnosis of "distrust or outright hatred" among the audience, the Bessie Smith Memorial Production Collective wrote in their letter, "Any white and/or heterosexual person experiencing such feelings did so as a result of her own fears and projections onto the Black and lesbian women present." The collective's letter conceded that there had been some "technical flaws" in the concert's sound engineering, but they argued that Lee had "exaggerate[d] their frequency and prevalence."[19] Concertgoer Kiki Herold, in a letter of her own, similarly allowed that "there were some technical difficulties" but characterized them as minor, writing, "It sure sounded alright to me."[20]

Sound and mediation were clearly problems for this night of the Varied Voices of Black Women tour, at least in the sense that different perceptions of the concert's sound created or amplified conflict among the attendees. Amy Horowitz, who worked with Roadwork to help book the tour, recalled that getting the sound right was in fact a struggle. The venues Roadwork could afford to book were usually not designed for musical performances: at the venue in Washington, DC, for instance, the theater's electrical circuit blew out when they plugged everything in for a sound check. In addition, the sound technicians in the women's music scene, who were accustomed to amplifying "a solo vocal with a guitar," now had to contend with a full band, drumkit, and electrified instruments, which presented new challenges.[21] But whether these sonic difficulties were the minor imperfections of a community learning in public or night-ruining emblems of the failure of multiracial feminism depended on who was listening. As these scenes from the tour demonstrate, contestations within feminism over voice, sound, and images anchored shared, if conflictual, endeavors in an era of feminist disappointment. In this chapter, by attending more closely to these concepts as shared grounds of feminist disagreement, we will see how even in this tumultuous period, with conflicts and divisions giving rise to raw and intense feelings, feminists were nevertheless at work on a shared intellectual and political project.

Feminist History and Its Disappointments

Before returning to the archive of feminist thought on voice, a word is warranted about my characterization of the late 1970s and early 1980s as a time of feminist disappointment. The era plays a definitive role in many of the staple narratives of feminist history—among them progress, loss, and return—but it bears different significance in each of these accounts.[22] In loss narratives, this is the moment when feminism splintered, lost its way, and encountered opposition from which it never recovered. According to another influential narrative, which combines elements of loss and return, the movement in this era entered a period of "abeyance": activists withdrew from political action and focused instead on more insular cultural projects that would keep their spirits up during a period of reaction and allow them to later pick up where they'd left off.[23] Other narratives highlight how this supposed moment of abeyance or defeat was a tremendously productive time for feminists of color: many of the founding texts and events for Black feminism and for what was then frequently called Third World feminism date from 1977–1983, beginning with the Combahee River Collective's "Black Feminist Statement" in 1977, making this period a crucial element in narratives of feminist progress toward greater inclusion.[24] This period also saw the emergence of sex-radical feminism, which famously had its coming out at the 1982 Barnard Conference on Sexuality, and of academic feminist theory, with a significant number of germinal publications and journals arriving on the scene in the early years of the 1980s.

It's important for us to listen closely to the polyphony of these different strains of feminism, and to attend to the varied counterpoints and moments of cadence where multiple voices intersect. Here another meaning of the word *voice* becomes useful: in Western musicology, the term can refer to a line in a multipart harmony. The work of harmonization, also known as voice leading, consists of arranging a piece so that each line of music moves euphoniously both on its own and in relation to the other lines. Often, in voice leading, it's possible to keep several notes constant from one chord to the next. In a situation where every note in a chord must move in order to build the next one, though, traditional voice-leading rules favor contrary motion, in which some voices travel upward to their new notes while others travel down.

Shared harmonious movement, especially in times of great change, doesn't always require that every element move in the same direction: in politics as in music, divergent movement can lend balance, tension, and stability while making substantive change possible. Popular distillations of feminist history often depict feminism as an initially white project that women of color then joined to critique or correct, a conception that reduces Black feminism to the limited and subordinate status of a response, a demand, or a corrective while also often leading to a dismissal of white women's feminist thought and history *tout court*.[25] In addition, this narrative is frequently invoked in such a way as to emphasize contrary motion while not the chord: that is, to emphasize dissensus while not taking seriously the ways Black feminists, Third World feminists, white feminists, and others understood themselves as engaging, however conflictually, in a common project. This chapter works to hear multiple strains of feminism as intertwined in a work of polyphony and harmony, where dissonance and contrary motion are not just tolerated elements or corrections but in fact the very elements that make the work worthwhile.

In mainstream accounts of twentieth-century feminist history that emphasize the work of white women, the early years of the 1980s are generally depicted as a dramatic decline. Such narratives often highlight Ronald Reagan's election in 1980 and the 1982 failure of the Equal Rights Amendment, but backlash-era disappointments actually began setting in for white-led second-wave feminism by 1977. That year brought the first post–*Roe v. Wade* Supreme Court ruling to permit limitations on access to abortion. The Equal Rights Amendment's halting progress toward ratification rattled to a standstill in 1977 as well: on January 18, Indiana became the thirty-fifth and final state to ratify the amendment, leaving the measure three states short of its needed total. Finally, a national conference in Houston that November, organized by a presidential commission with congressional support and federal funding to celebrate women's progress and discuss the status of American women from a liberal feminist angle, drew organized opposition from right-wing women. Over the course of the year, a series of statewide meetings leading up to the conference in November were thrown into crisis by coordinated opposition from conservative women working as part of Phyllis Schlafly's Eagle Forum. The National Women's Conference, which had aimed to solidify feminism as a bipartisan commonplace, instead became a platform for pitched public battles. When the time for the national event finally arrived, a "pro-family" rally across town, headlined by Schlafly herself, drew nearly as many people as the federally funded women's conference.[26] Feminists also watched with apprehension as the right wing launched new attacks on gay and lesbian rights: in 1977, Anita Bryant's Save Our Children campaign successfully repealed a pro-gay ordinance in Dade County, Florida, and a ballot initiative was introduced in California to bar gays and lesbians from teaching in schools.[27]

Understanding how the antifeminist backlash commonly seen as beginning in the early 1980s had actually coalesced by 1977 helps highlight how thoroughly the onset of that backlash coincided with the rise of multiracial feminist theory and activism, which likewise proceeded from important origins in 1977 and reached critical mass by the early 1980s. It might initially seem difficult to account for this simultaneity without concluding that mainstream white feminism and the feminism of women of color were linked by nothing but antagonism and exclusion. I propose, though, that a shared sense of disappointment in feminism generally and a common commitment to understanding the failure of feminist voice in particular were present as early as 1977 for both white feminists and feminists of color, and that these concerns furnished the grounds for productive coalitional efforts.

Disappointment, in fact, was an initial condition of possibility and driving force for multiracial conceptions of feminism, grounded in the intellectual work of Black feminists. Members of the Combahee River Collective wrote and spoke about feeling both disappointed in the National Black Feminist Organization, of which they had initially been a chapter, and disillusioned with other liberation movements in which members had been involved. "I don't think we were happy with NBFO," collective cofounder Barbara Smith would later recall. "I remember being incredibly disappointed with them and being very skeptical.... But those were complicated questions because we certainly did not want to alienate or cut off contact with other black feminists."[28] The collective's "Black Feminist Statement" itself narrates Combahee's emergence by first discussing Black feminists' involvement with "the second wave of the American women's movement" and "movements for Black liberation," explaining, "It was our experience and disillusionment within these liberation movements, as well as experience on the periphery of the white male left, that led to the need to develop a politics that was anti-racist, unlike those of white women, and anti-sexist, unlike those of Black and white men."[29] Close attention to this excerpt reveals that collective members' "experience and disillusionment within these liberation movements" for women's and Black liberation is distinguished from members' "experience on the periphery of the white male left": the recounted relationship to feminism and Black liberation is a relationship of proximity rather than exclusion, belonging rather than marginality. Combahee River Collective members were disillusioned not *by* these liberation movements but *within* them, an intimacy that brings their disillusionment close to disappointment.[30]

In 1977, when the collective authored their "Black Feminist Statement," they didn't yet see their disappointment as being shared with white women. In the statement, they discuss their struggles to organize Black women and contrast these with what they saw as continued expansion and momentum in white feminism: "We have tried to think about the reasons for our difficulties, particularly since the white women's movement continues to be strong and to grow in many directions."[31]

Already in 1977, though, white feminists were increasingly conscious of the difficulties facing their efforts. That year, the DC-based radical feminist news-letter *off our backs* published an article titled "What If the Revolution Isn't Tomorrow?"[32] The piece, written by longtime *off our backs* collective member Carol Ann Douglas, advised readers to prepare for a long process that would feel different from the previous phase of the women's movement, when victory had seemed euphorically within reach. "This is not a lament for the feminist movement," Douglas wrote, "because the feminist movement doesn't need laments. But it is becoming apparent that the feminist revolution will be a long-term struggle and perhaps some of us need to readjust our perspectives to accommodate that realization."

Articles published in *off our backs* over the preceding two years had largely treated the feminist movement's difficulties as attributable to solvable internal problems: the different factions of the movement (lesbian separatists, feminist witches, coffeehouse folksingers, leftist politicos) might have disagreed about where to take the movement, but people just needed to discuss the options and choose a winning strategy.[33] On the rare occasions when mounting right-wing opposition was acknowledged, it was downplayed.[34] Douglas's piece sounded a new realism. Disappointment, for Douglas—the shift away from expectancy and a proximate horizon of victory—called not for the melancholic affect of a lament but for a clear-eyed understanding of the temporal shift that had taken place, from a short-term revolution to a long-term struggle.

Douglas counseled coming to terms with difficulty, slowness, seriousness, and a big-picture historical perspective:

> We also need to appreciate that resistance in periods of reaction is perhaps even more difficult and important than participating in the high points, the moments when revolution seems just around the corner. We need to care for each other through the slow pe-riods, perhaps suppressing or going beyond some of our previous tensions. This struggle is going to take all of our lives, not just a few exciting, hectic years; we just need to take ourselves seriously and not assume that we are the only revolutionaries who ever met with setbacks or divisions. Even what appear to be sudden revolu-tions are generally preceded by decades of uprisings that didn't quite make it.[35]

Temporality looms large here, as Douglas prescribes an attitude change that would take into account political temporality characterized by a slow pace, long timescales, and the possibility of reversals, rather than a linear march toward a goal. The new temporality heralded in Douglas's piece demands seriousness instead of excitement, and an acceptance of falling short rather than confidence that victory is well within reach.

By 1980, when the difficulties facing both the mainstream women's movement and predominantly white radical feminism had become even clearer, it would be possible for at least some feminists of color to understand disappointment as a possible zone of connection and productivity between white women and women of color. Cherríe Moraga, in the preface she wrote in 1980 for the Third World feminist anthology *This Bridge Called My Back*, writes of her own mounting dissatisfaction with the women's movement amid the rise of lesbian separatism, which she sees as an "exclusive and reactionary" development in part because it doesn't account for women of color who choose to stay connected to men in their communities.[36] She juxtaposes her dissatisfaction to a "boredom setting in among the white sector of the feminist movement," finding possible common ground in this shared nonfulfillment. Moraga then cites an instance of interracial feminist discourse, in this case a conversation between herself and the white working-class lesbian writer Amber Hollibaugh: "I am involved in this book because more than anything else I need to feel enlivened again in a movement that can, as my friend Amber Hollibaugh states, finally ask the right questions and admit to not having all the answers."[37] Here, feminist boredom—one affective guise disappointment can wear—is felt across racial lines, and it spurs not just a *need* for a feminism that attains a condition of perfected incompletion but an opening, a possibility that through disappointment, this might finally be attainable.

Moraga's and Hollibaugh's coalitional "finally" names a familiar, chronic feminist desire for arrival, for a movement that reaches its potential once and for all—a desire that operates continually in a disappointed and persistent mode.[38] And this particular "finally," we see in Moraga's preface, grows *causally* out of disappointment, as if thwarted desire might itself hold the power to open up new possibilities for the movement that were closed off in headier times. We will now turn to a history of second-wave feminist ideas about voice, exploring how, as feminist disappointment increased, early ideas of voice as presence and participation gave rise to more critical conceptions of voice as sonic, mediated, and interacting dynamically with visuality.

Voice and Image in the Feminist Imaginary

The second wave began with a notion of voice as posited against a harmful visual realm. In the opening pages of *The Feminine Mystique,* Betty Friedan identifies the main enemy of privileged women in the United States as an *image:* "the image by which modern American women live."[39] Friedan writes that although an earlier image, one of the courageous and career-oriented woman, had prevailed in the years around the Second World War, by the mid-1950s "the new image of American woman, 'Occupation: housewife,' had hardened into a mystique" (44). The book's titular mystique takes its shape from the world of images.

The image is not all-powerful, though, and Friedan writes that its failure appears in auditory form: "In the mind's ear, a geiger counter clicks when the image shows too sharp a discrepancy from reality" (24). The image's wrongness registers in sound, a mechanical clicking from within, registering the presence of a harmful substance much as a Geiger counter detects radiation. The sonic shows up here as a conspicuous substitute for the visual, with "the mind's ear" offering an obvious invocation of a supplanted eye, and Friedan's sonic figures hint at sound's ability to identify and combat sexist images and their petrified mystiques.

The most promising sounds for Friedan, though, are not those of a synesthetic Geiger counter but rather the sounds of voices. Even voices are practically inaudible at first: the book opens with a characterization of housewives' malaise as an "unspoken problem" in which women are "afraid to ask even of [themselves] the silent question—'Is this all?'" (1). But American women are learning "to hear the strange, dissatisfied voice stirring within" (15), "that voice within women that says: 'I want something more than my husband and my children and my home'" (22). Voice, then, is announced at the very onset of second-wave discourse, ahead even of organized feminist activism in this era, as a metaphor for women's contributions that could counter and ultimately defeat limitations on their lives. And from the mid-1960s until the late 1970s, voice operated as an explicit and implicit article of feminist faith, the primary means by which women's absence or nonrecognition in public life, frequently described as silence, would be undone.

If the voice in Friedan is private, audible at best only to the woman herself, a more public version of it was soon evident elsewhere. As we already saw, many early feminist publications and institutions communicated their faith in a public, collective notion of feminist voice by including the word *voice* in their titles. The key theoretical texts about the movement's consciousness-raising method did not discuss voice directly, focusing on the sharing of "women's experiences" rather than on that sharing's sonic medium, but retrospective considerations of feminist voice would directly discuss its centrality to consciousness-raising, and the effects of the voice-based consciousness-raising process on the formation of feminist theory. Ann Rosalind Jones, for instance, writes that "the phonocentric emphasis in American feminist criticism, the celebration of the 'real woman's voice,' came partly out of the consciousness-raising process: we wanted to speak, we constructed occasions to speak, we heard ourselves quavering out difficult sentences, we waited to hear a supportive response. CR groups were de-repressive, permission-granting structures that opened up a new oral medium."[40] Drucilla Cornell offers a similar reflection, depicting feminist voice not merely as a preexisting entity, as Friedan had suggested, but also as an expressive medium that was brought actively into being in conjunction with others: "All those who came into feminist consciousness-raising groups were to be given a voice and heard with seriousness. It may sound strange to put it that way, as if such a group could give to women what they did not have—a voice. But that was exactly the point. . . . Voices were not just something we had, a natural attribute of our human being, but also something we helped each other develop."[41]

Feminist optimism about the power of voice also drove second-wave feminism's first mainstream pop anthem, which rose to the top of the *Billboard* Hot 100 chart in 1972. The lyrics of Helen Reddy's "I Am Woman" didn't include the word *voice,* but they scarcely needed to: the song's central invitation—"I am woman, hear me roar"—clearly announced female presence as a sonic force capable of breaking boundaries, fusing as it did a declaration of gendered human subjectivity with the nonhuman, prelinguistic assertion of a roar. Its claim of gendered personhood and nongendered animality took the form of a referred-to, but never directly audible, sound. The idea of the roar played out in the song's lyrics even as its subtle melody, tailored backup vocals, and soft-rock orchestration (twangy guitars, pensive flutes, bouncy trombones) telegraphed nothing remotely roar-like.

In insistently claiming a platform for a gendered human subject wielding an animalistic voice, "I Am Woman" joins a long conversation about voice, gender, political participation, and the human. That conversation goes back at least as far as Aristotle, who argued that man's status as a political animal is grounded in the deliberative powers of speech, as opposed to the solely affective function of voice. "Whereas mere voice is but an indication of pleasure or pain, and is therefore found in other animals . . . ," he wrote in the *Politics*, "the power of speech is intended to set forth the expedient and the inexpedient, and therefore likewise the just and the unjust"—distinctions essential to undertaking the collective activity that constitutes political life.[42] In adopting voice as a key figure for women's participation and suppression, Reddy and second-wave feminist thought more broadly drew on voice's history as a vehicle and a metaphor for subjectivity, presence, and political participation.[43]

Hannah Arendt, in *The Human Condition* (1950), invokes the Aristotelian speech / voice distinction to offer a challenge to its classical formulation that would become instrumental in feminist thought on voice. Arendt proposes speech as a core human activity, contrasting it to the more passive operation of voice, in a way that is directly descended from Aristotle: "In acting and speaking, men show who they are, reveal actively their unique personal identities and thus make their appearance in the human world, while their physical identities appear without any activity of their own in the unique shape of the body and sound of the voice."[44] For Arendt, though, the conjunction of these voluntary and involuntary aspects of action and speech is the point: it is this union of personal and physical identities that enables the subject of the acting and speaking to fully appear. Arendt's discussion leaves unrevised Aristotle's attention to "men" as the speakers, but her idea of uniting rational and embodied components of selfhood is audible in Reddy's "I Am Woman" and also helps make sense of the idea of voice as it functioned in early second-wave thought.

Early second-wave feminist texts did not directly cite Arendt—or Aristotle, for that matter—in explaining the appeal of voice as a figure for agency and political participation, or as a "guarantor of truth and self-presence," in the words of a recent theorist of voice.[45] Indeed, second-wave feminism's initial embrace of voice took place without any explicit reflection on it. From the late 1960s through the mid-1970s, voice remained a consistent undertone, quietly shaping the movement and anchoring its conceptual vocabulary, whether operating as a simple term to be deployed in titles and slogans or as the implicit medium through which women's "bitter experiences" and "feelings about our experiences" could be collated into organic theory and strategy for action.[46] In the few places where it was invoked explicitly, the reference was always approving, as when Adrienne Rich praised the feminist poet Susan Griffin's play *Voices* (1975) for its "affinity with the speaking voice," calling Griffin's work "a search for the words, the rhythms, in which the voiceless can be heard."[47]

If there is a theory of voice suggested in the conception that held sway in early second-wave feminism, it is this: The expressive and affective dimensions of communication signified by voice are not excessive components that are ultimately extraneous to clear communication. In fact, granting affective and personal elements of speech significance in the public sphere is necessary if the exclusion of women from political participation is to be undone. If the Aristotelian division between speech and voice presumed an ideal political subject who was able to separate rational thought from the material and affective realities of bodily life—a subject Aristotle envisioned as exclusively male—then the feminist embrace of intermingled voice and speech aimed to replace this model of subjectivity and citizenship with an embodied, affectively implicated version of political participation that took the exercise of voice as itself a foundational practice of feminist politics. What was missing, though, was any conception of mediation, labor, or difference as complicating this idealized exercise of voice. Feminists did not yet see voice as being, in contemporary anthropologist Laura Kunreuther's useful terms, "a medium that works in concert with writing, performance, and other media to constitute subjects."[48]

By the late 1970s, some feminist writers began expressing concern that voice and speech could not be so easily equated, and that neither possessed a privileged relationship to truth or liberation. A widely circulated 1977 essay by Adrienne Rich titled "Women and Honor: Some Notes on Lying" and a 1978 essay by her partner, Michelle Cliff, titled "Notes on Speechlessness" grapple with the capacity of women's language to mislead, deceive, and omit. In "Women and Honor," Rich writes of yearning for a candid and honorable standard of women's speech that could free women from the forms of deception forced upon them by patriarchy. "As we cease to lie with our bodies," she writes, "as we cease to take on faith what men have said about us, is a truly womanly idea of honor in the making?"[49] Cliff's response to the disappointment of voice is, even more strikingly, to redefine speech entirely, proposing that speech is only speech when it is true: "The obscuring and trivialization of what is real is also speechlessness. Speechlessness is not simple muteness—it is the inability to speak but also the inability to reveal."[50] For Cliff, dishonest words are not speech at all.

The word *voice* does not appear in these two essays, but it is present in their shared dream of alignment among women's speech, women's embodied experience, women's subjectivity, and the truth—"the truth of our bodies and our minds," in Rich's words.[51] These essays' worries about betrayal and suppression point toward an encroaching recognition of voice as an undependable ally in the feminist cause. This is no historical accident, as the essays emerge from a moment when right-wing women were starting to mobilize women's voices against feminism. At the enormous Eagle Forum rally in Houston in 1977, conservative radio talk-show host and recently elected congressman Bob Dornan told the attendees, mostly women, "Let your voice be heard in Washington."[52] Anita Bryant vowed that "in Houston and all over the nation the voice of motherhood will be heard."[53] There was, it increasingly seemed, nothing inherently liberating about the voices of women.[54]

A talk Rich delivered the following year both reiterated a persistent desire for women's voices to remain efficacious and introduced a new recognition of mediation and labor as forces framing and complicating any feminist conception of voice. In the essay "Motherhood: The Contemporary Emergency and the Quantum Leap," which grew out of a speech to an Ohio conference on "the future of mothering," Rich begins with a ringing endorsement of sonic speech: "One of the most powerful social and political catalysts of the past decade has been the speaking of women with other women, the telling of our secrets, the comparing of wounds and the sharing of words. . . . Let this be a time, then, for hearing and speaking together, for breaking silences."[55] Her call to unite *this* present time with "the past decade," along with her use of the present perfect continuous verb tense "has been," asserts that the hearing and speaking practices that were powerful in the past can still be effective, even in the face of what the essay acknowledges as "backlash, setback, . . . temporary defeat," and "emergency."[56]

Rich nevertheless strikes some subtly new notes about voice here. "And so I begin tonight," she goes on, "by urging each of you to take responsibility for the voicing of her experience, to take seriously the work of listening to each other and the work of speaking, whether in private dialogue or in larger groups." She refers here to speaking and listening as "work," not just a by-product of embodiment. By reframing *voice* as *voicing*, she further calls attention to the labor involved, discussing voice as not attribute but action. And although she casts voice and speech as having potency undimmed from "the past decade," they are nonetheless portrayed here—as they are not in earlier feminist texts by Rich and others—as explicitly mediated, not only by labor but also by difference, distance, and the necessary techne without which voices cannot cross such distances. "I hope that here, speaking to and hearing one another," Rich's text reads, "we can begin to fling cables of recognition and attention across the conditions that have divided us."[57] The image of cables evokes something more materially present than the mention of an invisible medium like radio waves would have offered, suggesting a hope on Rich's part that labor, mediation, and difference might not alter too drastically the activity of in-person spoken communication on which second-wave feminism had been built. Here, then, is an early indication of second-wave thinking about voice as being subject to mediation enacted through labor and inflected by difference.

Amid the early-backlash conditions of feminist disappointment, other feminists were signaling exhaustion with the old model of voice. Pat Parker's collection *Movement in Black* (1978) included "Don't Let the Fascists Speak" in addition to another poem whose speaker is "tired / of hearing about" common political buzzwords and concludes,

> I'm beginning to
> wonder if
> the tactics
> of this revolution
>   is to
> talk the enemy to death.[58]

Such exhaustion appears as well in Gloria Anzaldúa's foreword to the second edition of *This Bridge Called My Back,* published in 1983. Here, in an essay that toggles between English and Spanish, Anzaldúa equates spoken language with noise and talking with inaction:

> Perhaps like me you are tired of suffering and talking about suffering . . . de contar las lluvias de sangre pero no las lluvias de flores *(. . . of counting the rains of blood but not the rains of flowers).* Like me you may be tired of making a tragedy of our lives. . . . Basta de gritar contra el viento—toda palabra es ruido si no está acompañada de acción *(enough of shouting against the wind—all words are noise if not accompanied with action).* Dejemos de hablar hasta que hagamos la palabra luminosa y activa *(let's work not talk, let's say nothing until we've made the world luminous and active).*[59]

This passage conveys a clear exhaustion with voice and a skepticism about the power of speaking. The writer is "tired of suffering and talking about suffering," which she compares to "shouting against the wind" and calls mere "noise" without action. Talking reifies "our lives," selectively congealing the active and multifaceted flux of living into a tragic genre.[60]

This exhaustion with an older model of feminist voice may help explain the changing reception to Tillie Olsen's writing about silence between the second wave's early days and the late-1970s moment of feminist disappointment. In 1965, two years after Friedan's *Feminine Mystique* diagnosed a "silent question" simmering within unhappy housewives, Olsen published an essay in *Harper's* titled "Silences: When Writers Don't Write," about the losses entailed by some writers' long unproductive periods and about the factors—many of them connected to gender, parenting, or economic hardship—that kept writers from writing.[61] This idea made waves in 1965; her article, and the mimeographed syllabi of recovered women's writing she circulated among teachers of literature, gained her a passionate feminist following over the ensuing decade. Yet by the time Olsen's book *Silences,* an expansion of the *Harper's* piece, was published in 1978, the moment for merely lamenting women's silences and celebrating their voices had passed, and the book's reception was lukewarm at best. Most feminist scholars at the time, inside and outside the academy, politely averted their gaze. *Signs* did not review the book; nor did *Sinister Wisdom* or *off our backs.*[62] Even committed feminist scholars and Olsen partisans found it underwhelming: a review in *Women's Studies* by a scholar who professed deep admiration for "Tell Me a Riddle" criticized the new book's "fragmentary, repetitive, and discussive" qualities and concluded that "the cumulative impact is paralyzing."[63]

In the face of the exhaustion and paralysis spurred by the old conception of voice, some feminists investigated other approaches to the topic. In 1978, as the flagship women's studies journal *Signs* was ignoring *Silences,* it published an article in which Cornell University linguist Sally McConnell-Ginet surveyed existing research on gender differences in spoken language. McConnell-Ginet explained that in English these differences are limited to intonation, which she poetically termed "speech melodies" and "the tunes to which we set the text of our talk."[64] Perhaps most interestingly, she noted that what she called the dynamism, or relative mobility and range, of women's intonations is often understood as a marker of emotional expressivity, with women's speech heard by androcentric listeners as indicating excessive emotionality. Pushing back against this sexist interpretation, McConnell-Ginet argued that the qualities of women's speech that get heard as emotional expressivity may in fact be merely habitual speech patterns, or serve purposes other than conveying emotion. In this article, as elsewhere in feminist thought about voice beginning in the late 1970s, attention to voice as a set of sonic practices enables and even invites a more critical perspective toward the relationship between "voice" and women's expressivity.

Despite these clear signals of critical attitudes toward early second-wave approaches to voice (and its purported opposite, silence), feminists continued to organize conversations around these concepts throughout the late 1970s, but increasingly their participants declined to take up the phonocentric charge. Two such conference sessions stand as examples: "The Transformation of Silence into Language and Action," a panel convened at the Modern Language Association convention in December 1977, and "Woman and Culture: Her Silence, Her Voice," a session of a 1979 feminist theory conference held at New York University to commemorate the thirtieth anniversary of Simone de Beauvoir's *The Second Sex.*

"The Transformation of Silence into Language and Action," a panel organized by the Modern Language Association's Lesbians and Literature group, drew an audience of 700 people. The session was chaired by Julia P. Stanley and included talks by Mary Daly, Audre Lorde, Judith McDaniel, and Adrienne Rich. Lorde's presentation, which has endured as a classic feminist discussion of the importance of speaking up, also included several remarks about potential limitations of speech. "I have come to believe over and over again that what is most important to me must be spoken, made verbal and shared," she said, "even at the risk of having it bruised or misunderstood." On Lorde's account, speaking is worthwhile not for any promise of easeful or effectual communication; it can even subject one's meaning to injury and misconstrual. Its primary value is the benefit it offers to the speaker: "That the speaking profits me, beyond any other effect."[65]

The other main effect of speech, for Lorde, has to do with its ability to stage the unfinished, effortful activity of a heterogeneous critical community marked by difference: "But for every real word spoken, for every attempt I had ever made to speak those truths for which I am still seeking, I had made contact with other women while we examined the words to fit a world in which we all believed, bridging our differences. And it was the concern and caring of all those women which gave me strength and enabled me to scrutinize the essentials of my living."[66]

These critical examinations of what speech can do are admittedly milder than the skepticism about speech that Lorde's friend Pat Parker had written into "Don't Let the Fascists Speak." Yet Lorde's remarks contrast with the other panelists' approaches to the subject, including Stanley's opening remarks extolling speech about one's lesbian identity and Daly's speculative etymologies of words such as *hag* and *crone*. They contrast as well with Rich's talk on the panel, a very early version of what would eventually develop into her reflection on women and racism titled "Disloyal to Civilization" but which at this gathering took Olsen as a key point of departure to focus primarily on "writing and teaching, as a choice between collusion with silence, or revolt against silence."[67]

Lorde's address famously takes aim at silence on the grounds that keeping silent will attenuate neither risk nor fear: "My silences had not protected me. And your silence will not protect you."[68] Yet for all the attention Lorde pays to what it means to speak, she does not connect this act to the specific figure of voice or propose a faith in a personalized, identifiable vehicle of speech. In fact, the one mention of "voice" in her talk associates it not with untrammeled expression but with fear, the very thing that stands in the way of speech and visibility throughout the talk. "And, of course, I am afraid—you can hear it in my voice."[69] Speech for Lorde is meaningful because of the collectives it assembles, and it is rendered through a sonic voice that is vulnerable to faltering.

At the essay's rhetorical apex, Lorde contrasts silence not to voice but to visibility: "In the cause of silence, each of us draws the face of her own fear—fear of contempt, of censure, or some judgment, or recognition, of challenge, of annihilation. But most of all, I think, we fear the visibility without which we cannot truly live."[70] This synesthetic crossing subtly but profoundly redistributes the veneration of voice and opposition to images that had prevailed in second-wave feminist thought ever since Friedan pitted the *voice* of the dissatisfied woman against the sexist *image*. Lorde's introduction of visibility also opens up onto a discussion of Blackness, not only as one element in the dialectical flourishing of difference that anchors so much of Lorde's thinking overall but also as marking a particular sensory history: the history of Black people, and especially Black women, in relationship to visually based epistemologies and regimes of racialized difference. She elaborates:

> Within this country where Blackness creates a constant, if unspoken, distortion of vision, Black women have on one hand always been highly visible, and so, on the other hand, have been rendered invisible through the depersonalization of racism. Even within the women's movement, we have had to fight, and still do, for that very visibility which also renders us most vulnerable, our Blackness. For to survive in the mouth of this dragon we call america, we have had to learn this first and most vital lesson—that we were never meant to survive. Not as human beings. And neither were most of you here today, Black or not. And that visibility which makes us most vulnerable is that which also is the source of our greatest strength.[71]

In Lorde's telling, Black women have always been subjected to an "unspoken distortion of vision," a systematic visual misrecognition that gives rise to a stark insight into one's vulnerability to being destroyed. Recognition of this vulnerability is essential to survival, and it is applicable across difference, relevant to "most of you here today, Black or not," while retaining its roots in Blackness and its relationship to racialized visibility.

Lorde's call to visibility within a forum organized around silence and language offers evidence that even as outdated figurations of silence and voice continued to structure feminist thought, some feminists were calling for intensified attention to vision as another register in which oppression and liberation, especially engaging race as well as gender, could play out. A similar call for vision within a voice-centered forum took place the following year, at the *Second Sex* conference at New York University. There, veteran feminist and *Ms.* magazine editor Robin Morgan chaired a panel titled "Woman and Culture: Her Silence, Her Voice." The panelists, theorists and philosophers Evelyn Keller, Iris Marion Young, Hélène Cixous, and Sandra Lee Bartky, all found ways to sidestep or disregard the panel's titular frame. The precirculated papers that were discussed in the session contain no mentions of silence or voice. Bartky even addressed vision directly, calling—as Lorde and Parker had before her—for careful attention to the affordances of vision for feminist thought. Bartky offered a brief for "feminine narcissism," working to claim as useful the pleasure women can derive from being, literally, seen, and she concluded with a call for the elaboration of a new collective feminist subject of vision: "As part of our practice, a new witness must be created, a collective Significant Other, become part of the self but nourished and strengthened from without, from a revolutionary feminist community. This collective Other, while not requiring body display, will not taboo it either; it will allow and even encourage fantasy and play in self-ornamentation. Without falling into hypocrisy or sentimentality, our ideas of what is beautiful will have to be expanded and so altered that we will perceive ourselves and one another very differently than we do now."[72]

In the same moment, emerging conversations in sex-radical feminism and academic feminist theory were likewise coalescing around unanswered questions about vision and visuality. The landmark 1982 Barnard Conference on Sexuality, which was organized as a response to antipornography activism among feminists, aimed to rethink not just sexuality but vision and visuality as well. In her introduction to *Pleasure and Danger*, the anthology that grew out of the 1982 event, conference organizer Carole Vance noted with concern the proliferation of "polemical slide shows mounted by Right to Life groups or some feminist anti-pornography groups," and she argued that feminists were vulnerable to manipulation or outmaneuvering because the movement had not yet developed a critical approach to images.[73] The controversies over porn, sadism and masochism, and butch and femme identities showed how urgently feminism needed to cultivate "a more developed analysis of symbolic context and transformation, especially difficult in regard to visual material where our education, vocabulary, and sophistication are far less developed than in regard to literary texts. Our visual illiteracy," she concluded, "renders the image overpowering."[74]

To that end, film theorist Mary Ann Doane and artist Barbara Kruger organized a workshop at the conference that promised to "explore both issues of the relation between the woman and the image and issues surrounding the possibility of female spectatorship. What happens when the woman appropriates the gaze? Can feminists use the visual in non-problematic ways or is the image so ideologically loaded that it can only be deconstructed?"[75] Kruger's contribution of artwork to *Pleasure and Danger,* based on her presentation in this session, is accompanied by a text where she writes that her work constitutes a series of attempts "to welcome a female spectator into the audience of men."[76]

Many second-wave feminist thinkers, from Friedan to Rich, long embraced voice as a symbol of autonomy, self-presence, and political participation. For many feminists of color, meanwhile, the pitfalls of voice were quickly apparent: the voices of women of color could too easily be drowned out, as they are for Parker in "Don't Let the Fascists Speak"; misheard and misinterpreted, as Lorde acknowledges; or requisitioned for tragic tales, as Anzaldúa laments. Also, any concept of voice that relied on a conception of a liberal subjectivity expressible through speech that would be received as rational was an uneasy fit for Black women and other women of color, whose historical relation to such perceptions of subjectivity and rationality was strained from the start.[77]

As much as the feminist elevation of voice initially may have aimed to amalgamate a democratic ideal of rational speech with an embrace of embodied identity, this aspirational combination often rested on an idealized selfhood whose mere audible presence and inclusion, it was hoped, would change the world for the better. This was always unrealistic: voices simply don't work that way, and neither does democracy. But it was especially incongruous where women of color were concerned, because when the voices of women of color have been heard by power in the United States, they have more often been heard as noise than as rational speech.

Thus the desire feminist voice indexes—a wish for women's speech to produce political change merely through the sonic self-presence, whether private or public, that it enacts—had by the late 1970s proved to be an unrealistic fantasy that could only disappoint. The repeals, reversals, and challenges that were already eroding feminists' cultural and political victories revealed some of the limitations of voice. And the ascendant intellectual project of Black and Third World feminisms both enabled a more layered understanding of voice's operations and highlighted the importance of visuality as an additional arena that might differently encompass racialized histories and enable coalitions across difference.

An intensified attention to feminist visuality, and to the importance of images in discussions of both sexuality and race, is at the core of two poems written in the early 1980s, one by Rich and one by Lorde. It is to these poems, and the dialogue between them, that I will now turn.

Adrienne Rich and Audre Lorde in the Visual Field

Rich wrote "The Images" in 1976–1978 and published it in 1981, as the opening poem in her collection *A Wild Patience Has Taken Me This Far.*[78] In this poem, Rich asks whether it would be possible to reclaim the terrain of the visual from patriarchal violence, and whether images might offer greater liberation and empowerment than language. Speech serves in the poem not as a means of empowerment but as a burden from which images might set one free. Lorde's poem "Afterimages," written in 1981 and first published in 1982, can be read as a response to Rich's, and it challenges Rich's binary between speech and images, offering instead a striking exploration of the power of active seeing, careful listening, and the compassionate transcription of voice and silence to assemble difficult solidarities across differences of race and history.[79] Lorde's poem also highlights how Rich's poem blurs the workings of spectacular violence across registers and racial lines in ways that read today, at least in parts, as severely undertheorized—somewhat surprisingly so, given how concertedly Rich was thinking about race and difference and discussing these issues with Lorde.[80]

The opening stanza of Rich's "The Images" circulates through touch and sound to set a scene of two lovers lying in bed, listening to late-night sirens beneath them.

> Close to your body, in the
>   pain of the city
> I turn. My hand half-sleeping reaches, finds
>   some part of you, touch knows you before language
>   names in the brain. Out in the dark

a howl, police sirens, emergency
    our 3 a.m. familiar, ripping the sheath of sleep
  registering pure force as if all transpired—
the swell of cruelty and helplessness—
    in one block between West End
  and Riverside.

Here, as the poem begins, a variety of sensory interactions jostle one another. Touch offers direct access to interpersonal knowledge, preceding language and tendering comfort; an invasive sound "register[s] pure force," directly communicating crisis and pain from the outside world. In a single caesura-cleaved line—"names in the brain. Out in the dark"—cognition and linguistic identification are joined through juxtaposition, sound, and rhythm to an obscure cacophony of vulnerability that roils, unseen, outside the safety of the domestic scene in the few lines that follow:

    drawn against the updraft
  of burning life, the tongueless cries
of the city.

In the unsettling urban soundscape Rich presents, a direct knowledge of life is conveyed neither through language (whether spoken or written) nor through images but through touch and pure sound, without any perceptible mediating operations. Even the "cries / of the city" are "tongueless": inarticulate, but telling in their nonlinguistic quality. The image evokes, if distantly, both the rape of Philomela and the lynching of Emmett Till, a twinned allusion that is of immense importance to the Rich poem and to Lorde's response.

The titular "images" do not appear until the second stanza, where the speaker's reflections on the pain in the streets turn from formless sounds to visual objectification.

    but when did we ever choose
  to see our bodies strung
in bondage and crucifixion across the exhausted air
    when did we choose
  to be lynched on the queasy electric signs
of midtown

Here Rich makes the startling suggestion that pornographic imagery renders women akin to lynched bodies. Indeed, when Rich read the poem at Saint

Peter's Church in New York in 1979, an event where Lorde also read, Rich added extra emphasis to the word "lynched," enunciating it loudly and pausing after its bunched consonants. The image returns by the end of the second stanza: "in the name of freedom of speech/they are lynching us no law is on our side."

A disillusionment with the First Amendment, familiar from Pat Parker's "Don't Let the Fascists Speak," spills over into a disenchantment with words themselves: the next stanza begins with the line "I can never romanticize language again." Because words carry "power for disguise for mystification," the poem's speaker seeks to distance herself from words entirely, sidling up to pictures instead. Sitting "near the sea/among parched yet flowering weeds," she eyes a "thorned purple-tongued flower, each petal/protected by its thorn-leaf." This tongue brings not voice or speech but a jagged, sharpened self-defense. Drawing the flower in a notebook, she experiences its wordlessness as her own, and as exoneration:

> I was mute
>   innocent of grammar as the waves
> irrhythmically washing   I felt washed clean
>   of the guilt of words   there was no word to read
>   in the book of that earth no perjury

The speaker's disenchantment with language is then further crystallized by an encounter with an unidentified female figure.

> When I saw hér face, she of the several faces
>   staring   indrawn   in judgment   laughing for joy
> her serpents twisting   her arms raised
>   her breasts gazing
>   when I looked into hér world
> I wished to cry loose my soul
>   into her, to become
>   free of speech   at last.

For all the declared wish to be free of speech, Rich's orthography here, her unusual use of accents to mark emphasis, aims with precision to approximate speech in writing. And her aerated invocation of one of the most famous political speeches in American history ("free of speech   at last") seems to mark a persistent desire for language that might be able to liberate instead of imprison.

At the reading at Saint Peter's Church, Rich spoke of the poem as growing out of a trip she had taken to Crete, "where I saw for the first time, in large numbers, strong, positive images of women in the museums, among the ruins, enormous labryses painted on jars several feet tall, figures of the snake goddess—all kinds of intrinsically female images as the common images of that culture. And I realized how I had hungered for such images and how in our waking life, in this world, we do not see such images."[81]

But the poem's ancient image of a woman is not only *seen* here; she herself sees as well. Of her "several faces," the first one mentioned is "staring." And in the line "her breasts gazing," the word "gazing" syntactically attaches not only to the subsequent line about the speaker's gaze but to the breasts as well, suggesting that the goddess-like figure derives visual agency from, not despite, her hyperexposure. This possibility stands in direct contrast to the poem's overall fear about pornography's ill effects, and it brings to mind Nicole Fleetwood's concepts of hypervisuality and excess flesh as ways to trouble the field of vision through being especially visible.[82]

This female figure renders the speaker "a woman starving / for images"—or, if the enjambment here is read a different way, longing for these images to speak to her after all ("for images / to say"), which might amount to a reconciliation of image and speech:

> And so I came home   a woman starving
> for images
> to say my hunger is so old
> so fundamental . . .

The speaker wishes, or wants the images to tell her, that lost or suppressed visual representations of female power

> could rise   reassemble   re-collect   re-member
> themselves as I recollected myself in that presence
> as every night close to your body
> in the pain of the city, turning
> I am remembered by you, remember you
> even as we are dismembered
> on the cinema screens, the white expensive walls
> of collectors, the newsrags blowing the streets
> —and it would not be enough.
> This is the war of the images.

The war, then, plays out between, on the one hand, visual images of women that "dismember" the speaker, her lover, and women overall, and, on the other hand, images that might hold women's bodies together in a way that would not be new but would build on a long, suppressed history. It is not an equal fight, though, and the poem is far from optimistic that recovering previously suppressed images of women could ever carry the day. The speaker dreams of assembling a counter-repository of images from "all the lost/crumbled burnt smashed shattered defaced/overpainted concealed and falsely named/faces," a recovery effort that would mirror the interpersonal way the speaker and her lover "remember" each other through their proximity in bed. Yet that private, domestic sheltering, Rich writes, "would not be enough." All media—film, art, newspapers—mediate and dehumanize; language, whether spoken or written, distorts. The best one can hope for is a private, barbed, wordless, mutual self-defense: "We are the thorn-leaf guarding the purple-tongued flower/each to each."

There is little doubt that Audre Lorde was familiar with Rich's "The Images" by the time she wrote "Afterimages" in 1981. As noted earlier, Rich read "The Images" at an event with Lorde in New York in May 1979. The two poets' friendship and professional collaboration were well established by the late 1970s; in 1979, in addition to reading together at Saint Peter's Church and both speaking at the *Second Sex* conference at New York University, the two conducted a conversation with each other that was published in *Signs*.[83] This deep and ongoing dialogue between the two poets, the pronounced overlap in concerns and imagery between the two poems, and the poems' titles all support a reading of Lorde's poem as being, at least in part, a response and a successor to Rich's.

Lorde's poem, like Rich's, investigates alternative possibilities for visuality. Yet while Rich largely limits her consideration of visuality to the different ways contemporary women can be *seen* (with the Greek figure as the ancient exception proving the present-day rule), Lorde writes into her own poem a powerful enactment of the principle Hortense Spillers would announce at the Barnard Conference on Sexuality the following year: "The subject is certainly seen, but she or he certainly sees."[84] "Afterimages" outlines a robust argument for seizing sight as a source of power amid violence and destruction. In addition, Lorde's poem critiques Rich's equation of pornography with lynching and of sexual images with "dismember[ing]," by directly confronting racial as well as sexual difference. And Lorde points toward a more complex engagement with visuality than most other feminists, including Rich, had been able to conceive.

"Afterimages" is organized around a syncretic act of seeing historically. The poem's speaker, watching television, sees a white Mississippi woman bemoaning the destruction caused by a flooded river, and this footage calls forth in the speaker's memory another image of loss connected with a river in Mississippi: Emmett Till's corpse. The speaker combines these two visions, image and afterimage, across decades and contexts, superimposing Till's body upon the contemporary woman's grief:

> A white woman stands bereft and empty
> a black boy hacked into a murderous lesson
> recalled in me forever
> like a lurch of earth on the edge of sleep
> etched into my visions
>
> . . .
>
> fused images beneath my pain.

The speaker of "Afterimages" conjures images from the past that arrive to animate and thicken a present moment—an operation that should already be familiar to us from "Don't Let the Fascists Speak." In Parker's poem, though, the images allegorize a broader conclusion that it falls to the speaker to analyze before the poem can conclude. In Lorde's, it is the images themselves, along with the act of juxtaposing them, that carry their own significance.

Lorde's poem explores the speaker's history of interactions with "pictures of black broken flesh," engagements both imposed and willed. The initial encounter takes place through no action of the speaker's own, but the speaker—and specifically her eyes, her faculty of sight—turns the excruciating images into a source of strength. The poem begins:

> However the image enters
> its force remains within
> my eyes
> rockstrewn caves where dragonfish evolve
> wild for life, relentless and acquisitive
> learning to survive
> where there is no food
> my eyes are always hungry
> and remembering
> however the image enters
> its force remains.

An image may be painful, it may impose itself with cruelty and violence, but the power with which it insinuates itself into the speaker's vision becomes her own power, helping her survive. Lorde metaphorizes the speaker's eyes as sites for evolution, homes for life-forms that have "learn[ed] to survive/where there is no food." But far from being merely passive sites of change, the eyes are also alive and active themselves, "always hungry/and remembering," both habitat and creature.

Lorde contrasts these eyes, in their boldly seeing survival, with Emmett Till's "gouged out eyes/sewed shut," which appeared in the summer of 1955 in

> newspapers protest posters magazines
> Police Story, Confidential, True
> the avid insistence of detail
> pretending insight or information
> the length of gash across the dead boy's loins
> his grieving mother's lamentation
> the severed lips, how many burns
> his gouged out eyes
> sewed shut upon the screaming covers
> louder than life
> all over

The speaker tried not to look—"I walked through a northern summer/my eyes averted/from each corner's photographies"—but the image worked its way in, searing itself into the speaker's sight: "His broken body is the afterimage of my 21st year." These grotesque images cross over into sound, but the sound is that of "screaming," rather than a speaking voice.

Lorde's critique of Till's appearance across multiple media, of "the secret relish/of a black child's mutilated body" that underlies the images' replication, is reminiscent of Rich's denunciation of "the cinema screens, the white expensive walls/of collectors, the newsrags blowing the streets." Yet in implicating "protest posters" as well as newspapers and magazines, Lorde embarks on a more ambivalent exploration of suffering and spectacle. The historical display of Till's body, of course, was first of all a tactical one, famously chosen by Mamie Till Mobley as a call to ethical witness and public action. But the poem insists that to recirculate images of violence, even with the intention of raising awareness or spurring action, is still to recirculate images of violence. This recirculation is bound to pain many viewers, to titillate others, and to contribute, however inadvertently, to an association of that suffering body with vulnerability to violence.[85] In the poem, witnessing these images impresses upon the speaker the ubiquity of anti-Black violence, and it accustoms her to that violence—

wherever I looked that summer
I learned to be at home with children's blood
with savored violence
with pictures of black broken flesh
used, crumpled, and discarded
lying amid the sidewalk refuse
like a raped woman's face.

—but as the anguished string of past participles makes clear, it does not de-sensitize her. This speaker is lingering amid the persistent aftermath of vio-lence, dwelling there, though not by choice.

Inverting Rich's metaphor, Lorde connects images of Till's broken body to a "raped woman's face." Whereas Rich wrote of women being "lynched/on the queasy electric signs/of midtown"—"lynched," that is, in image alone—Lorde anchors her own metaphoric web with perhaps the most well-known lynched body of the twentieth century. Lynching is a spectacular crime, in-tended as imagistic terror, which is presumably why it struck Rich as an ap-propriate metaphor. But lynching is not *only* an image; it is also actual violence against a Black body, violence so horrifying in its scale that it seems to repel metaphor, conjuring an irreducible corporeality. In Lorde's poem, Till's body becomes a sacramental one, returned to infuse feminism with the reality of racist terror.

The hurt-drenched seeing that follows in the wake of the initial looking and looking away, the production of "fused images beneath my pain," proves gen-erative. This, too, is a major change from Rich's poem, where images of violence and dehumanization cancel out the possibility of old counterimages' resur-facing to any meaningful effect. In the aftermath of that speaker's encounter with the Cretan icon, she does not play an active role in reconvening old images; her hope is rather that these historical images would "reassemble re-collect re-member/*themselves*" (emphasis added). Lorde, in contrast, does not imagine such a passive seeing subject, nor such ultimately agential images. For her—as for the speaker of "Don't Let the Fascists Speak," who viewed "images/of jews in camps–/of homosexuals in camps–/of socialists in camps–" beneath more contemporary "faces in/a college classroom"—the seeing subject super-imposes historical and present images, producing a visual palimpsest that reveals the workings of history, opens a space for the past to reshape the present, and serves as a potential source of strength for those who see. This is a question not just of the historicity of images but of seeing historically.

The speaker's act of seeing historically, in "Afterimages," enables Till to live on as more than battered flesh; he "rides the crest of the Pearl, whistling," sounding again the piercingly insouciant paravocal utterance that his killers tried to silence. This practice of seeing transforms images of pain and degradation into sustenance for the seeing subject, illuminating a methodology for Lorde's 1982 proclamation that "one of the most basic Black survival skills is the ability to change, to metabolize experience, good or ill, into something that is useful, lasting, effective."[86] But it also returns sound to the historical scene.

Seeing historically makes space for complicated relations across difference that aren't reducible to blame but exceed any easy solidarity. The poem imagines that the white woman who has lost her home in the flood is an alternate incarnation of Emmett Till's accuser, Carolyn Bryant, and that the same river where Till's body was cast has reared up to take its revenge, freeing the speaker of any burden of empathy or charity:

> 24 years his ghost lay like the shade of a raped woman
> and a white girl has grown older in costly honor
> (what did she pay to never know its price?)
> now the Pearl River speaks its muddy judgment
> and I can withhold my pity and my bread.

Yet even alongside this statement of *possible* noncare, the speaker offers empathy to the white woman anyway, understanding her not just as an heir to or grown-up version of Bryant but also as a victim of sexism silenced by her husband, who abruptly cuts her off from speaking to the television reporter:

> a man with ham-like hands pulls her aside
> snarling "She ain't got nothing more to say!"
> and that lie hangs in his mouth
> like a shred of rotting meat.

In connecting this unnamed woman with Bryant, the poem not only finds the flood woman a holder of a shared blood-guilt, but it also, conversely, finds a way to attenuate Bryant's own culpability, writing of her as a silenced white girl who was "never allowed her own tongue / without power or conclusion / unvoiced": more a pawn of white male power than an accomplice to it, permitted to speak only if she gives the white supremacist patriarchy what it needs. There is a difficult solidarity at work here, a solidarity focused on systems of power, rather than individual perfidy or malice, while nevertheless stopping short of forgiveness.

It is a solidarity that proceeds by attending to and transcribing someone else's sonic voice. Lorde transcribes the unnamed woman's words from the television with care, setting down the sounds of her accented speech—"'we jest come from the bank yestiddy'"—while noting the tone of her "flat bewildered words" and the "despair [that] weighs down her voice." It is a markedly sonic voice, then, that the husband proceeds to silence with a snarl.

Lorde's decision to mitigate Bryant's culpability is even more striking in light of the role Till's story already played in feminist politics. In the 1975 best seller *Against Our Will: Men, Women, and Rape,* Susan Brownmiller had argued that "what began in Bryant's store should not be misconstrued as an innocent flirtation.... Emmett Till was going to show his black buddies that he, and by inference, they, could get a white woman.... The accessibility of all white women was on review." Brownmiller continued, "We are rightly aghast that a whistle could be cause for murder, but we must also accept that Emmett Till and J. W. Milam shared something in common. They both understood that the whistle was no small tweet ... it was a deliberate insult, just short of physical assault, a last reminder to Carolyn Bryant that this black boy, Till, had in mind to possess her."[87]

Brownmiller's glaringly racist revision of the Till story, by a founder of the group Women Against Pornography (of which Rich was also an active member), brings even more plainly to the surface what is so disturbing about Rich's equation of pornography with lynching in "The Images." If sexual objectification in whatever guise is on par with lynching, then the injustice of Till's murder dwindles, because he committed, or "had in mind to commit," an equivalent assault. The ethical and historical errors of this line of thought hardly need be spelled out. Rich's use of lynching as a metaphor might on its own seem mere hyperbole, or a tone-deaf consideration of spectacle and intimidation, but in light of Brownmiller's book, we can discern even more clearly how Lorde's exhuming of Till, her concerted re-presentation of his body, offers a pointed critique of Rich's poetic logic.

Lorde's poem understands that in the always historical drama of images, the one who sees must seek sustenance in whatever is at hand. The poem's closing lines gesture back to its opening stanza, where enjambment asserted a relationship between vision and nourishment, connecting the speaker's eyes with a *lack* of food: "where there is no food / my eyes are always hungry." By its closing lines, "my visions," and the pain-soaked "fused images" they assemble, are revealed to be a form of food after all:

> etched into my visions
> food for dragonfish that learn
> to live upon whatever they must eat
> fused images beneath my pain.

The speaker's eyes found nothing to eat, but the actively superimposed visions, produced by the deliberate work of seeing historically, prove to be a source of sustenance. The practice of active seeing, when undertaken in tandem with transcriptive attention to the sonic voice of an unforgivable other, produces a difficult and nourishing solidarity.

From Historical Seeing to "the Dancing Voice Embodied"

Lorde's "Afterimages" anticipates an endorsement of active and syncretic seeing that we find in Hortense Spillers's essay "Interstices" of the following year, and it also anticipates Spillers's insight there that attention to the visual enables a fuller reckoning with voice in all its sonic, embodied, mediated complexity. "Interstices" poses an expansively gendered spectator not as a question or even as an intervention but as an already existing fact. "The subject is certainly seen," Spillers declares, "but she or he certainly sees." One's relation to the visual is particular and conditioned by multiple factors—this may be the double meaning of *certainly* that leads her to repeat the word—yet that must not detract from the task at hand, which is to recognize *seeing* as itself productive: "It is this latter seeing," she continues, "that negotiates at every point a space for living, and it is the latter, though an armed force will help, that we must willingly name the counter-power, the counter-mythology."[88]

Here Spillers articulates with poetic compression a strong claim for the visual, and especially for seeing, as a space of active engagement that generates political effects. It is connected to what Nicole Fleetwood would later theorize as "the visual, visible, viewed and viewing black subject," and to what Nicholas Mirzoeff would analyze as countervisualities: practices of active seeing in opposition to structures of authority that rule by categorizing and segregating based on sight. "The right to look," Mirzoeff suggests, "claims autonomy from this authority, refuses to be segregated, and spontaneously invents new forms."[89]

In the early 1980s, amid myriad disappointments, vision eclipsed voice as the central concept in feminist thought. Many factors contributed to this shift, including the inability of voice to do everything early feminists asked it to do and the reality of vision as a site of oppression along racial as well as gender lines. Through the idea of vision, feminists metabolized disappointment and managed, like the dragonfish of Lorde's poem, to make lasting sustenance out of a challenging period's seemingly meager meal.

But that was not the end of the story. In "Interstices," Spillers not only talks about seeing but also directs attention to "the domain of music and America's black female vocalists," proposing that early female blues singers offer an important archive documenting Black women's experiences of sexuality. She speaks of the blues singer as "the dancing voice embodied," and as "a living body, insinuating itself through a material scene" amid "a dance of motives, in which the motor behavior, the changes of countenance, the vocal dynamics, the calibration of gesture and nuance in relationships to a formal object—the song itself—is a precise demonstration of the subject turning in fully conscious knowledge of her own resources toward her object."[90]

In other words, in a moment when feminists have loosened their grip on an outdated notion of voice in order to ask expansive questions about vision, Spillers demonstrates how keen attention to vision and active seeing does not lead to merely swapping out voice in favor of vision but rather enables and demands accounting for the voice as sonic, subject to mediation and performance, inflected by race as well as gender, ineluctably embodied, and understandable through the transcriptive practices that allow "the song itself" to travel between performance, sheet music, and transcribed lyrics in an academic lecture later published as a pathbreaking essay.

Perhaps the best way to understand feminism's ongoing hope for the right questions, its perpetual quest for the perfect object or figure of thought that might solve once and for all (or even just for now) the problems that feminism both addresses and presents, is to listen all the way back through the century to W. E. B. Du Bois where he writes, referring to the multiple objects that arose in the aftermath of Emancipation, "All these we need, not singly but together, not successively but together, each growing and aiding each."[91] The dialectical fusion of senses and scenes is part of what Spillers assembled an audience for at Barnard. If the subject certainly sees, then the subject, through that seeing, not only accesses possible counterpower or a space for living or sustenance but also becomes subject to a call to witness and heed something beyond the imagined voice of self-presence, something discernible and transcribable in scenes including a blues performance, a nightly news report, and a poet's recitation recorded for later radio broadcast amid technical difficulties.

The project of rethinking voice, a project that was held in common across multiple feminist tendencies, gives us insight into the productions of those moments in political history when activist movements can't agree on a way forward. Stories about feminist history often narrate the late 1970s and early 1980s as a time of fracture, when a once-unified movement became riven by internal differences around race, professional positioning, ideology, and erotics. Yet amid all of this ostensible fracturing, a shared metaphoric shift cut across many sectors in feminism. A dynamic discussion about voice and image as productively interlinked through the mediating operations of transcription, technology, and the body emerged through a common effort, and thus became a location of possible if not always actualized solidarity, even as other avenues seemed to be closing off. Through amplifying attentiveness to sight and sound, a period of political disappointment gave rise to metaphors and concepts that were more important than abeyance, more long-lasting than dejection, and more connected and productive than narratives of fragmentation suggest.

CHAPTER 5

THE ANCESTORS' BREATH

AIDS and Aural Coalitions

In her essay "Coalition Politics: Turning the Century," the musician and veteran civil rights activist Bernice Johnson Reagon issues a call for building coalitions and for thinking beyond the boundaries of individual life-spans.[1] Much of what she says in this essay, based on a workshop she led at the West Coast Women's Music Festival in 1981, is now classic advice for anyone who wishes to work in coalition with others: recognize the necessity of working across difference; expect discomfort; maintain a nurturing home base that can recharge you for the challenging work of building solidarity, but keep in mind that all such protected spaces are vulnerable to attack, and that only through joining forces with people different from yourself can substantive change possibly be brought about. Reagon also discusses the importance of staying alive long enough to do this kind of work: "None of this matters at all very much if you die tomorrow—that won't even be cute," she says, advising her audience to ask movement elders how they have managed to keep going.[2]

Toward the end of this piece, though, as Reagon expands on her advice about coalition building and intergenerational dialogue, she adds a call to consider the effects of one's actions beyond the boundaries of a single lifetime. "Most of us think that the space we live in is the most important space there is, and that the condition we find ourselves in is the condition that must be changed or else," she says. "But most of the things you do, if you do them right, are for people who live long after you are long forgotten," she goes on to say. Building connections beyond one's individual life-span, by saying or doing things that others can benefit from when one is no longer alive, is described here as a practice of generosity: "Whatever it is that you know, give it away, and don't give it away only on the horizontal. Don't give it away like that, because they're gonna die when you die, give or take a few days. Give it away *that* way (up and down)."[3] The phrase "up and down" takes her advice beyond merely connecting with people in the future, suggesting instead a bidirectional generosity that extends equally toward those who came before, the movement elders she'd spoken of earlier and perhaps even those who have already died.

The appearance of "up and down" within parentheses aligns it with other parentheticals that appear throughout the talk as published in the 1983 Black feminist anthology *Home Girls,* most of which seem to indicate audible responses of the festival audience: "(Applause)," "(Laughter)," "(Laughter and hoots)." A smaller number of parentheticals seem to set off spoken asides— "the definition of 'women' that's in the dictionary (which you didn't write, right?)"—but the clear majority can be understood as offering faint echoes on the page of the original workshop's collective sonic atmosphere.[4] Whether Reagon spoke the words "up and down" as an aside or added them when she was preparing this text for publication—to transcribe, perhaps, a hand motion she'd made at the workshop—her parenthetical comes to us in the text as an incomplete indication of what happened in the workshop and a reminder of her published piece's intermedial status: something that doesn't quite fit the textual frame ungrounds the written form ever so slightly, invoking but not satisfactorily reconstituting the collective initially addressed. It points toward, but can't fully grant access to, the event of the 1981 workshop, the sounds and motions of that physical assembly. Reagon's parentheses can be approached as tiny rips in the text, hinting at the presence of the document's capacious outside, context that a printed essay can hold space for but not encapsulate. Placing our ears to these rips, we try to tune in.

This exceeding—of generation, of form—is sonically called for and performed in a song Reagon was singing around the same time with the a cappella group she founded and led. The Sweet Honey in the Rock song "Breaths," which was composed in 1980 by group member Ysaye Barnwell and today remains one of the group's best-known songs, similarly addresses generosity and coalition exceeding individual life-spans, and it enticingly sets forth listening as a practice for enacting expansive alliances.[5] The lyrics, drawn from a poem by Birago Diop, encourage listeners to

> Listen more often to things than to beings
> Listen more often to things than to beings
> 'Tis the ancestors' breath when the fire's voice is heard
> 'Tis the ancestors' breath in the voice of the waters[6]

Sounds of nature, the lyrics proclaim, offer audible evidence that "those who have died have never, never left / The dead have a pact with the living," and the song urges its audience to draw near to and care for ancestors by listening closely for them. What's being advocated here can be described as listening as a practice of solidarity across difference—in this case the difference between beings and things, between living and dead.

"Breaths" is a midtempo a cappella song in which musical form fuses with paramusical soundings. In the song, what these sounds attaching to musical form render audible is not primarily disappointment, as we heard in Chapter 2, but the persistence of messages from past times and lives, whether disappointed or not. The song's main musical elements are relatively simple and concise: The melody occupies the compact span of a perfect fifth, devoid of challenging leaps or other technical demands, and it is sung by two lead voices that move almost unwaveringly in parallel thirds, with their two melodic lines, alike in contour and direction, separated by a narrow and mostly constant interval. Backing singers provide a bassline and ostinato on sonorous syllables, wordlessly maintaining a buoyant rhythm.

The song's most memorable parts are the places that approximate the ancestors' breaths referenced in the lyrics. At the end of each refrain, the lead singers leave off words momentarily to turn their voices into fire, wind, and water:

> 'Tis the ancestors' breath
> In the voice of the waters
> Ah—wsh.

The backing singers keep up the rhythm in these moments, grounding and framing the sibilant evocations of ancestral breath. At the song's conclusion, the backing voices, too, gradually stop singing notes and join in on the nature sounds, such that the melody and harmony both give way to sequences of unpitched *ah*s and *wsh*s. Finally the song sizzles out on a procession of *wsh—wsh—wsh—wsh—wsh—wsh*.

This song is the opening track on Sweet Honey in the Rock's live album *Good News*, released in 1981. When the live album was recorded in Washington, DC, three days after Ronald Reagan was elected president in November 1980, real-life good news was already in short supply for Sweet Honey in the Rock's left-of-center listeners. The cover of the album was laid out like the front page of a newspaper with an above-the-fold photo of the band, the album title doubling as a banner headline, the clear implication being that Sweet Honey in the Rock could offer good news in sonic form at a time when it was otherwise in short supply. At a moment of political defeat, listening for those who had come before appeared as a practice of disappointment and even a possible source of good news.

What's at stake in both "Breaths" and Reagon's talk on coalition is the idea that collective practices can and should exceed the boundaries of individual lifespans. This notion has been quietly present at least in the background of the historical disappointments this book has engaged with so far, and as we turn to the AIDS crisis in this final chapter, it becomes even more pronounced, because of the accelerated pace and staggering scale of death in the early years of AIDS in the United States.

The filmmaker Julie Dash made a music video for "Breaths" in 1994 that makes explicit the link between intergenerational listening and AIDS.[7] Dash's video interweaves footage of several women on a grassy hillside—including a dancer, a sign language interpreter, and a woman spreading incense—with shots of the natural world: cloud-scattered sky, rippled surface of water, soaring bird. Shots of outdoor altars, votive candles, and different forms of incense give the video the feel of a ritual object, an offering, a rite of remembrance.

In the breaks between verses, Dash splices in footage of the Names Project's AIDS memorial quilt, and atop the sung ostinato she layers recitations of names of people who have died from AIDS. Dash's use of the AIDS quilt in this video augments the song's focus on active connections between the living and the dead while also highlighting the difficult questions mourning can present for political work. Unlike more confrontational AIDS activist tactics of the same era such as the kiss-in or the die-in, the AIDS memorial quilt was viewed warily by some activists. Quilts were familiar staples of straight families' homes, of den sofas and children's bedrooms, while collective quilting projects were solidly established as traditional, wholesome American endeavors. Calling on these connotations, the Names Project made AIDS grief accessible to people otherwise sheltered from the virus, and in using the homey form of the quilt, it proposed the possibility of a domestic reincorporation for queer mourners. Yet these very qualities, and the way the quilt gave a platform to static memorializing rather than dynamic action, led some AIDS activists to view the project as quietist. One activist said he wished somebody would "just burn that stupid blanket." Another told an interviewer, "I was a little contemptuous of the Quilt, 'cause in some ways, it seemed to divert energy from anger. It seemed to say 'mourning is the valid response,' and *not* say the other thing that needed to be said with that: . . . 'turn your mourning into anger.'"[8]

These responses indicate that some activists were uncomfortable with mourning as an endpoint, preferring the active energies of rage. This attitude was common in the AIDS movement, according to the curator and art critic Douglas Crimp, who in a famous essay from the period diagnosed a discomfort with mourning he had noticed in himself and his fellow activists. "For many AIDS activists," he wrote, "mourning is not respected; it is suspect." Crimp wrote of the importance of mourning and argued for a deeper understanding of how grief and anger could productively coexist: "Militancy, of course, then, but mourning too: mourning *and* militancy."[9]

From the beginning of this book, I've pursued a conception of disappointment as nonidentical with mourning, because the absolute end death denotes is not synonymous with the forms of nonfulfillment that disappointment encounters as historically contingent. Turning to the AIDS crisis of the 1980s and 1990s brings us up against the limits of this distinction. The AIDS activist movement responded to and met with multiple disappointments in the realm of policy, legislation, and ongoing social stigma, but death overshadowed it all: the epidemic's relentless rhythms of illness and death make it impossible to consider disappointment in isolation from these forces. Death had pervaded political nonfulfillment in other eras and movements as well, from the lynching of Black people and the assassination of activists to the casualties of botched abortions. But pushing health-care systems to save people's lives was the central issue in AIDS activism, and deaths were the principal currency of its disappointments. Although disappointment as such is not coextensive with mourning, the archive of the AIDS crisis asks us to consider the importance of mourning practices as responses to disappointment.[10]

As Dash's video attests, the mounting deaths of the AIDS crisis rendered Reagon's calls for intergenerational listening and generosity especially resonant. Dash's pairing of Sweet Honey in the Rock's ancestor invocations with AIDS mourning also reveals a particular conception of an "ancestor" for whom to listen—an ancestor who might not be distant generationally (as in the conventional understanding of ancestor) but rather achingly proximate: not necessarily an elder but possibly a peer who had died young. The realm of the dead drew closer, and the project of building coalitions with the dead grew ever more imperative.

Over the course of this book, we have developed an understanding of sonic and transcriptive practices as crucial means of assembling potential solidarities and coalitions. This chapter will discuss art and activism of the AIDS crisis—including the work of Crimp, Cathy Cohen, Marlon Riggs, and David

Wojnarowicz—with particular interest in the ways disappointment seeds new coalitions, such as the staging and transcribing of collective audition beyond the boundaries of individual life-spans. The discussion of Riggs's and Wojnarowicz's coalitional listening practices, which can be understood as sonic versions of the transhistorical superimpositions we saw play out visually in Chapter 4, will elaborate how listening to, with, and for one's forebears; making oneself audible across distinctions between life and death; and hazarding imperfect transcriptions of these relations are practices that can remake selves and identities in response to disappointment, rearranging social collectives through sound, attention, and generosity.

AIDS and Disappointment

Some might wonder what a discussion of the AIDS activist movement—an effort commonly discussed as a success—is doing in a book on political disappointment. Triumphalist narratives about AIDS activism abound, yet these tend to erase advocates and stakeholders who remained outside the networks of power, while ignoring populations for whom the development of expensive antiretroviral therapies has still not put an end to the AIDS crisis.[11]

That said, AIDS activists in the 1980s and 1990s, especially from the group ACT UP (AIDS Coalition to Unleash Power), did successfully pressure pharmaceutical companies and governments to develop treatments to save the lives of people infected with HIV. Yet even amid these successes, disappointment was in the DNA of the movement, which emerged in recognition of the degree to which the post-Stonewall project of gay liberation had not succeeded.[12] The unfinished quality of that project had already been made clear by a spate of antigay ballot initiatives beginning in the late 1970s, and the 1986 US Supreme Court ruling *Bowers v. Hardwick,* which upheld laws against sodomy, came as an added shock. The US government's widespread indifference about the deaths of thousands of gay men from a mysterious illness drove the point home even more soberingly: gay lives were considered neither worth saving nor worth grieving. In light of this, grieving itself became a political act.[13] Disappointment in the failures of gay liberation was inextricable from this work of mourning and from the AIDS activist movement as a whole.

The movement was hit with an additional wave of disappointment in the early 1990s, after the first several years of activism had brought about sped-up drug trials, increased visibility, and new lines of communication with political and scientific leadership. Despite these advances, a cure was still not forthcoming. People with AIDS kept dying, in ever-increasing numbers, and the toll on the living was heavy as well. "By the early 1990s," sociologist and former ACT UP member Deborah Gould writes, "many activists started to feel desperate. It was becoming ever more clear that the battle was going to be long and hard and that many people in the movement and many other loved ones would not make it."[14]

Gould describes the mood within the movement in the early 1990s as "despair" and argues that it had the effect of "fracturing solidarities." Douglas Crimp writes similarly of the arrival of new difficulties in the early 1990s, but he interprets the moment differently. In a 1992 essay bearing the sardonic title "Right On, Girlfriend!," Crimp articulates the mood within the movement not as outright despair but as a diminution of hope, and he argues that solidarities in this moment were not thoroughly fracturing, but rather were being rearranged and reorganized through new collective practices, with active coalitions producing new collective identities.

Crimp begins his account by discussing one high-profile AIDS death in late 1990—that of film historian Vito Russo—and writes of a mounting disappointment and hopelessness among activists:

> Vito's death coincided with the waning not only of our optimism but also of a period of limited but concrete successes for the AIDS activist movement. During that period—roughly, the first two and one-half years after the founding of ACT UP in the spring of 1987— we had succeeded in focusing greater public attention on AIDS, in shifting the discussion of AIDS from one dominated by a punitive moralism to one directed toward combating a public health emergency, and in affecting policy in concrete ways, particularly drug development policy.
>
> During the past two years, however, we have experienced only disappointment and setbacks.[15]

Crimp's discussion of disappointment serves to introduce his description of a change in tactics he has noticed among queer and AIDS activists, and specifically a shift in expectations about what the disclosure of identity, whether one's own or others', could achieve. In crisis was the old gay-liberation hope that merely coming out and pushing others to do the same would be enough to change the culture: "Our outing fantasy—that the revelation of homosexuality would have a transformative effect on homophobic discourse—was only a fantasy after all, and a dangerous one at that."[16] As with the feminists before them, who in the early 1980s confronted the reality that merely raising one's voice would not be enough to reshape policy, AIDS activists in the early 1990s were learning that self-narration was not all-powerful: that as Audre Lorde had warned, although silence might not be protective, speech offered no guarantees either.

One response to this disappointment was a redrawing of alliances within the movement. ACT UP had always been a loose coalition of semi-independent affinity groups, organized variously around shared friendships, genders, racial and ethnic identities, favored tactics and issues, and so forth. In response to the escalating sense of crisis in the early 1990s, ACT UP's constituencies began to fight with one another. "This level of specialization does not necessarily result in factionalism," Crimp writes. "But conflict does exist, and much of it concerns competing identities and contradictory identifications across identities. There are conflicts between men and women, between lesbians and straight women, between white people and people of color, between those who are HIV-positive or have AIDS and those who are HIV-negative."[17]

On Crimp's account, these conflicts sharpened precisely as disappointment made it increasingly difficult to have faith in the coherence of a shared queer identity. Early in ACT UP's existence, he writes, "everything about us was queer. We camped a lot, laughed a lot, kissed each other, partied together."[18] Crimp's earlier "Mourning and Militancy" had included a eulogy for a lost pre-AIDS utopia of carefree gay sex, and "Right On, Girlfriend!" at first tracks, in a similar register, the loss of the first-person-plural queer community that had replaced and compensated for the former sexual paradise.

But then something even more transformational comes about. "New political identifications began to be made ... across identity," Crimp writes, offering the important clarification, "I am not speaking of identity as nonrelational. Because of the complexities of the movement, there is no predicting what identifications will be made and which side of an argument anyone might take." He speaks of collective identifications as being not preordained but assembled through practice. Such identifications form among individuals with a range of experiences and characteristics—for example, "a white, middle-class, HIV-negative lesbian" and "a poor black mother with AIDS" might connect personally and be motivated to work together on an issue important to both of them. Crimp notes that "a politics of alliance based on relational identities" can clash with "old antagonisms based on fixed identities," but he also offers a story of success, about a group of queer ACT UP members who mobilized to change New York City policy on hypodermic needle exchange. These activists' recognition of shared interest based on vulnerability to HIV and to "stigma, discrimination, and neglect" remade their identities beyond simple queerness.[19]

I have discussed Crimp's article at length because he was writing it from within the AIDS movement's most disappointed moment, a period that also saw the creation of the works by Marlon Riggs and David Wojnarowicz that this chapter will discuss next. But Crimp's article is also significant for its connection with Cathy Cohen's landmark 1997 article "Punks, Bulldaggers, and Welfare Queens: The Radical Potential of Queer Politics?," which, like Crimp's essay, highlights disappointment's key role in calling forth new alignments, identities, and collective practices.[20] In "Punks, Bulldaggers, and Welfare Queens," Cohen discusses how, during the early 1990s, many people had embraced the antiessentialist nomenclature *queer* in an effort to replace static and potentially divisive identity categories (such as *gay* and *lesbian*, which in the mid-1980s were often mutually exclusive categories grounding largely separate political and cultural spaces) with an umbrella designation that, in its reclamation of a slur, also telegraphed a rejection of an assimilationist strategy that had already failed.[21] *Queer* represented the hope for a productive coalition of the nonnormative that could build insurgent solidarity on grounds of deviance, marginalization, and fluid alliances as opposed to purportedly stable identity categories.[22] Yet in practice, Cohen wrote, *queer* had often reified a monolithic queer/straight binary that disregarded consequential racial and class differences and failed to account for all the different axes along which people were regularly subject to power. Thus *queer* both raised the possibility of meaningful queer coalitional alignments and failed to actualize them, since acknowledging differences is a necessary element in building coalitions.

Cohen, writing a few years after "Right On, Girlfriend!," cites Crimp's argument about identities as relational and able to be remade through collective practice, and she offers his needle exchange advocacy case study as a possible example of how to make good on the radical potential of *queer*. "We must thus begin to link our intersectional analysis of power with concrete coalitional work," she writes, suggesting that such work can lead to "the destabilization and remaking of our identities."[23] Shared vulnerability to stigma, illness, and death could and should give rise to coalitions and redraw individual and collective identities.

In the art of the AIDS crisis, listening shows up as an important practice through which coalitions can be assembled with those who have gone before and those who are yet to come, not just amplifying preexisting voices and identities but building new collectivities.[24] For the remainder of this chapter, through discussions of Riggs's and Wojnarowicz's art, we will linger with political listening not in the conventional sense, where the privileged commit to "hearing the voices" (ostensibly transparent and self-disclosing) of the marginalized, but political listening built on generosity, distanced intimacy, and attentive presence in the face of profound difference.[25] This listening is not solely a receptive endeavor. As the artists in this chapter will clarify for us, such listening can entail reactivating sonic traces of the past, listening to the present as if through the ears of those who have gone before, and performing for ancestors to hear us, ultimately assembling intergenerational ensembles. This may initially sound overly mystical, but Riggs and Wojnarowicz will provide examples of how it can work in practice. At a moment when the AIDS movement was grappling with multiple disappointments, Riggs and Wojnarowicz assembled auditory coalitions that dissolved and reconfigured collective identities, reaching toward models of care and coalition that would continue to encompass them even after their own deaths.

"Older, Stronger Rhythms": Marlon Riggs's Sonic Superimpositions

A journey from voicing a Black gay identity to remaking relationality through active coalitional listening shapes Riggs's late-career filmmaking, especially the progression from his documentary *Tongues Untied* (1989) to *Black Is . . . Black Ain't* (1995). Where *Tongues Untied* focuses on the specificity of Black gay men's experiences and is presented as a call to speech and visibility, *Black Is* takes as its subject Black identity as a whole, making a case for an inclusive, pluralist, coalitional conception of Blackness while shifting from sound as metaphor ("voice," "silence") to an interest in the materiality of sound. Where *Tongues Untied* labors to offer a story about survival, *Black Is* tears at that story's seams to ask how to leave things behind, how to set things up to act on the present even after one's death, and how to seed coalition and collaboration beyond individual life-spans.

Tongues Untied begins with a black screen and a single voice intoning a rhythmic chant: "Brother to brother / brother to brother."[26] As these hitched-rhythm words loop around, their clipped beats outlining quick odd-meter measures of 5/8, they are picked up by additional voices speaking in unison. A series of quick cuts next show us several Black men, alone or in small groups. The shots all emphasize the ways these men look at each other or fail to look, the ways they are seen by others or remain unseen. In one instance, a group of three men are shown standing in a park, wearing expressions of incredulity, rejection, and disgust as they turn their heads almost directly toward the camera. A possible object of their gaze is revealed in the next shot. This is another group of three men; their chic attire and fluid gestures set them apart from the first group, but they do not seem to realize they're being watched. As the sequence continues, the depiction of visual nonrecognition among Black men unfolds further, with more unmet looks and curtailed glances. The opening statement is clear: relations between individuals ("brother to brother") and between groups are stymied by distance and nonrecognition that amount to a failure of visibility and visuality. Nobody is being truly seen, and nobody is really seeing.

The next sequence presents this problem of nonrecognition as an auditory one as well. A single word, "Silence," is both printed on-screen and spoken assertively, announcing silence as something discernible visibly as well as audibly. "Silence is what I hear after the handshake and slap of five," begins the spoken text, drawn from an essay by Joseph Beam titled "Brother to Brother"—a connection that further ties together the previous sequence on visibility (whose soundtrack, recall, was a vocal repetition of the essay's title) and this one on silence. The speaker goes on to lament the reluctance to discuss, even among close friends, the pain of facing homophobia from other Black people and of being devalued by white supremacy.

Thus the film first presents stymied visibility as a problem and then equates this with a silence that can and must be broken through acts of intersubjective visual recognition and sonic voice. Yet to court visibility and to end this silence will demand more than mere self-disclosure. The self is far from simple, formed as it is at the unsteady intersection of multiple histories, aesthetics, relationships to power, political demands, and bodily vulnerabilities. Accordingly, just at the moment that the film seems to arrive at a triumphant scene of recognition, the consummation is thrown into doubt by the possibility of death and a foregrounding of sound as not always reducible to communication.

The scene in question begins late in the film, with an exchange of meaningfully wordless gazes between two men at a bar. As a man in a yellow shirt enters the room, the poet Essex Hemphill lifts his eyes and levels a long, assured gaze straight out—at the camera, at the man, at the viewer—while a voiceover line, "His eyes howl at me," reiterates the early pairing of sight and sound.

The two men cruise each other with looks and slight smiles while two saxophones perform a sultry counterpoint on "Black Is the Color of My True Love's Hair," layered over a steady pattern of drumbeats spaced out to sound like a beating heart. This tensely seductive sonic superimposition then gives way to a joyous mashup between a doo-wop quartet and a contingent of gay-pride marchers: "Out of the closet, into the streets," runs one call-and-response chant, and a moment later: "We're Black, we're gay." The visuals switch back and forth between the marchers in a city street and the quartet singing in a black-walled room, but both scenes' sounds often play simultaneously, yielding a clash of ragged polyrhythms and pointed lyrical overlap. "Hey boy, can you come out tonight?" a singer croons melismatically as the marchers chant, "Out of the closet."

This superimposed sound suggests that the audiovisual connection whose absence was earlier lamented has now been made. The markedly victorious tone of the chant, combined with the sung exhortations that seem to both announce an emergence and invite one still to come, together convey a celebration with an edge of aspiration, an incomplete or unstable arrival. A shot of Christian counterprotesters at the pride march, with their signs proclaiming homosexuality "an abomination," likewise underlines the coexistence of joy with ongoing struggle.

Throughout this section of *Tongues Untied*, sound and silence operate not as metaphors for presence or communication, as they did at the film's outset, but as objects in their own right, first by way of this sonic superimposition and then, in the very next sequence, by the reduction of language to its sonic material. In a sensual, slow-motion scene, two men embrace to the sounds of a poem and a slowed-down heartbeat. But then a percussive word, its meaning initially obscure, fades up in the soundtrack. "*Navathinkavafa*. [Beat.] *Navathinkavafa*." It is not until Hemphill's face appears, reciting a poem's first lines—"Now we think/as we fuck/this nut/might kill us"—that the string of consonants sidles up to meaning.

A second man continues chanting "*navathinkavafa*" between Hemphill's lines, the antiphony repeatedly toggling the passage between pure sound and clear meaning. Then a third voice joins in, emitting truncated sighs that interrupt the poem's lines about fear of AIDS halting interpersonal intimacy—"We stop kissing/tall dark strangers"—and about people attaching instead to media, objects, and the past: "pictures./Telephones./Toys./Recent lovers." The sighs and quick exhalations speed up, cutting more and more frequently into the poem, until these noises become the main event, with Hemphill's words mere occasional punctuation, in an erotic near echo of the closing of Sweet Honey in the Rock's "Breaths."

AIDS again announces its presence through sound in the sequence that immediately follows the poem, where Riggs speaks about his diagnosis and anticipation of death. "Still, I listen to the beat of my heart, let this primal pulse lead me," Riggs recites as the heartbeat sound returns. "Though lately I've lived with another rhythm. At first, I thought just time passing. But I discovered a time bomb ticking in my blood." A slideshow of AIDS obituaries for Black men flashes across the screen, and the high-pitched ticking of a watch is added to the portentous heartbeat. Riggs's voice lowers and slows: "Faces, friends disappear. I watch. I wait. I watch. I wait."

The faces of the dead flash past at increasing speed for nearly thirty seconds, the rapid series both soliciting and eluding recognition. As these faces flip by, first we hear the heartbeat along with the ticking, then just the ticking, and then, finally, nothing, as the slideshow comes to a rest on a photograph of Riggs's face gazing at the camera. "I listen," we hear Riggs say, "for my own quiet implosion." By giving us an auditory representation of his infected blood's circulation, and by proleptically inserting his image into a gallery of the dead—that is, by listening into his sick present and envisioning his future death—Riggs begins to unground the very conceptions of identity, voicing, and recognition that had seemed to structure the film, and to assemble instead a coalition that exceeds any individual life-span.[27] This becomes even clearer a moment later, when, in a further expansion of historical scale, he superimposes the photograph of his face with a faded photo of Harriet Tubman, which morphs into a photo of Frederick Douglass, then one of Sojourner Truth. These ancestors sonically challenge the temporalities of disease and death: "But while I wait," Riggs says, "older, stronger rhythms resonate within me, sustain my spirit, silence the clock."

Next, a freedom song rewritten as a gay-pride song—"Ain't gonna let homophobia turn me around," a chorus sings—accompanies archival footage of civil rights marchers, including Martin Luther King Jr., that cross-fades with more recent video of Black gay-pride marchers. Through musical reperformance and visual superimposition, Riggs articulates coalition audiovisually and explores layered rhythms of defiance that temporarily overtake the ticking of both clock time and sick time. The late-1980s exuberance of the AIDS movement, the faith that collective action and loving community would be enough to conquer the virus, is on full display in this ultimately hopeful closing sequence—yet so too is an awareness of the proximity of death. Expanding out from the film's initially abstract metaphors of silence, this extended sequence enacts transhistorical superimpositions both visually and sonically that temper the impending threat of death with a consciousness of liberation struggles' centuries-long timelines.

Visual and sonic superimpositions return to shape Riggs's final feature film, *Black Is . . . Black Ain't*, from its initial moments.[28] In the midst of a seemingly direct opening sequence where the filmmaker is shown explaining the project to a group of teenagers ("This is a documentary we're doing for public television; it's called *Black Is . . . Black Ain't*"), a dreamy, elongated synth chord arises in the soundtrack, and cross-fading visuals meld shots of a digital filmmaking slate, handheld tracking shots of a nondescript hallway, and close-ups of Riggs sitting in what the soundtrack begins to make clear is a hospital bed.

Riggs's voice is heard saying, as if from a great distance, "We've finally begun production on the new project," and visual and audio superimpositions depict the filmmaking process as inextricable from Riggs's illness. Red LED time-code numbers scroll past on the digital slate, and when its clapper slams shut with an audible snap, a voice murmurs in a near whisper, "Two hundred twenty-five." This number has no obvious referent at first, not corresponding to the numbers on the slate; then the spoken number appears on the screen, white digits wavering over a view of a nurse's station in a hospital, and then the slate reappears with its swiftly ascending numbers. Riggs says, "I thought the number *would* be higher," delivering this line with the same hushed, wistful intonation as the previous line about the film; the tone of his voice, along with the on-screen numbers, splices together two seemingly separate conversations and demands that the viewer-listener hear them as linked. "T cell count back down, weight down too," murmurs the other, more official-sounding voice. The shots continue oscillating—vertiginous views wobbling around hospital spaces, digital slates clapping shut to indicate a rolling camera—and the garble of voices over a hospital intercom intercedes as Riggs speaks with emphasis and bewilderment: "My weight and T cell count are the same. What's happening to my body?"

Sonic and visual superimpositions, then, work from the beginning of *Black Is . . . Black Ain't* to register a poignant intertwining between physical dissolution and creative coalescence: an artwork is coming together and a body is coming apart, two key sets of numbers going down as another climbs. The repeated appearance of the digital slate also underscores the role of sound as a means of aligning disparate but connected registers: in the history of filmmaking, the clapperboard was initially introduced to provide a crisp audiovisual index point for synchronizing a film's video and audio tracks, and the digital slate used in the sequence still serves this purpose, in addition to keeping a record of shot titles and timestamps.

Black Is . . . Black Ain't uses sonic and visual layering not only to link the film's content and its technologies of production but also to seed collaborations

5.1　Film still from Marlon Riggs, *Black Is ... Black Ain't,* 1995. Image © Signifyin' Works.

that extend beyond individual life-spans. Immediately after the opening sequence just described, an on-screen title appears, explaining, "During the
making of this film, [Riggs] died of AIDS." The next screen's title continues,
"This film was completed in tribute to his vision and humanity." Riggs con-
ceptualizes, scripts, and shoots the film before his death, stars in it as he is
dying, and, as I will argue, continues to codirect it, in collaboration with his
colleagues, even after his death.

Some of the most affecting sections of the film show Riggs in a hospital bed,
clearly working to complete as much of the film as possible in the time he has
remaining, and to make sure his collaborators have what they need to finish
the project once he is gone. In one such scene, he explains to editor Christiane
Badgley the significance of some footage he has already shot. "When you see
the scenes of me naked, running through the woods, which I will hope you
will use an abundance of," he says in a voice-over as one of these wooded scenes
plays, "those things had a powerful image for me in terms of searching through
clutter in my life, searching through the clutter of the project, searching
through the attempts by society at large to cover you and to confine you in
some space in which you're not seen for the naked truth of who you are. Those
scenes are critical in their metaphoric importance."

As Riggs speaks, viewers may at first think we are being addressed directly—we hear him say, "When you see the scenes of me naked," as we are indeed seeing these scenes—but we then realize that we are instead listening in on a production meeting between Riggs and his collaborator, watching at once a cinematic scene and the process that informed the use of that scene in the completed film. "And I can say that—or write it, actually, as text, 'cause I don't know if I want to record more narration," he continues. Badgley replies, "Well, we've been recording this. We can, you know, we can work with it." Riggs and Badgley are implicitly acknowledging that the work of the film will continue beyond his death, and they are laying the groundwork for their collaborative process to outlive him. Indeed, Riggs's repetition of the word *will*—"which I will hope you will use an abundance of"—indicates that he envisions his own preferences and input continuing into the future.

Riggs was already in the early stages of AIDS-related dementia when that scene was filmed, Badgley said later, explaining,

> Filming him in that hospital served multiple purposes. I wanted to talk to him about the script; I wanted to make sure that everything that I was going to be doing was in agreement with what he wanted and was following his instructions. I wanted to check the tone of everything. I also wanted to have material from him that I could use for narration, because we had gone into a studio to do narration, but his voice was—that was one of those settings where he couldn't really function normally, and his voice became very unnatural, and kind of—he didn't sound like Marlon, he sounded strange. . . . I knew if I was in the hospital just chatting with him, that tone could work for narration. And then ultimately it became clear, even though that wasn't an intention of his in the script of the film, that we needed to have his illness be part of the film, because he was dying.[29]

Thus the scene of hospital-bed narration connects to the superimpositions at the beginning, reiterating the ways the film's overt content is intertwined with its conditions of production, conditions that include illness, death, collaboration, and the changing sound of one's voice.

When Riggs spells out the link between his illness and the film's focus on Black identity, both the text of his explication and the visual superimpositions that accompany it invite the differences and suspended tensions between the narratives to linger. "The connection between AIDS and Black folks, and Black folks' identity, is metaphoric," he says in a voice-over, as the visuals show a slow zoom in on a dark, empty hospital room, superimposed with still photos that show Riggs directing film shoots. "Both of them," Riggs goes on, "are a struggle against the odds in the face of adversity, in the face of possible extinction." This is straightforward enough, and the still images that follow, which show Riggs with IV ports taped to his chest, and in a hospital bed attached to a ventilator, amply support Jennifer Denise Williams's contention that "Riggs's body . . . functions as the site upon which blackness and AIDS coalesce, thus incorporating AIDS into an experience of black embodied trauma."[30] For Riggs, as Williams points out, the connection between Blackness and AIDS is not merely metaphoric but literal as well. Indeed, although transcripts of the film render his line as "is metaphoric," when listened to closely, that key word sounds more like "isn't" than "is," at least to this listener: there is an audible hitch in the spoken rhythm, an extra beat's worth of nasal consonant that seems to precede and exceed the initial *m* of "metaphoric." Riggs's explication of the link between the film's two main narratives as potentially both metaphoric and literal is grounded in his own singular body, as Williams aptly argues, and also in the possibility that a word spoken aloud could be heard differently by different listeners. The auditory imprecision additionally mirrors the workings of metaphor as such, which is itself a sort of transformational coalition, a relation whose power derives from linking disparate elements without downplaying the dissonance involved.

"How do we keep ourselves together as a people in the face of all our differences?" Riggs continues, as photos show him hooked up to oxygen while gingerly embracing visitors, posing with them, playing Scrabble on his hospital tray. "How do we maintain a sense of communal selfhood, if you will?" Riggs suggests throughout *Black Is . . . Black Ain't* that sound is a crucial means of actualizing such heterogeneous collectivities. In one sequence, he traces a 1960s trajectory of iconic Black-pride sounds: the choral refrain of Nina Simone's "To Be Young, Gifted and Black," a crowd echoing Stokely Carmichael's "Black Power" chant, Black Panthers chanting "Free Huey." Sound, for Riggs, registers historical iterations of group identity. And its absence, conversely, marks the shortcomings of such identity: "All the time we were saying it loud and proclaiming the beauty of our Blackness," he says in this sequence, "a deep wedge of silence divided me from my father." In contrast to *Tongues Untied*, where silence sometimes referred to an unwillingness to say certain things, here he really does mean silence as silence: "We didn't talk, literally."

Sound also anchors a hospital-bed scene in which Riggs portrays what on-screen text identifies as "the world's pre-eminent authority on Black music, esteemed scholar of Afro-rhythmic tonal permutations, and distinguished fellow at the Bootsy Collins Foundation for Musical Kinesthesia and Funky Badness." "Black *muuu*-sic," he intones in a mock-stuffy voice. "What's it all about?" Across a series of quick cuts, he proceeds to sing tiny and increasingly parodic snippets of spirituals, jazz, freedom songs, blues, opera, funk ("turn / this mother / *out*," he sings, waving his arms in the air), and finally something that his gestures suggest is intended as an experimental electric guitar solo but that the on-screen titles identify, hilariously, with a lone question mark. This madcap history of African American music comes across as another set of unfinished production notes, perhaps his sketching out the shape that a sequence outlining the history of Black music with archival sound and video might have finally taken. Its presence in the film feels loose and provisional, from a poorly miked interjection of Badgley's early on to the closing off-camera words— "What's the sign for 'cut'?"—delivered amid laughter from the crew and from Riggs himself, who cracks up as he offers a few final strums on his air guitar.

To better understand the importance for Riggs of sound and transhistorical listening, we turn now to his essay "Letter to the Dead," which was first published while he was working on *Black Is . . . Black Ain't*.[31] In this essay he addresses departed friends and colleagues one by one, reflecting on the "silence" that has fed his own denial about AIDS and similar denial among other Black gay men. This silence is finally broken—and rendered, like the link between Blackness and AIDS, more than metaphoric—when Riggs writes of a time in the hospital where he was first diagnosed with HIV, when he began to sing spirituals aloud. At first, he writes, he sang to be heard by a deceased friend named Lewayne, but then he started to consider the possible presence of other listeners:

> Surely, I thought some nurse would have rushed to the door and hushed me, or some less polite fellow patient simply demanded that I shut up all that noise. But no one came and no one protested, so from my hospital bed I continued to sing, with all my might:
> *I shall not*
> *I shall not be moved*
> *I shall not*
> *I shall not be moved*
> *Just like a tree*
> *that's standing by the water*
> *Oh I shall not be moved!*

Did you hear me, Harriet?

Did you hear my voice drop to a quieter song sung just for you—the song of someone escaped from captivity yet uncertain of his way:

I don't believe
you brought me this far
just to leave me
Oh, my God!
I don't believe
she brought me this far
just to leave me

Did you hear, Harriet, the trembling trepidation in my voice (trembling which even now in remembering threatens to repossess me)? And didn't you, like the good shepherd that you are / have always been, didn't you come—and take my hand?

Beneath the continuous blare of Geraldo and Joan and Oprah and Donahue, The Young and The Restless, and All My oh-so-tedious Children, I heard you, Harriet, paid strict attention to your silent command: stand up and walk![32]

Harriet Tubman's face had figured, recall, into the end of *Tongues Untied*. She reappears in this essay as a listener whose audition secures for Riggs's songs of survival a historic status. He expects to be heard and shushed by others in his own time and place, by a patient or a nurse, but these people seem not to be listening. Only Harriet—legendary wayfinder, crosser of borders, determined guide—hears. And under (not over) the noisy clamor of daytime television, Riggs hears Harriet too, hears her wordless messages of communion and command.

Like Reagon adding "(up and down)" to her essay on coalition, Riggs inserts a parenthetical here—"(trembling which even now in remembering threatens to repossess me)"—that breaks the text's frame slightly, bringing us into something material from the text's production. Riggs is trembling as he writes of an earlier moment in which trembling affected his voice. Through the memory and retranscription of a trembling that once shook his sonic voice, Riggs's status as a sovereign subject is likewise shaken. The evocation of sonic-haptic trembling connects Riggs to another ancestor, too: James Baldwin, who in *The Fire Next Time* wrote, "Yes, we were trembling. We have not stopped trembling yet, but if we had not loved each other, none of us would have survived."[33]

Tubman returns in one of the final scenes in *Black Is . . . Black Ain't*, where Riggs recounts a dream about her. As a chorus hums "Lift Ev'ry Voice and Sing," Badgley's off-camera voice asks, "Marlon, what kind of dreams have you been having lately?" His energy is at a low ebb, and he at first offers a vague response: "It's like MTV, I just watch it sort of flashing." Badgley prompts him again, more pointedly: "What about this dream that you were having not too long ago, when you were dreaming about Harriet Tubman?"

"Mm-hm," he responds, remembering now. "Just her coming and standing by me, not saying anything, so I had to become aware of her presence, and then just looking into my eyes, and then looking at the river in front of us." This dream is seemingly silent, which is why I here consider the description in tandem with his essay's sonic scene, to more fully apprehend the sensory spread of this transhistorical encounter. "She didn't say anything," Riggs re-iterates; "it was with her eyes. She just looked at me and then turned and looked at the river and we started walking. Harriet and I walked across the river."

"And what do you think that dream is about?" Badgley asks.

The imagery might seem straightforward to us: a trusted guide and com-forter visits a dying man to accompany him as he crosses from this world. Yet Riggs reads the significance of his dream as being not about death but about surviving and collaborating. "If I have work, then I'm not going to die," he replies, "'cause work is a living spirit in me—that which wants to connect with other people and pass on something to them which they can use in their own lives and grow from." He stands poised at the edge of the river, giving it away *that* way (up and down): collaborating with Tubman, with Badgley, and with others who will outlive him but come to know him through his films. Tubman's silence, in this dream as in "Letter to the Dead," is a form of expectant listening that calls forth and amplifies Riggs's own continued reverberations.

The idea of breaking silence, which was *Tongues Untied*'s central mission, de-velops, by that film's end and even further throughout *Black Is . . . Black Ain't*, into a practice of listening beyond the bounds of individual life-spans. Here listening takes center stage as a practice of transhistorical, intergenerational col-laboration and coalition whose power is undimmed even as death draws near. Such collaborations and coalitional listening also resound through the work of David Wojnarowicz, where the conjunction of intimacy and distance across the threshold of death makes difficult demands of the living.

"Peter I Have to Touch You":
Distanced Intimacy and David Wojnarowicz

I think what I really fear about death is the silencing of my voice.... I feel this incredible pressure to leave something of myself behind.

—David Wojnarowicz, in Rosa von Praunheim, *Silence = Death*

In a text that appears in several of his visual and multimedia artworks from the late 1980s and early 1990s, David Wojnarowicz writes of an aspiration to erase the distinction between himself and a dying other: "If I could attach our blood vessels so we could become each other I would. If I could attach our blood vessels in order to anchor you to the earth to this present time I would. If I could open up your body and slip inside your skin and look out your eyes and forever have my lips fused with yours I would."[34]

His text is a love letter both tender and terrible, an expression of intimacy that conjures with gory specificity a compound body, at once alive and dying. Wojnarowicz imagines rerouting death through an act of coalitional seeing, and through the speaker's loving choice to forfeit the prerogatives of the living. In this fantasy of becoming coalitional, becoming metaphoric, veins and arteries and eyes are all conceived as tethers or transoms of a transfusion that undoes the borders of a particular self. And the text itself embodies this painfully physical yearning, its comma-free sentences unspooling like veins or viscera that keep encountering abrupt cutoffs: "When I put my hands on your body on your flesh I feel the history of that body. Not just the beginning of its forming in that distant lake but all the way beyond its ending."

In Wojnarowicz's artwork, one-to-one intimacy is often juxtaposed with incandescent large-scale visions of a destructive, disintegrating America in ways that open the possibility of solidarity beyond the borders of individual identities and life-spans. Throughout his work, by acting as a witness to death at industrial and individual scales, Wojnarowicz imagines transcending the limitations of embodiment and enacting forms of intimate coalition beyond the boundaries of self and history.

In one of the most poignant sections of Wojnarowicz's book *Close to the Knives: A Memoir of Disintegration* (1991), he tells a story of taking his beloved friend Peter—the photographer Peter Hujar—to a doctor on Long Island who has supposedly worked out a promising treatment for AIDS. Midway through the drive from Manhattan, Peter announces that he has to pee. Peter orders David to pull over by the side of the highway, but David insists on finding a gas station—which turns out not to have a bathroom. David goes to help Peter out of the car so he can relieve himself outside. But Peter is already suffering from AIDS-driven dementia, and David's task is not simple.

> After pulling off his blankets, I reached toward him to help him out. "Don't touch me." Peter I have to touch you to help you out. "Don't touch me it hurts." . . . When he was done I buttoned his pants back up and led him back to the car. The attendant stared at us as I helped him back into the seat. Then the layers of blankets. "I don't want the seat belt on." I said, "You have to have the seat belt on; what if there's an accident?" "I don't care." I continued putting it on. "I don't want the seat belt on. . . ." "We're not going anywhere unless it's on." He resigned himself to having the seat belt on, "Don't touch me."[35]

Wojnarowicz's narrator seems to dissolve the boundaries of self and other. Peter pees, David buttons his pants; Peter sits, David fastens the seat belt. The very mechanics of the dialogue, run together as it is in a single paragraph, downplay distinctions between the two men, pushing against Peter's attempts to assert a division even as it documents those attempts. This passage contains no instances of "Peter said" or similar speech indicators, and only one "I said." At first Peter's spoken words are distinguished from David's by punctuation, with only Peter's speech taking quotation marks, but then Wojnarowicz abandons even this distinction. This intimacy is not pleasant, and it scarcely looks reciprocal. It's conducted across the widening distance of illness, dementia, and encroaching death, yet it simultaneously takes place at extremely close range.

Many of Wojnarowicz's best-known works focus on a single figure: Wojnarowicz's face partially buried in coarse desert dirt, or his face with his lips sewn shut, or Peter Hujar's face just after his death. This selective canonization, though, barely hints at a mode that was even more common in his work for much of his career. In a great deal of Wojnarowicz's artwork from the late 1980s and early 1990s, intimate encounters are superimposed on or spliced into visions of large-scale organization. Unlike Riggs's visual language of overlays and crossfades that bring disparate elements into harmonious proximity, Wojnarowicz's superimpositions feature obstinate borders, ominous circuitry, and seemingly unbridgeable distance. In his *Sex Series* of 1989, for instance, circular cutouts featuring photographic negatives of erotic pairings are set against backgrounds of natural and built environments. The intimacy depicted within the insets is rendered eerie and unreal by the high-contrast negative treatment, while the unceremonious juxtapositions—porthole-scale sex scenes prosaically sited amid New York bridges, a freight train, a robotic-looking water tower—evoke a feeling of enclosure and hopelessness, as if tenderness and connection were nothing more than fragments of a distorted nightmare being dreamed by industrialized society.

Yet Wojnarowicz spoke about these pieces as a prosocial and ultimately political response to the constancy of death: "It came out of loss," he told the writer Cynthia Carr in 1990. "I mean every time I opened a magazine there was the face of somebody else who died. It was so overwhelming and there was also this huge backlash about sex, even within the activist community. . . . And [*Sex Series*] essentially came out of wanting some sexy images on the wall—for me. To keep me company. To make me feel better. It was fairly democratic."[36] For Wojnarowicz, to affirm interpersonal intimacy and erotic connection in the face of wide-scale mortality is not just to seek comfort at the level of the self, though it certainly is that; it is also a mode of pursuing fairness and democracy, of modeling a concerted intersubjective attention that could, or ought to, serve as the basis for a politics.

Such trans-scalar intimacies are central to much of Wojnarowicz's visual art, including *Wind (for Peter Hujar)* (1987); *Water* (1987); *Something from Sleep* (1987–1988); and *Bad Moon Rising* (1989). His paintings, prints, and multimedia works often employ gridded schemas to convey a sense of organization that simultaneously unites and separates things as tiny as cells and as vast as the cosmos. These grids echo the crumbling warehouses of the postindustrial Hudson River piers, those vast abandoned buildings on Manhattan's West Side where gay men, including Wojnarowicz, went to find sex and make art during the 1970s and 1980s. Within the famed cruising grounds, telescoping series of rooms upon rooms stood as mute testament to superseded shipping protocols and long-gone agglomerations of goods, as well as more recent, more intimate transits. Wojnarowicz's fascination with the piers owed not only to the passing encounters they housed, and not only to the older operations whose specters still inhabited their honeycombed spaces, but also to their massive scale and slow disintegration, the way people and stray dogs and unknown sounds could surface and then be lost again in the vast warrens, and the sense they offered of remoteness from any enclosing context. "What I loved about them," Wojnarowicz recalled in the late 1980s, after many had been demolished, "was that they were about as far away from civilization as I could walk, and I really loved that sense of detachment. It was like sitting with the entire city at your back and looking across the river."[37]

This pairing of intimacy and distance can be seen in a work from 1988 in which the outline of two men kissing is cut out from a gridded contact sheet, showing exposures made in various spots around the derelict piers, a room with a black-and-white checkerboard floor and a pool table, and a few other locations. The kiss and the grid present competing bids to shape and make order of what is otherwise a motley array of images. In much of Wojnarowicz's visual art, as in his writing, networks wed intimacy and distance, tenderness and vast systems.

This distanced intimacy is also evident in Wojnarowicz's extensive listening practices. In his early-1980s No Wave band, 3 Teens Kill 4, he not only contributed spoken and sung vocals but also, as he would tell people, played the

5.2   David Wojnarowicz, *Untitled,* 1988. Courtesy of the Estate of David Wojnarowicz and P·P·O·W, New York.

tape recorder: he regularly collected found sounds—from the nightly news, passersby ranting, kids playing in the street—and he'd play his tapes into a microphone at concerts, placing his reenacted, mediated listening at the center of the songs. Wojnarowicz's sound-archiving practices continued long after he left 3 Teens Kill 4. Throughout his life, he held on to recordings of that band and the found-sound tapes, and to that collection he added recordings of interviews he'd given, phone calls he'd made and received, radio shows he'd listened to, and messages people had left for him on his answering machine. In the 2021 documentary *Wojnarowicz: Fuck You Faggot Fucker*, which builds much of its soundtrack out of these tapes, the answering machine recordings stand out as everyday expressions of warmth and intimacy—not the sharpened and condensed act of looking back later to reconjure a relationship, as the more recent interviews in the film do, but audio time capsules, capturing the casual tenderness of speaking to somebody who's not right there to hear you but who might be soon. An answering machine message is an anticipation of a conversation you hope to have later; played back after the fact, it becomes an archive of that anticipation, a storehouse of intimate intention. And these messages' deployment in the documentary shows how elastic that timeline can be.

The most significant objects in Wojnarowicz's sonic archive, though, are the tape journals he recorded in the early and late 1980s. These journals also provide the most poignant records of his practices of listening beyond the boundaries of individual life-spans. His first tape journal dates from March 1981, shortly after the beginning of his defining friendship with Hujar, and he made another one in April 1982, consisting largely of heroin-smudged ramblings recorded during his short-lived dalliance with the drug. His art career took off a few months later, and he recorded no more tapes for over six years.

When he turned on the tape recorder again, in November 1988, Hujar had recently died and Wojnarowicz had been diagnosed with AIDS-related complex. These were two of the first things he mentioned when he started recording again: "I was diagnosed with ARC sometime in the summer; it's now near the end of November. I'm living at Peter's house—Peter Hujar. I helped take care of him, and he died of AIDS."[38] Illness, time, place, care, and death locate the sound within a personal history even as they emphasize commonalities between Wojnarowicz and Hujar: shared diagnosis, shared apartment. Wojnarowicz's decision to make sure he gives Hujar's full name suggests that he is contemplating the possibility of the tape's someday being heard by people who do not know him well enough to know who he means when he says "Peter." He then proceeds to tell a long story about the previous day. The story begins with his sour thoughts about the art world, his wish to destroy his artworks and withdraw from that politically fraught milieu with all its tangled power relations. These thoughts escalated, he relates, until he began to speak aloud a wish to vomit all over his artwork, all over the street, all over the world. Finally he really started puking. And now, reflecting back on it the next day, he can't tell whether he made himself throw up with his thoughts, or whether, alternatively, he was feeling sick anyway, perhaps because of AIDS or some unrelated stomach bug, and the physical feeling of sickness put the thought of puking into his mind.

This is the question he has gone to the tape recorder to talk out: Do his thoughts and feelings produce his physical reality, or does the symptom come first? "And somehow I needed to feel like—I don't know, I felt like I'd rather that it was that I had some kind of bug that caused all these thoughts," he says. But he can't dismiss the thoughts, since "all these thoughts are based on feelings that I carry." Whether they caused the nausea or they were what his mind made of nausea, the feelings and thoughts are his. *My mind remembers / and my innards churn:* like Pat Parker in "Don't Let the Fascists Speak," Wojnarowicz is faced with unruly viscera and their obscure knowledge. Where does the sickness originate, he wonders, in his body or his mind? The confusion unsettles him further: "And I felt like a fucking mess."[39]

Twenty minutes after finishing his story, Wojnarowicz turns the tape back on to talk about an act of seeing. "Another thing I remembered yesterday laying on the bed after puking," he says, "was suddenly feeling like I was seeing through Peter's eyes. All those months of him being ill and never knowing exactly what he felt, never knowing what was going on inside his mind other than the times he would talk about it. Suddenly I just felt like I'm seeing—that I had his eyes and I'm looking at the whole place, and everything just made me nauseous—every surface, every extension of the outside. I just felt a lot of fear about the whole violence of that moment."[40] In this experience, his earlier fantasy about letting a loved one fuse with his own body returns. To him, illness is dissolving his physical boundaries in all directions: his insides are exiting his body ("I want to throw my guts up out the window, and onto the street," he recalls thinking), and the organs of another have entered. Rather than this being an ecstatic escape or return, though, it is suffused with fear and violence.[41] In his text about entering the skin of a dying loved one, the dream had been to keep them alive by joining bodies together. But if the loved one is already unrecoverable, then feeling such a corporeal connection to them can bring up nausea instead of comfort. The violence, Wojnarowicz senses, is the reiteration of his own mortality and impending death. That reality is never distant from Wojnarowicz, especially after his diagnosis. But he would also find, in listening, a less frightening way to join senses with those who had gone before.

A few journal entries later on the same cassette, Wojnarowicz recounts a story he heard about the importance of listening to the dead. A writer, Michael DeCapite, had an aunt who died, and the next night she came to him in a dream offering to tell him the winning lottery numbers. DeCapite, worried that he would forget the numbers upon waking, told her to come back later. The aunt said, "Fuck you!" and left. "The next morning he woke up," said Wojnarowicz, "and he remembered the dream. And he thought, Shit, he should have taken the numbers."[42] DeCapite's aunt had something valuable to offer him, but listening to her would have meant leaving his own temporality and subjecting himself to hers, and he couldn't make the time.

As we listen to Wojnarowicz's taped monologues, we become aware that listening practices can incline us to act in certain ways and can nourish our literal ability to do so, and that they can also obligate us, making us subject to ethical demands for coalitional action we might otherwise have considered ourselves free from.[43] In fact, this may be already implicit in the ethical demand to do the listening that we heard from Sweet Honey in the Rock toward the start of this chapter.

Wojnarowicz listens to the dead—we can presume as much from his collection of answering machine tapes, which include tapes of Peter's voice—but he also listens *for* them, in the sense of "on behalf of." In one especially moving tape journal, which Wojnarowicz made in February 1989 while driving through New Mexico, he offers his ears to his dead friends, which brings him into contact—much as seeing through Hujar's eyes did—with his own proximity to death. Instead of spurring nausea, though, it brings him a rare sense of peace.

Driving through the desert, Wojnarowicz hears Tracy Chapman's "Fast Car" come on the radio, and he turns on his tape recorder and starts talking. This portion of the tape begins with a quick squeak, as the recording function comes up to speed from a dead stop, then Chapman's acoustic guitar lick, then the dull thud of the recorder being put back down somewhere in the car. "It's a sunny day riding back to Albuquerque, in between Gallup and Albuquerque," he says as the lick revolves in the background. He coughs briefly, then continues in a duet with Chapman's song, pausing sometimes to let her singing come through. In the book *Weight of the Earth*, which collects transcriptions of all Wojnarowicz's tape journals, this entry begins with a brief acknowledgment of the song—"['Fast Car,' by Tracy Chapman, is playing on the radio.]"—and then offers Wojnarowicz's spoken words in an unbroken block.[44] But I hear his words and Chapman's song as counterpoint, and I want to retranscribe this tape in a way that takes seriously the sonic intertextuality, the layered call-and-response, as a listening and a collaboration that encompasses Chapman, Wojnarowicz, and those who have gone before.

> It's a sunny day riding back to Albuquerque, in between Gallup and Albuquerque. [*coughs*] Sometimes a song comes on the radio, and it's a day filled with fast trucks, a day of sunlight, and (*Somebody's got to take care of him*) all these clouds, just huge clouds. [*The song's guitar lick kicks back in.*] And you can turn your head from left to right, 360 degrees, and all you see is sky—sometimes the most amazing cliff formations and red sandstone and red dirt. (*Leave tonight or live and die this way*)
>
> But in these moments when a song comes on the radio, something that you like driving to, it's kind of hard (*I remember we were driving*) to suddenly think of people like Peter or Keith or Paul, all of them having died from AIDS, and—(*And I-yee-I had a feeling that I belong*) Just thinking about Peter, just knowing that he's never gonna hear this song, and he'll never . . . (*be someone, be someone, be someone*)[45]

When he makes this tape, Wojnarowicz has for nearly a decade been saving sounds, holding on to the sounds of neighborhood children since grown up, the voices of his dead friends leaving messages, radio interviews broadcast and largely forgotten. These tapes he keeps are all indirect records of his listening practices: at least once, he listened to each sonic event and decided it was worth saving for possible future playback.

This "Fast Car" tape is different. Here we get not just an offstage listening implied by the fact that Wojnarowicz pressed Record or took a tape out of his answering machine for safekeeping, but a direct record of his own attending to sound. For starters, we can hear that he listens as a way out of a rigidly bounded present moment. Almost immediately upon beginning, he expands from a particular time—"It's a sunny day riding back to Albuquerque"—to a more general, recurrent condition: "Sometimes a song comes on the radio." He also listens as a way out of possessive individualism: the first two paragraphs (as I've broken up the transcription) contain no first-person pronouns, with everything he says filtered through a "you" or verbs with no specified subject: "to suddenly think," "just thinking." It is as if the thoughts are thinking themselves, rather than any separate thinking self. In the moment of turning on the tape recorder, what he bears to impress there is an absence of any strictly bounded self, an attitude of awe and reverence toward the encompassing landscape and sky, and the pleasure of a listening that accompanies, even directs or draws, movement and action: "something that you like driving to." He listens to register the pleasure of consonance between the sonic world and the rest of the field of perception, between the song's fast car and the highway's fast trucks and, unspoken, the fast car within which the listening takes its mobile place beneath the sky.

Having listened his way into such spaciousness and connection, he now feels acutely the absence of his friends who have died. It comes up sharply because this pleasure of listening is unavailable to them. Peter and Keith and Paul will never hear this song, which was recorded after they were already gone. Wojnarowicz can listen to it on their behalf, and I think he is doing so; he's trying to notice everything because that ability, simply to hear a song and watch the sky and cover the miles, is already out of reach for people he loved, and it will soon be out of reach for him too, but if he can really attend to it simultaneously with the fact of his own death, if he can balance on the point between hearing and not hearing, seeing and not seeing, wholly inhabiting a present that includes a future obliteration, it will amount to something like an offering for his ancestors, and for the ancestor he soon will be.

> And then suddenly feeling like it's a moment of, of a mortality hallucination, where I realize just how alive I am and also the impermanence of it. (*Still ain't got a job, and I work in a market*) Yeah, I'm alive, but, you know, I could be dead in another year from now or two years from now. (*I'll get promoted and we'll move out of the shelter*) And I won't see this road, and I won't see this sunlight, and I won't see these [*pause*] fast trucks driving by—the long, long road up ahead of me, and a long, long road in the rearview mirror. (*Driving in your car, speed so fast it felt like I was drunk, city lights lay out before us*)

He listens in order to collaborate with what he's hearing, to echo and amplify and improvise on the song. The way Chapman's chorus hits—its memory of togetherness and speed accentuated by the switch from sparse fingerpicking to strummed chords—calls forth Wojnarowicz's own memories of companionship. His narration shadows Chapman's, at times anticipating, at times following an emotional volta or turn of phrase. In this way, death's transformation shades the singer's hope to move out of the shelter, sharpening the edge on the song's bleak and repeatedly extended optimism, just as the speed and magic of the sung car lend added romance to Wojnarowicz's highway mise-en-scène. For the singer of "Fast Car," a memory of driving, the sensation of automotive freedom, powers a belief that the future is primarily a matter of will and determination: "We gotta make a decision / Leave tonight or live and die this way." By the end of the song that possibility has proved disappointing:

> I got a job that pays all our bills
> You stay out drinking late at the bar
> See more of your friends than you do of your kids
> I'd always hoped for better...
> I got no plans, I ain't going nowhere.[46]

All the singer has left is the memory of freedom's hope, of having believed that things could improve. That memory no longer has the power to drive any escape by the narrator. But it can shape a song that helps its listeners feel more keenly their own location between the long, long road up ahead and the long, long road in the rearview mirror.

A practice of coalitional listening—listening with and for the living as well as the dead, up as well as down—remakes Wojnarowicz's own identity over these two and a half minutes of tape journal. At first he experiences himself as nonspecific, a *you* driving in the perpetual present of a *sometimes* amid a subjectless *just thinking*. Then, paradoxically, the act of making space for his ancestors grounds him, takes him from *these moments* to *a moment*, from a nonspecific *you* to an all-too-solid *I* who is alive and thus hurtling, at unknown but inexorable velocity, toward death. Rather than nausea as on the earlier tape, this coalitional listening summons for Wojnarowicz a sense of well-being that extends far beyond his own existence. His tone of voice is gentle here, and his tempo is relaxed: "And time just moves so slow, and time moves so fast, and then time stands still for some, and time (*feeling that I belong*) just speeds up for others. (*had a feeling I*) For me at this moment, I'm in quite a dislocation of time; I'm both outside of time and inside of time at the same time. And all the world looks pretty great."

The unsullied contentment he voices here is especially striking when compared with the most extensive sound work he made during his career, the evening-length performance *ITSOFOMO (In the Shadow of Forward Motion)* that premiered at the Kitchen in New York in 1989, the same year that he made the "Fast Car" tape. In contrast to the "Fast Car" tape's elegiac equanimity,

ITSOFOMO, which Wojnarowicz created in collaboration with the composer Ben Neill, is a chaotic, ominous work. Wojnarowicz's monologues, which he delivered live in the initial performances, speak of rage, violence, and looming destruction; his delivery ranges from low, sullen grumbles to outraged shouts, with layers of echoey reverb amping up the sense of dread. The rest of the work's musical vocabulary includes high trills on trumpet, intermittent tambourine hits that sound like a rattlesnake contemplating a strike, thunderous bass drum and timpani fusillades, and, at the most intense moments, looped audio from a rural North Carolina "hollerin'" contest featuring yodel-like calls that farmers in the region used for long-range communication before telephones became common. Those calls, which formerly let farmers exchange greetings and information across long distances, sound in *ITSOFOMO* like alarms, threats, or sometimes the yelping of an animal in unabating pain. That is to say, they mirror Wojnarowicz's vocals, both in the sense of urgency and in the capacity to convey information and emotion across great divides.

Wojnarowicz, Neill, and percussionist Dan Yellich performed *ITSO-FOMO* around the country before Wojnarowicz's death in 1992. In the decades since, Neill and Yellich have revived the piece several times, including at the Whitney Museum of American Art in 2018 and at the Getty Center in January 2021, with Neill mixing in recordings of Wojnarowicz's voice. In these recordings reactivated live and in the *ITSOFOMO* soundtrack that was recently rereleased, as well as in the tape journals that in the four years leading up to this writing were made publicly available in written transcriptions and vinyl pressings, the living engage in collaborations with Wojnarowicz, listening to and for him, heeding his wish for ongoing hearing.

The coalitional listening that Wojnarowicz engages and invites is akin to the listening practices in Marlon Riggs's work as discussed earlier in this chapter, and it is connected as well to the historical seeing Pat Parker and Audre Lorde enacted in the poems discussed in Chapter 4. In "Afterimages" in particular, Lorde superimposed historical and present-day images to reveal the workings of history, transform painful images into sustenance, and open a space where the past could arise and assist in the reshaping of the present. Such historical seeing also made space for complicated relations across difference that were irreducible to easy alignment or blame—what we can now understand as a jagged, unsettled coalition of imperfect practice and difficult solidarity. Alongside the historical seeing elaborated by Parker and Lorde, Riggs and Wojnarowicz reveal coalitional listening as another way of inhabiting and altering history through superimposition. The ancestral lineage Wojnarowicz inhabits through his listening is largely one based in interpersonal intimacy, while Riggs situates his own relationships with friends and colleagues explicitly within the long African American freedom struggle, which guides him to take his place alongside Harriet Tubman at the river's edge and finally step in.

This river flows all the way back, back beyond Ella Sheppard of the Fisk Jubilee Singers and her careful work to listen to the songs of her community's elders and ancestors as sung by young students who, having gone off to college in a bid to outlive the past, soon found that their purchase on a future depended on their willingness to listen closely to that past and grant it new resonance. It flows on to W. E. B. Du Bois, who listened to children singing to the sunshine with a brightness he could only borrow, and to Charles Chesnutt, who intuited that a musical stillness could hold space for the disagreement without which nothing else could move. It flows up past Huddie Ledbetter making a choice to bring the labored soundscape of the prison farm onto the stages of the Popular Front, even as those who heard the record of forced labor weren't sure how to transcribe it; and it flows past Tillie Olsen boasting about her "tape-recorder ear" even as she revealed in her fiction a lingering unease about the ethics of transcribing amid sentimental projection. Gathered by this river are the marchers of Mississippi, among them Stokely Carmichael exploring muteness as a political stance and Martin Luther King Jr. training a movement's ears to the tramp, tramp, tramp of marching feet; assembled there are hopeful and disappointed feminists seeking a workable voice, Adrienne Rich grappling with the effects of labor and mediation in self-expression, Hortense Spillers spotlighting a 360-degree scene of embodied performance, and Audre Lorde and Pat Parker braving an overlay of traumatic pasts on the present and daring to take all of it as a form of nourishment.

Each of these models helps to flesh out the project this book has been pursuing from the start. It is an endeavor of paying homage to a lineage of political aspiration, action, and thought; of articulating an ancestral ensemble to whom it might be possible to listen closely and hold oneself accountable; and of letting superimposition, attention to transcription, and close listening transport us beyond our "little meager human-body-mouth-talking all the time" to explore ways of being in transhistorical coalition that could reshape the past and reclaim a future.[47] Listening to and with and for those who have come before, holding space for the occluded or possible audition of what is no longer strictly extant (Did you hear me, Harriet?): these are practices of the untimely desires for transformation I have tracked throughout this book as disappointment.[48] Listening with these desires, we come to understand that disappointment is a coalitional practice of caring attention: attention to those who came before, attention to ideals still unrealized, and attention to what still resonates and demands a hearing, not when it is convenient for us but now, defined as we are by our own ongoing experiences of untimely desire.

CODA

In this book, I've argued that political disappointment was the defining political experience of the twentieth century in the United States, that it shaped the century's literature and art, and that a shared experience of loss offered grounds for solidarity across difference. In the recurrent rhythms of disappointment and the ongoing efforts to cope with nonfulfillment, this book's archive demonstrates the paradoxical generativity of loss, showing how letting loss resonate produced new forms, practices, and collectivities that span and survive the century. Without negating any concrete historical conditions of defeat or ambivalent attainment, this productivity nevertheless exceeds individual moments and tenders a gesture toward what still might come: an openness to an unfixed future is disappointment's paradoxical halo.

In the ongoing erratic motion of history, disappointed writers, musicians, artists, and activists of the twentieth century find grounds for the possibility, if never the secure guarantee, of things being different, and of some potential arena for further action. In their disappointment, these thinkers repeatedly ask, What might come next? Grace Paley's narrator in "Wants" sees the trees finally budding. W. E. B. Du Bois hears a chorus of children cheering the weary traveler. Ella Sheppard vows to sing all along the way. Tillie Olsen's characters transmit their values to their children. Stokely Carmichael, even as he announces that the system has failed, vows that his people will not just demand, but achieve, Black power. Marlon Riggs understands his work as extending beyond his life-span, and David Wojnarowicz finds release and perfection in the flows of time that greet a body poised between living and dying.

Through all the disappointments of the last century, then, there breathes some hope. This manifests less as "a faith in the ultimate justice of things," as Du Bois heard in the Sorrow Songs, and more as a curiosity toward and unknowing about what might come next, and an awareness of history as changeability: an understanding that the passage of time and the workings of historical forces would bring about conditions that were somehow different from the present. The writers and artists I have analyzed question seriously whether conditions are improving—they often note that in the short term things are getting worse—but they do not rule out the possibility that conditions *might* improve someday, "anon in His good time."[1]

This is the aspect of disappointment that feels most remote for us now. When I first embarked on this project, in the middle of Barack Obama's presidency, political disappointment was pervasive on the left. A Black former community organizer, adept at rousing whole arenas with a United Farm Workers chant, was in the White House. Yet for all the symbolic changes this had brought to the political scene, the substantive conditions of American life—racism, economic inequality, carceral and imperialist violence—remained largely unaltered. The contrast between expectation and actuality fueled the explosive emergence of movements such as Occupy Wall Street, Black Lives Matter, and Me Too, formations that combined online self-expression with real-life collective mobilization. These movements successfully brought their issues and analyses into public discourse, but a stubborn gap persisted between affecting the discourse and changing institutions.

All of this initially felt familiar to me as a product and scholar of the twentieth-century Left. A moment of possible transformation was not panning out as hoped, but people would muddle through and make something out of it. Legislative half measures and ongoing political contradictions would spark ever more deeply considered desires and demands, connect us to our activist forebears, and remake our collective identities. As I mapped out this book, I expected to conclude that the twenty-first century's disappointments were nothing new, and that we were tasked with critiquing and adding to a meaningful archive of responses to nonfulfillment by understanding it, as our predecessors had, to be a matter of historical contingency. This was to be my way of situating present disappointments within a longer arc of history, and also my rebuttal to an Obama-era intellectual and aesthetic celebration of failure as resistance, a trend perpetuated by scholars and artists I respected but that nevertheless made me worry about a possible abdication of civic engagement. My argument would serve, too, as a delayed riposte to talented organizers I'd worked with who always spun any defeat, no matter how crushing, into a positive: we'd shown how scared the bosses were of our cause, or we'd trained new activists, or we'd gotten people talking about our issues. I wanted more; I felt it was important to reckon with the actual stakes and casualties of political defeat, and I believed the archive of the twentieth century offered us models for honestly acknowledging our losses.

Halfway through drafting the book, though, it became harder for me to believe that twentieth-century political disappointment had an easy analogue in the present. The force with which Donald Trump's election hit me was paired with the shock of my move from New York City to the relentlessly gerrymandered, permanently deep-red state of Indiana, a place that nourishes grim resignation in anybody to the left of Richard Nixon. My new home felt extreme, but I also realized that the distressingly bare conditions of Hoosier existence, where government's main purpose appeared to be helping corporations squeeze every last drop of productive life from a low-wage workforce, were much more representative of Trump-era America than were coastal liberals' plucky postcard-writing parties and hat-knitting bees. Living in Indiana, where antiabortion clinics abound and mammoth pickup trucks with Punisher skull stickers belch unregulated exhaust, I had a real sense that the gloves had come all the way off. It was easy to feel that the basic foundations for even being able to imagine a nondystopian collective future were dissolving. Since that time, the coronavirus pandemic, the letdown of the Joe Biden presidency, and the drastic realignment of US politics by a far-right Supreme Court have only intensified this sense. And of course, for many low-income communities and communities of color, obstacles to thriving such as inadequate health care, vulnerability to environmental harm, and disenfranchisement are nothing new. Nor are reasons to be skeptical of, if not pessimistic about, liberal claims about progress. Yet disenfranchisement and vulnerability became more broadly—if still not at all evenly—distributed over the years that I was writing this book, prompting me to reconceptualize some of my starting assumptions. The element of disappointment that maintains faith in a future window of possibility started to feel like a relic of the past.

The past six years have seemed an eternity. As somebody invested in doing cultural history, I'm obliged to say that it's still too soon to state definitively whether we are seeing the twilight of nightfall or the flush of some faint-dawning day. But many major developments, including accelerating climate catastrophe, the engineering of minority rule at state and federal levels, and the technologically enabled disintegration of a shared basic conception of reality on matters like health care or election outcomes, appear increasingly difficult to reverse anytime soon. The kind of disappointment we face today strikes me as deeper and more lasting than what came before.

Asali Solomon's 2021 novel *The Days of Afrekete* registers this sense powerfully. In this book, Solomon looks back on the Obama era from the vantage of Trump's America as a way to stage a confrontation between a feeling of temporary disappointment and a sense of irreparable injustice. *The Days of Afrekete* is set in the middle of Obama's second term, a fact Solomon emphasizes. The plot concerns a Black woman named Liselle, whose white husband, the now inaptly named Winn, has just conceded defeat in a campaign for the Pennsylvania state legislature. Liselle is aware, however, that the failure is more thoroughgoing than any of the supporters or even her husband knows: he is about to be indicted by the FBI for unspecified acts of corruption he may have committed during his campaign. What looks to Winn and the book's other characters to be merely a quotidian, historically specific defeat is instead understood by our protagonist as a more permanent devastation. When Winn natters on about a possible future campaign, Liselle inwardly scoffs: "His loss had been definitive. . . . Politics did not need him."[2]

Liselle sees her own future in bleak terms as well: her husband in jail indefinitely, their comfortable Northwest Philadelphia house repossessed, her family forced to move back into Liselle's childhood home, her lifelong upward trajectory of ever more money, more comfort, more power suddenly and gravely reversed. All through the dinner party that anchors the book, she expects the FBI to knock at the door. When a knock finally arrives, though, it is Liselle's long-ago ex-girlfriend Selena, the only Black woman she dated in her time as a college lesbian. Unlike Liselle, Selena has never harbored any illusions about America or democracy. Her troubles began in elementary school, when, upon learning about Native American genocide, she began to have nightmares in which her parents' Thanksgiving tablecloth was "covered in bloody handprints." "I still don't get what this has to do with you," Liselle years later tells Selena, who replies, "Look. . . . Maybe it's not happening here and now, but it happened to someone. And if it happened to someone, it might as well have been me."[3]

Selena's inability or refusal to separate herself from the foundational violence of American history condemns her to an adulthood spent shuttling in and out of psych wards. Yet her acceptance of present and future disasters offers some paradoxical comfort. Contemplating climate change, she reflects, "The end of this world was not a delusion but an imminent fact. A calm settled over her body at this thought."[4] This may explain why, when Liselle needs help understanding how everything could fall apart so thoroughly, she calls Selena and utters the code word, drawn from their undergraduate study of Audre Lorde, that they had agreed would serve as their SOS signal: "Afrekete."

By the time Selena arrives, on the last page of the book, Liselle's dinner-party playlist has come to an end. Rather than cue up a new album on whatever app has been piping the music through the house, she instead opens her cabinet of vinyl and pulls out Stevie Wonder's *Innervisions* (1973). "Don't You Worry 'Bout a Thing" is one of blithe Liselle's favorite tracks and a means of refusing to hear the future: "These days when she played it, Liselle often tried to stop time, superstitiously starting it again before the silence or the next song."[5] She listens only to what she wants to hear. (As Solomon likely knows, Stephen Colbert asked Wonder to play "Don't You Worry" on television the night before the 2016 presidential election to calm the worries of Colbert and his liberal audiences.[6]) Rather than simply cueing it up to loop on her phone or tablet, Liselle habitually restarts the song by hand, laboring to maintain an unfixable present of consolation. At the end of the book, though, she just lets it play through, because "her ankle hurt and she was tired": she is too worn down to keep doing the work of believing things will get better.[7]

Winn and his supporters wrongly understand his defeat in the state legislature race as temporally contingent, even reversible: one supporter asks for a return of her campaign contribution, mistaking it for a loan. But at the end of the book Liselle understands what Selena has known all along: disappointment is baked into the very foundations of the American project. *The Days of Afrekete* faces head-on a twenty-first-century political disappointment in which embracing the end of the American project, even the end of the world—aided by interpersonal intimacy and encounters with literature—is the best one can do.

A similar embrace of dissolution drives the band Big Thief's song "Not." When the song came out in 2019, I was living with my partner and our young child in Los Angeles, where I had a fellowship. Everything was vibrant and sweet-smelling, every day was shot through with ecstasy and sunshine and trilling fountains in Spanish-style plazas, roosters sang to us in the morning and coyotes at sunset, the horn flourishes of virtuoso *banda* musicians drifted up to our hillside cottage from parties at night, and I thought for a few delirious months that we might get to stay in LA and build our lives there. The wider world felt unfixable, but after several years of Indiana rawness I found California a syrupy narcotic, and I wanted to drift forever in its plume.

Into this fog barreled "Not," an uncompromising avalanche of negative determination from which the only positive presence that emerges is noise. The song begins with an electric guitar strumming a power chord topped by a minor third, an interval so slim and unstable it continually threatens to cave in under its own weight; it's plumped up unsustainably with distortion and fuzz. One bar later, taut sixteenth notes on a high-hat clamp down the beat even as the sandwiched cymbals rattle slightly open.

"It's not the energy reeling," Adrianne Lenker sings, part whisper and part whine,

> nor the lines in your face
> nor the clouds on the ceiling
> nor the clouds in space.

With audible breaths every three words, these are midstopped lines, cleaved by ancient-feeling caesuras and by the way Lenker's voice breaks on the word *space*, as she registers the labor of skipping upward and works it anyway. Nearly every verse in the song starts with a version of this lyrical pattern: it's not the *x*, nor the *y*, nor the *z*.

The guitar starts to solo before we even hit a chorus, which feels too early, but this song has no patience for repetition; no sooner does it set up a structure than it undermines, dismantles, unravels it. The guitar vaults to feedback behind an onslaughting verse that keeps veering into the infinite:

> It's not the formless being
> Nor the cry in the air
> Nor the boy I'm seeing
> With her long black hair

As the cry shakes the air, or doesn't, the lover wavers into unclear view: grave and thoughtful, uncoiffed, fluid gender appearing here as an elision of form or an outrippling circle of sound. The cry and the fluid gender all render as flux in the feedback, which masses bulk from wave and air. The bass is Crazy Horse–plump, Lenker's voice reedy and sure, the chords oscillating over and over back to the opening minor third.

Two minutes in, the guitar drops out, the bass sounds like a rubber band on a shoe box, and then that feral, alien guitar swoops back in and suddenly Lenker is feral too: "It's not the hunger revealing," she sings, tearing "hunger" from the back of her throat so roughly that it sounds like "hunk of" instead, "nor the ricochet in the cave. Nor the hand"—another growl on "hand," body bursting through the unreality of Platonic cavern shadows—"that is healing, nor the nameless grave." Step by step, Lenker is challenging listeners to think beyond physical forms and needs, then beyond shadows and representations, then again beyond embodied intersubjectivity, then again beyond the collective end of death. No meditation retreat has ever been so thorough.

In light of this contemporary sense of evacuation, shared by Big Thief's "Not" and Solomon's *The Days of Afrekete*, it's tempting to look back on twentieth-century disappointment, all those resolute refixings of gazes upon the horizon, and conclude that these people had it wrong. The horizon was not open; the future was not unfixed; American democracy had never been a set of ideals that might be mobilized to hold this nation to its never-realized promises. In other words, we might look back on all this disappointment and conclude that disillusionment would have been better suited to the reality. A great deal of contemporary literature and music, and for that matter political culture across the board, operates in a bleak mode: conditions are only getting worse, and usually in ways that have been preordained for centuries.

But it's hard to relinquish the idea that inchoate possibility might emerge from that very bleakness. As autumn wildfires exploded across California, I drove an hour into the LA suburbs to see Big Thief play in an Orange County office park. The sound in the room was thicker and rounder than anything I'd heard streaming from my speakers all year. During a very slow song, a fan in a tube top and combat boots crowd-surfed languidly while the band grinned in surprise. Finally, the opening chords of "Not" tore through the room. Everybody put up their phones for half a minute to shoot video, then put them down, conquered by the room and the thick sound and their own bodies in space.

The fiercest line of the song, when sung live, is different from the fiercest line on the record. I was certain this song's molten core was the line about revealing, its anti-credo against articulate or redemptive embodiment. But onstage at the peak of a final chorus, Lenker howled *"not dying"* at top volume, which made the rest of the song, the rest of the concert, a commentary on that pair of words, whose meaning amid the other negations was impossible to precisely pin down. Unless it was this: when the rigor of systematic negation comes up against the ultimate negation of death, what arises is so transformative that it might spark something nobody had expected, as simultaneously reassuring and demanding as the art of Marlon Riggs and David Wojnarowicz, as quotidian and unbounded as Du Bois setting his face toward morning and raising a cry to God the reader.

It could indeed be the case that the disappointed artists and thinkers of the twentieth century mistakenly saw possibility where there objectively was none, though it's difficult to see how we could render a final verdict with confidence at this point. Still, the ethical obligation to hold space for them regardless, to listen for them with care, is not contingent on their having accurately assessed the conditions and histories of their own time, let alone of ours. Caring for and listening to our ancestors, recognizing their untimely desires as linked with if not precisely cognate to our own, locates us within a capacious, productive heritage of nonfulfillment and aspiration. Attending to the ways those we accept as forebears lingered with loss and found new forms and practices to accommodate, process, and transform their disappointment, we, too, can seek forms and practices suitable to our time, working in coalition with the dead as well as the living. Listening across history, opening ourselves to the demands of those who have gone before, allowing historical superimpositions to resonate and ring out, and issuing transcriptions of all these untimely operations, we can refine and enlarge our own confrontations with a seemingly unbearable present. At the risk of sounding too hopeful, it may even help us think our way beyond America at last.

NOTES

Introduction

1. Where desire unfulfilled instead refuses to acknowledge loss, it seeks to force an opening. It musters rural armies; it batters the windows with a flagpole; it insists: there was no loss, and if there was, it will be undone, and if it is not, it will destroy us, so we may as well destroy everything. Part of my argument in this book will be that acknowledging nonfulfillment is precisely what allows political desire to change and learn, to remain alive and active, and to engender new productions.

2. That word *solidarity* is my proposed addition to Judith Butler's important discussion of loss in *Precarious Life*. There Butler posits vulnerability to one another, and hence openness to loss and grief, as possible grounds for "a more general conception of the human," while also acknowledging that such a commonality is dependent on recognition of others as capable of experiencing losses and acknowledgment of others' losses as grievable. In what follows, I will discuss the importance of recognition for one's own losses as well. Judith Butler, *Precarious Life: The Powers of Mourning and Violence* (New York: Verso, 2004), 31.

3. To be clear, the window closed in stages: the withdrawal of federal troops from Southern capitals in 1877 cleared the way for widespread disenfranchisement; the Supreme Court in 1883 struck down civil rights protections and gutted the Fourteenth Amendment; Congress later repealed the postwar civil rights protections, leaving the Fifteenth Amendment without any legal means of enforcement; lynchings increased throughout the century's final decades; and in 1896 *Plessy v. Ferguson* seemed to issue the final word on the matter. In 1901, the last Reconstruction-era African American member of Congress, George H. White of North Carolina, gave his farewell address and left the chamber. There would not be another African American in Congress until 1929; the next Black Southerners in Congress would be elected in 1973, and the next Black North Carolinian, Eva Clayton, would be elected in 1992.

4. See, for instance, Daniel Immerwahr, *How to Hide an Empire: A History of the Greater United States* (New York: Farrar, Straus and Giroux, 2019); and Stephen

Kinzer, *The True Flag: Theodore Roosevelt, Mark Twain, and the Birth of American Empire* (New York: Henry Holt, 2017).

5. W. E. B. Du Bois, *The Souls of Black Folk,* Norton Critical Edition (1903; New York: W. W. Norton, 1999), 11, 12.

6. Du Bois, 12.

7. Du Bois, 12.

8. Ernst Bloch, *The Principle of Hope* (Cambridge, MA: MIT Press, 1986); Jamie Owen Daniel and Tom Moylan, eds., *Not Yet: Reconsidering Ernst Bloch* (New York: Verso, 1997).

9. Du Bois, *Souls of Black Folk,* 12.

10. Sigmund Freud, "Mourning and Melancholia," in *Essential Papers on Object Loss,* ed. Rita V. Frankiel (New York: New York University Press, 1994), 38–51, 43. For more on this intriguing echo, and on resonances between Freud and Du Bois more generally, see Jonathan Flatley, *Affective Mapping: Melancholia and the Politics of Modernism* (Cambridge, MA: Harvard University Press, 2008), especially 105–157; Julie Beth Napolin, "Listening to and as Contemporaries: W. E. B. Du Bois & Sigmund Freud," *Sounding Out!* (blog), September 24, 2018, https://soundstudiesblog.com/2018/09/24/du-bois-freud-and-psychoanalytic-listening/; and Peter Coviello, "Intimacy and Affliction: DuBois, Race, and Psychoanalysis," *MLQ: Modern Language Quarterly* 64, no. 1 (2003): 1–32.

11. Du Bois, *Souls of Black Folk,* 15.

12. Nahum Chandler makes this point elegantly and incisively in *"Beyond This Narrow Now": Or, Delimitations, of W. E. B. Du Bois* (Durham, NC: Duke University Press, 2022).

13. Du Bois, *Souls of Black Folk,* 15–16.

14. Du Bois, 156.

15. Du Bois, 155.

16. See Michael Gallope, *Deep Refrains: Music, Philosophy, and the Ineffable* (Chicago: University of Chicago Press, 2017); Vladimir Jankélévitch, *Music and the Ineffable,* trans. Carolyn Abbate (Princeton, NJ: Princeton University Press, 2003); Roger W. H. Savage, *Music, Time, and Its Other: Aesthetic Reflections on Finitude, Temporality, and Alterity* (New York: Routledge, 2017); Ashon Crawley, *Blackpentecostal Breath: The Aesthetics of Possibility* (New York: Fordham University Press, 2016); Jacques Attali, *Noise: The Political Economy of Music* (Minneapolis: University of Minnesota Press, 1985); and Ellen Willis, *Beginning to See the Light: Sex, Hope, and Rock-and-Roll* (1981; Minneapolis: University of Minnesota Press, 2012).

17. On the aural imaginary, see Roshanak Kheshti, "Touching Listening: The Aural Imaginary in the World Music Culture Industry," *American Quarterly* 63, no. 3 (2011): 711–731.

18. See, for instance, Rebecca Harding Davis, *Life in the Iron Mills* (1861; first Feminist Press edition, New York: Feminist Press, 2020); Harriet Jacobs, *Incidents in the Life of a Slave Girl* (1861; New York: Signet Classics, 2010); and Ralph Ellison, *Invisible Man* (1952; New York: Random House, 2002).

19. "What Are the Contents of the Golden Record?," Jet Propulsion Laboratory, NASA, accessed September 9, 2022, https://voyager.jpl.nasa.gov/golden-record /whats-on-the-record/.

20. I draw here on Michael Gallope's insight about "the paradox of the ineffable"— that is, that "music appears as a sensuous immediacy at the same time that it always remains mediated by forms and techniques" (Gallope, *Deep Refrains*, 10)—and suggest that it is generalizable to sound in general. This tension is also explored in Jonathan Sterne, *The Audible Past: Cultural Origins of Sound Reproduction* (Durham, NC: Duke University Press, 2003).

21. Ellison, *Invisible Man*, 8.

22. Toni Cade Bambara, *The Salt Eaters* (1980; New York: Vintage Contemporaries, 1992), 245, 248; Carter Mathes, "Scratching the Threshold: Textual Sound and Political Form in Toni Cade Bambara's 'The Salt Eaters,'" *Contemporary Literature* 50, no. 2 (2009): 363–396.

23. Sheila Smith McKoy, "The Future Perfect: Reframing Ancient Spirituality in Toni Cade Bambara's *The Salt Eaters*," *Journal of Ethnic American Literature*, no. 1 (2011): 111–126; T. S. Eliot, *The Waste Land* (New York: Liveright, 2013).

24. Henry Louis Gates Jr., *The Signifying Monkey: A Theory of Afro-American Literary Criticism* (New York: Oxford University Press, 1988), 174.

25. Recent scholarship on interactions between sound, literature, and music that has influenced my thinking here includes Brent Hayes Edwards, *Epistrophies: Jazz and the Literary Imagination* (Cambridge, MA: Harvard University Press, 2017); Julie Beth Napolin, *The Fact of Resonance: Modernist Acoustics and Narrative Form* (New York: Fordham University Press, 2020); and Anthony Reed, *Soundworks: Race, Sound, and Poetry in Production* (Durham, NC: Duke University Press, 2021).

26. Alexandra T. Vazquez, *Listening in Detail: Performances of Cuban Music* (Durham, NC: Duke University Press, 2013), 8.

27. Over a week of events, as the Republican Party gathered to formally nominate George W. Bush for president, hundreds of activists were arrested at marches, in parks, and on street corners. In an especially striking crackdown, police raided a warehouse where artists were building giant puppets for a public pageant. Seventy-nine puppet-makers were arrested, and the city destroyed their work. Kris Hermes, *Crashing the Party: Legacies and Lessons from the RNC 2000* (Oakland, CA: PM Press, 2015).

28. Hermes, *Crashing the Party*.

29. Grace Paley, "Wants," in *Enormous Changes at the Last Minute* (New York: Farrar, Straus and Giroux, 1974), 1–6, 4.

30. Paley, 5.

31. Paley, 5.

32. "Cruel optimism" is, of course, a reference to Lauren Berlant; I engage Berlant's work on this concept more thoroughly later in this introduction. Here I am in the same territory as Jonathan Flatley when he writes of melancholia as "the site in which the social origins of our emotional lives can be mapped out and from which we can see the other persons who share our losses and are subject to the same social forces." Jonathan Flatley, *Affective Mapping: Melancholia and the Politics of Modernism* (Cambridge, MA: Harvard University Press, 2008), 3. Flatley's work on melancholia as a lens through which to recognize shared losses has been extremely helpful to this project. Where Flatley and others speak of melancholia, however, I am interested in thinking in terms of ongoing desire, which does not presume in advance any particular affective experience or presentation.

33. Paley, "Wants," 6.

34. See, for instance, Richard H. Crossman, ed., *The God That Failed* (1949; New York: Columbia University Press, 2001).

35. Saidiya Hartman, "Venus in Two Acts," *Small Axe* 26, vol. 12, no. 2 (June 2008): 1–14, 13; Christina Sharpe, *In the Wake: On Blackness and Being* (Durham, NC: Duke University Press, 2016); Rinaldo Walcott, *The Long Emancipation: Moving toward Black Freedom* (Durham, NC: Duke University Press, 2021).

36. Hartman, "Venus in Two Acts," 14, 13.

37. Ernst Bloch and Theodor W. Adorno, "Something's Missing: A Discussion between Ernst Bloch and Theodor W. Adorno on the Contradictions of Utopian Longing," in *The Utopian Function of Art and Literature: Selected Essays,* by Ernst Bloch, trans. Jack Zipes and Frank Mecklenburg (Cambridge, MA: MIT Press, 1988), 1–17, 4.

38. Bloch, *Principle of Hope;* José Esteban Muñoz, *Cruising Utopia: The Then and There of Queer Futurity* (New York: New York University Press, 2009); Crawley, *Blackpentecostal Breath.*

39. Ernst Bloch, "Can Hope Be Disappointed?," in *Literary Essays* (Stanford, CA: Stanford University Press, 1998), 339–345, 340, 341.

40. Bloch, 341.

41. Lisa Duggan and José Esteban Muñoz, "Hope and Hopelessness: A Dialogue," *Women and Performance: A Journal of Feminist Theory* 19, no. 2 (2009): 275–283, 278–279.

42. Frank B. Wilderson III, *Afropessimism* (New York: Liveright, 2020); Jared Sexton, "Afro-Pessimism: The Unclear Word," *Rhizomes,* no. 29 (2016), http://www.rhizomes.net/issue29/sexton.html.

43. Muñoz is of course key here, but provocative and generative instances of such utopianism can also be found in Jill Dolan, *Utopia in Performance: Finding Hope at the Theater* (Ann Arbor: University of Michigan Press, 2005); Tavia Nyong'o, *Afro-Fabulations: The Queer Drama of Black Life* (New York: New York University Press, 2018); and Josh Kun, *Audiotopia: Music, Race, and America* (Berkeley: University of California Press, 2005).

44. In addition to some of the works I've already mentioned, I want to flag Sianne Ngai's *Ugly Feelings* (Cambridge, MA: Harvard University Press, 2005) and Joshua Chambers-Letson's *After the Party: A Manifesto for Queer of Color Life* (New York: New York University Press, 2018).

45. Lauren Berlant, *Cruel Optimism* (Durham, NC: Duke University Press, 2011), especially chapter 7, "On the Desire for the Political."

46. Bloch and Adorno, "Something's Missing," 16–17.

47. Bloch and Adorno, 17. For a generative variation on this conception of hope, see the elegant concept of "melancholic hope" that Joseph R. Winters proposes in *Hope Draped in Black: Race, Melancholy, and the Agony of Progress* (Durham, NC: Duke University Press, 2016).

48. See especially Judith Butler, *Gender Trouble: Feminism and the Subversion of Identity* (1990; New York: Routledge, 1999); Judith Butler, *The Psychic Life of Power: Theories in Subjection* (Stanford, CA: Stanford University Press, 1997); and Judith Butler, "Melancholy Gender—Refused Identification," *Psychoanalytic Dialogues* 5, no. 2 (1995): 165–180.

49. Melanie Klein, "Mourning and Its Relation to Manic-Depressive States" (1940), in *Love, Guilt and Reparation and Other Works, 1921–1945* (New York: Free Press, 1975), 344–369.

50. Klein, 348.

51. Klein, 360.

52. Klein, 360.

53. Segal writes of "what I believe is present in the unconscious of all artists: namely, that all creation is really a re-creation of a once loved and once whole, but now lost and ruined object, a ruined internal world and self. It is when the world within us is destroyed, when it is dead and loveless, when our loved ones are in fragments, and we ourselves in helpless despair—it is then that we must re-create our world anew, re-assemble the pieces, infuse life into dead fragments, re-create life." Hanna Segal, "A Psycho-analytical Approach to Aesthetics," in *Essential Papers in Object Loss*, ed. Rita V. Frankiel (New York: New York University Press, 1994), 486–507, 491–492.

54. Segal, 498.

55. Nicholas Abraham and Marina Torok, "Mourning or Melancholia: Introjection versus Incorporation" (1972), in *The Shell and the Kernel: Renewals of Psychoanalysis* (Chicago: University of Chicago Press, 1994), 1:125–138, 127.

56. Abraham and Torok, 127.

57. Abraham and Torok, 128; emphasis in the original.

58. Jonathan Flatley, for instance, writes in *Affective Mapping* of melancholia as the widespread depressive, yet potentially resistant, response to modernity's failure to live up to its promises. David L. Eng and David Kazanjian similarly employ melancholia as a keyword for cultural reckonings with political loss, where the term is seen as indexing "both a formal relation and a structure of feeling, a mechanism of disavowal and a constellation of affect"—a constellation that also encompasses mourning, as well as "nostalgia, sadness, trauma, and depression." David L. Eng and David Kazanjian, "Introduction: Mourning Remains," in *Loss: The Politics of Mourning*, ed. David L. Eng and David Kazanjian (Berkeley: University of California Press, 2003), 1–25, 2–3. And Anne Cheng's influential idea of racial melancholia links melancholia closely with mourning and grief as a way of thinking about racialized subject formation: "The model of melancholia can help us comprehend grief and loss on the part of the aggrieved, not just as a symptom but also as a dynamic process with both coercive and transformative potentials for political imagination." Anne Anlin Cheng, *The Melancholy of Race* (New York: Oxford University Press, 2001), xi.

59. Dana Luciano writes, for instance, of "the absolute metaphorics of loss," predicated on a "presumably absolute division—that between life and death." Dana Luciano, "Passing Shadows: Melancholic Nationality and Black Critical Publicity in Pauline E. Hopkins's *Of One Blood*," in Eng and Kazanjian, *Loss*, 148–187, 157–158. It's worth noting here that Christian conceptions of the afterlife, which often reject the notion of death's finality, may well be instrumental in some scholars' impulse to apply the concept of mourning across the board. Conceptual historian Reinhart Koselleck proposed that in Western thought, the primary arena for potential completeness of life transitioned around the seventeenth century from a Christian hereafter to the space of life on earth. Reinhart Koselleck, "'Space of Experience' and 'Horizon of Expectation': Two Historical Categories," in *Futures Past: On the Semantics of Historical Time* (Cambridge, MA: MIT Press, 1985), 255–275. But political and eschatological conceptions of time and change have a long history of intermingling, with Walter Benjamin's Marxist mysticism and Crawley's Blackpentecostal otherwise thinking as but two examples. I'm not calling for a disentanglement of the two modes, as if such an extrication were even possible. Nevertheless, in thinking about political losses and how they are experienced, it's worth reiterating that political losses occur in historical time and, unlike the death of a person, are not necessarily permanent. They also do not always entail the loss of something that was ever truly present; a political loss, as Du Bois reminds us, can involve an ideal that has never delivered on its promise. I'm grateful to Anthony Pinn for this last insight—that mourning and melancholia may not be

the appropriate figures for political nonfulfillment in cases where dispossession is "already and always."

60. Meg Russell, *Must Politics Disappoint?* (London: Fabian Ideas, 2005); Wilson Carey McWilliams, *Beyond the Politics of Disappointment? American Elections, 1980–1998* (New York: Chatham House / Seven Bridges, 2000).

61. This focus is not meant to be exhaustive. In addition to writing and cultural production, for instance, Jodi Dean proposes social media activity, study, community building, and "punching a Nazi in the face" as forms of political work that can be imagined "under conditions where political change seems completely out of reach." Jodi Dean, *Comrade: An Essay on Political Belonging* (New York: Verso, 2019), 8. Yet it's also the case that literature and recorded sound tend to be much more durable than a Twitter post or a blow to the face.

Chapter 1. Failures of the Reconstruction

1. The chapter "The Coming of the Lord" in Du Bois's *Black Reconstruction* remains a brilliant evocation of the sense of possibility and redemption that accompanied Emancipation. W. E. B. Du Bois, *Black Reconstruction in America; an Essay toward a History of the Part Which Black Folk Played in the Attempt to Reconstruct Democracy in America, 1860–1880* (1935; New York: Atheneum, 1969).

2. Du Bois, 126.

3. W. E. B. Du Bois, *Dusk of Dawn* (Oxford: Oxford University Press, 2007), 13.

4. See, for instance, Richard Hofstadter, *Age of Reform* (New York: Knopf, 1955); and Robert Nisbet, *History of the Idea of Progress* (New York: Basic Books, 1980), especially chap. 8, "The Persistence of Progress."

5. Du Bois, *Dusk of Dawn*, 14.

6. See, for instance, Sigmund Freud, "Thoughts for the Times on War and Death," in *Standard Edition of the Complete Psychological Works of Sigmund Freud*, vol. 14, *On the History of the Psycho-analytic Movement, Papers on Metapsychology and Other Works, 1914–1916* (London: Hogarth, 1957), 275–300. By the early twenty-first century, the intellectual consensus no longer included any expectation of an inexorable tilt toward improvement over time. One recent corollary of this change is a skepticism within literary and cultural studies regarding linear time, now often spoken of as being the exclusive domain of oppressive forces such as racism, capitalism, nationalism, and heteronormativity—"the rational time of capital, nation, and family" in one representative (if necessarily partial) formulation—while nonlinear temporalities are lauded as being associated with queerness, resistance to capitalism and nation, and freedom for people of color. See Roderick A. Ferguson, in Carolyn Dinshaw et al., "Theorizing Queer Temporalities," *GLQ* 13, no. 2–3 (2007): 177–195, 180. See also, for instance, Elizabeth Freeman, *Time Binds: Queer Temporalities, Queer Histories* (Durham, NC: Duke University Press, 2010); Judith [Jack] Halberstam, *In a Queer Time*

and Place (New York: New York University Press, 2005); and other works discussed in this chapter's section on Charles Chesnutt.

7. On the nadir, see Rayford Logan, *The Negro in American Life and Thought: The Nadir, 1877–1901* (New York: Dial, 1954). On the nonadvancement of conditions for African Americans after the Civil War, see Saidiya Hartman, *Scenes of Subjection: Terror, Slavery, and Self-Making in Nineteenth-Century America* (New York: Oxford University Press, 1997); Christina Sharpe, *In the Wake: On Blackness and Being* (Durham, NC: Duke University Press, 2016); and Eric Foner, *Reconstruction: America's Unfinished Revolution, 1863–1877* (New York: Perennial Library, 1989).

8. Pauline Hopkins, *Contending Forces: A Romance Illustrative of Negro Life North and South* (1900; New York: Oxford University Press, 1988), 15. Daphne Brooks stakes a claim, in *Liner Notes for the Revolution: The Intellectual Life of Black Feminist Sound* (Cambridge, MA: Belknap Press of Harvard University Press, 2021), for Pauline Hopkins as a key theorist of Black feminist sonic modernity; I'm grateful to Brooks for reminding us of Hopkins's musical activities, which often take a backseat in discussions of her writing and editing careers.

9. Francis J. Garrison to Charles Chesnutt, November 9, 1901, Box 4, Folder 5, Charles Chesnutt Collection, Fisk University.

10. For Chesnutt and the sonic elements of stenography, see Charles W. Chesnutt, "Some Uses and Abuses of Shorthand," in *Charles W. Chesnutt: Essays and Speeches*, ed. Joseph R. McElrath Jr., Robert C. Leitz III, and Jesse S. Crisler (Stanford, CA: Stanford University Press, 1999), 74–78.

11. Anthony Reed's and Emily Lordi's comments on an earlier version of *Political Disappointment* helped me clarify this awareness of the conflicts and contestations over transcription that play out in the archive.

12. Du Bois, *Dusk of Dawn*, xxxiii.

13. W. E. B. Du Bois, *The Souls of Black Folk*, Norton Critical Edition (New York: W. W. Norton, 1999), 156.

14. An earlier version of the essay was first published in the *Atlantic* in 1899 before it was included in *The Souls of Black Folk*.

15. Du Bois also writes about this experience in *Dusk of Dawn*, 16.

16. Du Bois, *Souls of Black Folk*, 52.

17. Du Bois, 53.

18. Aldon Morris explains that quantitative methods in the social sciences were developed in Europe in the middle of the nineteenth century and were taken up in the United States only later, as American scholars, including Du Bois, received quantitative training in Europe that they then brought back to American institutions. Aldon Morris, *The Scholar Denied: W. E. B. Du Bois and the Birth of Modern Sociology* (Oakland: University of California Press, 2015), 20–21. Morris emphasizes, further, that these quantitative methods never

accounted for the whole of Du Bois's research: "Du Bois emerged from *The Philadelphia Negro* as the first number-crunching, surveying, interviewing, participant-observing and field-working sociologist in America, a pioneer in the multimethods approach" (47).

19. Du Bois, *Souls of Black Folk*, 54.

20. W. E. B. Du Bois, "Bibliography of the Negro Folk Song in America," ca. 1903, W. E. B. Du Bois Papers, MS 312, Special Collections and University Archives, University of Massachusetts Amherst Libraries, http://credo.library.umass.edu /view/full/mums312-b227-i009.

21. William Francis Allen, Charles Pickard Ware, and Lucy McKim Garrison, eds., *Slave Songs of the United States* (New York: A. Simpson, 1867), iv–v.

22. Allen, Ware, and Garrison, v.

23. *Encyclopedia Britannica*, s.v. "gamut," July 20, 1998, https://www.britannica.com /art/gamut.

24. Allen, Ware, and Garrison, *Slave Songs*, iii.

25. Helen W. Ludlow, "The Hampton Students in the North," in *Hampton and Its Students*, by M[ary] F[rances] Armstrong, Helen W[ilhelmina] Ludlow, and Thomas P. Fenner (New York: G. P. Putnam's Sons, 1874), 127–150, 128.

26. Thomas Fenner, "Preface to Music," in Armstrong, Ludlow, and Fenner, *Hampton and Its Students*, 172.

27. Brent Hayes Edwards, "The Seemingly Eclipsed Window of Form: James Weldon Johnson's Prefaces," in *The Jazz Cadence of American Culture*, ed. Robert G. O'Meally (New York: Columbia University Press, 1998), 580–601, 593. Edwards expands on the role of the figure of the Black body in transcription in *Epistrophies: Jazz and the Literary Imagination* (Cambridge, MA: Harvard University Press, 2017), 70–73.

28. Theodore F. Seward, preface to *Jubilee Songs: As Sung by the Jubilee Singers*, comp. Theodore F. Seward and George L. White (New York: Biglow and Main, 1872), 2–3, 3.

29. Seward, 3.

30. Saidiya Hartman's *Scenes of Subjection* remains indispensable for its detailing of the many efforts to discipline formerly enslaved people and their children into rule-bound subjects.

31. John Lovell, *Black Song: The Forge and the Flame: The Story of How the Afro-American Spiritual Was Hammered Out* (New York: Macmillan, 1972), 407.

32. Theodore F. Seward and George L. White, comps., preface to *Jubilee Songs: As Sung by the Jubilee Singers*, complete ed. (New York: Biglow and Main, 1884), 2–3, 3.

33. Armstrong, Ludlow, and Fenner, *Hampton and Its Students*, 172.

34. John Wesley Work II, *Folk Song of the American Negro* (Nashville: Press of Fisk University, 1915), 114. Spence was principal of Fisk from 1870 to 1875 and

continued at Fisk in numerous other capacities, including director of the
Mozart Society, until his death in 1900.

35. Quoted in Ronald Michael Radano, *Lying Up a Nation: Race and Black Music*
(Chicago: University of Chicago Press, 2003), 270.

36. [Jonathan Baxter Harrison], "Studies in the South," *Atlantic Monthly*, October
1882, 479.

37. John W. Work, "Jubilee Songs," *Fisk Herald*, March 1898, Fisk University
Archives and Special Collections.

38. Work does not mention here the spread of parodic "Jubilee songs" that appeared
in minstrel shows and were published in sheet music adorned with racist
caricatures, but Du Bois flags this aspect in his own treatment.

39. Du Bois, *Souls of Black Folk*, 154–155, 157.

40. Du Bois, 162.

41. For a fuller discussion of Hegel's influence on Du Bois's thought, see Shamoon
Zamir, *Dark Voices: W. E. B. Du Bois and American Thought, 1888–1903* (Chicago:
University of Chicago Press, 1995).

42. Du Bois, *Souls of Black Folk*, 162. Joseph R. Winters's discussion of these
questions in *Hope Draped in Black: Race, Melancholy, and the Agony of Progress*
(Durham, NC: Duke University Press, 2016) has been very helpful to my own
thinking about them.

43. Du Bois, 163.

44. Du Bois, 163.

45. Cheryl A. Wall, "Resounding *Souls:* Du Bois and the African American Literary
Tradition," *Public Culture* 17, no. 2 (May 2005): 217–234, 225.

46. Du Bois, *Souls of Black Folk*, 15–16.

47. Du Bois, 12, 15.

48. Du Bois, 164. The book itself, though, is not quite done. "The After-Thought"
that closes the volume is redolent with nonmusical sound, beginning as it
does, "Hear my cry, O God the reader." It goes on to pray, "Let the ears of a
guilty people tingle with truth, and seventy millions sigh for the righteousness
which exalteth nations, in this drear day when human brotherhood is
mockery and a snare" (164). I will take this up at the beginning of Chapter 2;
for now, it's enough to note that "The After-Thought" demonstrates that
Du Bois is thinking about a broad spectrum of sound, not only the Sorrow
Songs.

49. Ella Sheppard Moore, "Historical Sketch of the Jubilee Singers," *Fisk University
News* 2, no. 5 (October 1911): 41–58, 42.

50. See, e.g., Sandra Jean Graham, *Spirituals and the Birth of a Black Entertainment
Industry* (Urbana: University of Illinois Press, 2018), 40.

51. Moore, "Historical Sketch of the Jubilee Singers," 48.

52. Andrew Ward, *Dark Midnight When I Rise: The Story of the Jubilee Singers Who Introduced the World to the Music of Black America* (New York: Farrar, Straus and Giroux, 2000), 110.

53. I am grateful to Anthony Reed for his insight about the different ways this elision could have felt to different singers.

54. Theodore F. Seward, "Preface to the Music," in *The Story of the Jubilee Singers; With Their Songs*, rev. ed., by J. B. T. Marsh (Boston: Houghton, Mifflin, 1880), 121–122, 121.

55. Hortense Spillers, "Mama's Baby, Papa's Maybe: An American Grammar Book," in *Black, White, and in Color: Essays on American Literature and Culture* (Chicago: University of Chicago Press, 2003), 203–229, 214.

56. Sharpe, *In the Wake*, especially chapter 3, "The Hold," 68–101.

57. For instance, Bruce Barnhart, in his consideration of jazz's influence on African American modernist novels, argues that if art "too slavishly recapitulates the form, logic, and temporality of the society from which the recognition is desired"—a dominant temporality that for Barnhart involves "objective clock time" and "linear, progressive time"—then "it fails to trouble the exclusionary machinations of this society and ends up reproducing these maneuvers and their underlying justifications." For Barnhart, "too much conformity" to linear and clock time leaves a work of art unable "to produce the deformation and rupture" that liberatory art demands. Bruce Barnhart, *Jazz in the Time of the Novel: The Temporal Politics of American Race and Culture* (Tuscaloosa: University of Alabama Press, 2013), 25, 7, 20. Additional critics' warnings about linear time will be discussed in the next section of this chapter.

58. For an excellent survey of racist pseudoscience in academic and popular discourse, see John S. Haller, *Outcasts from Evolution: Scientific Attitudes of Racial Inferiority, 1859–1900* (Urbana: University of Illinois Press, 1971).

59. Charles W. Chesnutt, "The Future American: A Stream of Dark Blood in the Veins of the Southern Whites," *Boston Evening Transcript*, August 25, 1900, 15. SallyAnn H. Ferguson reads this essay in connection with what she calls Chesnutt's exclusive "focus on the social condition of light-skinned blacks" and his frequently stereotypical depictions of darker-skinned characters, concluding that Chesnutt "is essentially a social and literary accommodationist." Ferguson, "Chesnutt's Genuine Blacks and Future Americans," *MELUS* 15, no. 3 (1988): 109–119, 110, 109. The present chapter seeks to complicate this view.

60. Charles W. Chesnutt, *The Marrow of Tradition* (1901; New York: Penguin, 1993), 65.

61. Charles W. Chesnutt, "Charles W. Chesnutt's Own View of His New Story, *The Marrow of Tradition*," in *Essays and Speeches*, 169–170, 170.

62. Chesnutt, 169.

63. Chesnutt, *Marrow*, 198. Subsequent page references from the novel will be given in the text.

64. Ellis also views Tom as "a type of the degenerate aristocrat" and muses that "if, as he had often heard, it took three or four generations to make a gentleman, and as many more to complete the curve and return to the base from which it started, Tom Delamere belonged somewhere on the downward slant, with large possibilities of further decline." Chesnutt, *Marrow*, 95–96. Eric Sundquist further argues that the book's riot shows how "it was racist whites who had degenerated from the comparative paternalistic manners of their fathers and, more to the point, from the dignity of human behavior." Sundquist, *To Wake the Nations: Race in the Making of American Literature* (Cambridge, MA: Belknap Press of Harvard University Press, 1993), 408.

65. See, for instance, Julia H. Lee, "Estrangement on a Train: Race and Narratives of American Identity," *ELH* 75, no. 2 (2008): 345–365.

66. See Wai Chee Dimock, *Through Other Continents: American Literature across Deep Time* (Princeton, NJ: Princeton University Press, 2006).

67. Even if the first "about eleven o'clock" might have meant something closer to 10:45, the "now eleven o'clock" at the end of the scene must be more precise, because the characters are now measuring a journey's duration in half-hour increments.

68. Daylight Saving Time would not be implemented in the United States until 1918, but in New Zealand it was proposed in 1895, and again in 1898 (in a paper titled, marvelously, "On Seasonal Time"), by George Vernon Hudson. I have, however, found no evidence to suggest that Chesnutt was aware of or had taken an interest in Hudson's proposal.

69. See Joseph McElrath Jr., "Why Charles Chesnutt Is Not a Realist," *American Literary Realism* 32, no. 2 (2000): 91–108; and Ryan Simmons, *Chesnutt and Realism: A Study of the Novels* (Tuscaloosa: University of Alabama Press, 2006).

70. Chesnutt Collection, Cleveland Public Library.

71. See letters in Chesnutt Collection, Fisk University Library, especially Houghton, Mifflin to Chesnutt, October 22, 1901; and Chesnutt to Houghton, Mifflin, October 25, 1901, Box 4, Folder 5.

72. Chesnutt to Mr. Horace Talbert, April 3, 1913, Box 2, Folder 8, Chesnutt Collection, Fisk University Library.

73. Perhaps the extra hour constituted a form of wish fulfillment not just for his characters but for himself as well. *Marrow* was edited and published in something of a hurry, and toward the end Chesnutt himself was, like many writers facing a deadline, trying to buy himself more time. "I have n't [*sic*] sent in the manuscript of which I spoke to you, because I am doing a little more work on it," Chesnutt wrote to George Mifflin on July 3, 1901. "Every day's delay improves it, I feel safe in saying, but I will send it in for consideration in a very few days now." Charles W. Chesnutt, *"To Be an Author": Letters of Charles W. Chesnutt, 1889–1905,* ed. Joseph R. McElrath Jr. and Robert C. Leitz III (Princeton, NJ: Princeton University Press, 1997), 159. These "very few days"

became several weeks. By early October, the book was in proofs, and Chesnutt continued requesting corrections, to his publishers' chagrin: "We have now received back from you all the proof of 'The Marrow of Tradition.' We have arranged to publish it on the 23rd of this month, which is a later date than we should like to have set, but the numerous corrections have prevented our completing the work sooner." Houghton, Mifflin to Chesnutt, October 8, 1901, Box 4, Folder 5, Chesnutt Collection, Fisk University Library. It is not difficult to imagine how an error—especially an error that fantasized about finding an extra hour in a frantic day—could have initially gone unnoticed in the rush to completion. It is less simple to consider why, in the months of edits that followed, such a slip, if slip it was, would have gone unremarked.

74. Jared Sexton writes evocatively of such a disruption: "Whatever else there may be in black culture or cultures—in the most capacious, differentiated, global sense—a narrative of *antagonism* is inscribed there, powerfully and profoundly. And yet . . . that narrative is inscribed obliquely or obscurely, even and perhaps especially when addressing itself to intramural affairs, owing perhaps to an incommensurability between antagonism and narrative form itself. . . . How to theorize for battle, to go to war in theory, to fight without experiencing a breakdown or detour in language? How to stay within the anxiety of antagonism (and the narrative crisis it precipitates), to be guided by it, and, again, even to will it?" Jared Sexton, "Afro-Pessimism: The Unclear Word," *Rhizomes*, no. 29 (2016), http://www.rhizomes.net/issue29/sexton.html.

75. Sharpe, *In the Wake*, 73. This connects, as well, to the line in Frank B. Wilderson III's acknowledgments to his book *Red, White & Black* where he thanks Saidiya Hartman and Adrian Bankhead for "helping the manuscript to stay in the hold of the ship, despite my fantasies of flight"—that is, to reside in the generativeness of the nonprogressive, to allow a suspension wherein the possibility of nonprogress can be faced in all its disagreeableness rather than managed and tamed through tidy binaries of values or fantasies of forward motion. Frank B. Wilderson III, *Red, White & Black: Cinema and the Structure of U.S. Antagonisms* (Durham, NC: Duke University Press, 2010), xi.

76. "Far from a temporal free-for-all, afterhours structures a countertemporality that unwinds the reified clock of rationalized time and marks time instead by musical sets and the flows of musical time." Shane Vogel, "Closing Time: Langston Hughes and the Queer Poetics of Harlem Nightlife," *Criticism* 48, no. 3 (2006): 397–425, 407.

77. Barnhart, *Jazz in the Time*, 25.

78. Michelle Wright, *Physics of Blackness: Beyond the Middle Passage Epistemology* (Minneapolis: University of Minnesota Press, 2015), 43, 44.

79. Wright, 146.

80. Sharpe, *In the Wake*, 3, 10.

81. Sharpe, 18.

82. See LeRoi Jones [Amiri Baraka], "The Myth of a Negro Literature," in *Home: Social Essays* (New York: Morrow, 1966), 105–115; and Ferguson, "Chesnutt's Genuine Blacks."

83. Lloyd Pratt, *Archives of American Time: Literature and Modernity in the Nineteenth Century* (Philadelphia: University of Pennsylvania Press, 2010), 168.

84. This is treated most notably in Neill Matheson, "History and Survival: Charles Chesnutt and the Time of Conjure," *American Literary Realism* 43, no. 1 (2010): 1–22; and in Jennifer L. Fleissner, "Earth-Eating, Addiction, Nostalgia: Charles Chesnutt's Diasporic Regionalism," *Studies in Romanticism* 49, no. 2 (2010): 313–336.

Chapter 2. Transcribing Losses

1. W. E. B. Du Bois, *The Souls of Black Folk*, Norton Critical Edition (New York: W. W. Norton, 1999), 164.

2. Ps. 61:1 (KJV). For a fuller discussion of this epigraph in conjunction with "The After-Thought," see Julie Beth Napolin, *The Fact of Resonance: Modernist Acoustics and Narrative Form* (New York: Fordham University Press, 2020), 115–148.

3. In focusing on such moments, I'm building on important work such as Alexandra T. Vazquez's study, in *Listening in Detail: Performances of Cuban Music* (Durham, NC: Duke University Press, 2013), 132–133, of the grunts in Dámaso Pérez Prado's mambo recordings, a variable noise that makes "enigmatic trouble" and that she hears as "a mobile detail that has the potential to undo many of the assumptions made of music, its movements, and its makers"; Fred Moten's consideration of screams and shrieks in the opening chapter of *In the Break: The Aesthetics of the Black Radical Tradition* (Minneapolis: University of Minnesota Press, 2003); and Édouard Glissant's writing about the scream and the shout: "Since speech was forbidden, slaves camouflaged the word under the provocative intensity of the scream. No one could translate the meaning of what seemed to be nothing but a shout. . . . This is how the dispossessed man organized his speech by weaving it into the apparently meaningless texture of extreme noise." Glissant, *Caribbean Discourse: Selected Essays*, translated by J. Michael Dash (Charlottesville: University Press of Virginia, 1989), 123–124.

4. Tillie Olsen, "Tell Me a Riddle," in *Tell Me a Riddle* (1961; New York: Delta, 1989), 63–116, 108. The scene discussed here plays out on 108–115.

5. See, for instance, Lydia A. Schultz, "Flowing against the Traditional Stream: Consciousness in Tillie Olsen's 'Tell Me a Riddle,'" *MELUS* 22, no. 3 (Fall 1997): 113–131.

6. The inextricability of these two realms is highlighted by Deborah Rosenfelt in "From the Thirties: Tillie Olsen and the Radical Tradition," *Feminist Studies* 7, no. 3 (1981): 371–406.

7. George Barnett Smith, *Victor Hugo, His Life and Work* (London: Ward and Downey, 1885), 232.

8. Panthea Reid, *Tillie Olsen: One Woman, Many Riddles* (New Brunswick, NJ: Rutgers University Press, 2010), 79.

9. Many decades later, the unfinished novel was published as *Yonnondio: From the Thirties* (New York: Delacorte, 1974).

10. Reid, *Tillie Olsen*, 115.

11. Wilson Record, *The Negro and the Communist Party* (Chapel Hill: University of North Carolina Press, 1951), 115.

12. Robin D. G. Kelley, *Hammer and Hoe: Alabama Communists during the Great Depression* (Chapel Hill: University of North Carolina Press, 1990), 122.

13. For instance, as Benjamin Filene writes, "rather than preaching mass revolution, the Popular Front urged Americans to embrace cultural diversity and to bond together in common cause. Culture came to be seen less as a didactic tool for arousing class conflict than as a force for fostering community and revealing people's shared humanity." Filene, *Romancing the Folk: Public Memory and American Roots Music* (Chapel Hill: University of North Carolina Press, 2000), 70. See also Richard Reuss and JoAnne Reuss, *American Folk Music and Left-Wing Politics, 1927–1957* (Lanham, MD: Scarecrow, 2000); and Michael Denning, *The Cultural Front: The Laboring of American Culture in the Twentieth Century* (New York: Verso, 1996).

14. See Kelley, *Hammer and Hoe*; Record, *Negro*; Matthew Frye Jacobson, *Whiteness of a Different Color: European Immigrants and the Alchemy of Race* (Cambridge, MA: Harvard University Press, 1998); and Mark Solomon, *The Cry Was Unity: Communists and African Americans, 1917–36* (Jackson: University Press of Mississippi, 1998).

15. See Jacobson, *Whiteness*, 252–254, for party members put on trial for white chauvinism.

16. Quoted in Jacobson, *Whiteness*, 254.

17. Record, *Negro*, 133.

18. Kelley, *Hammer and Hoe*.

19. Richard Wright, "I Tried to Be a Communist," pt. 1, *Atlantic Monthly*, August 1944, 61–70, 69. Just afterward, Wright describes how, on a trip to New York for the star-studded American Writers Congress—a marquee event in this new cultural approach—his white comrades, apparently freed now from the party's previous commitment to prioritizing racial inclusion, admit that they have neglected to line up lodging that would be accessible to an African American Communist.

20. Alan Calmer, "Portrait of the Artist as a Proletarian," *Saturday Review of Literature*, July 31, 1937, 3–4, 17.

21. See Sonnet H. Retman, *Real Folks: Race and Genre in the Great Depression* (Durham, NC: Duke University Press, 2011); and Filene, *Romancing the Folk.*

22. Reuss and Reuss, *American Folk Music,* 76 (Eisler made his visits to the Composers Collective, a professionally oriented subgroup of the big-tent Workers Music League); Charles K. Wolfe and Kip Lornell, *The Life and Legend of Leadbelly* (New York: HarperCollins, 1992), 192.

23. Leadbelly, "Julie Ann Johnson (998-A-2)," on *The Remaining Library of Congress Recordings: Vol. 4 (1935–1938)* (DOCD-5594, Document Records, 1997).

24. Leadbelly, "Julie Ann Johnson (998-A-2)."

25. David King Dunaway and Molly Beer, *Singing Out: An Oral History of America's Folk Music Revivals* (New York: Oxford University Press, 2010), 26.

26. Quoted in Filene, *Romancing the Folk,* 72.

27. See chap. 2, "Theater Folk: Huddie Ledbetter on Stage," in Paige McGinley, *Staging the Blues: From Tent Shows to Tourism* (Durham, NC: Duke University Press, 2014).

28. Zora Neale Hurston to John A. Lomax, August 30, 1935, in Ellen Harold, "Zora Neale Hurston," Association for Cultural Equity, 2008, http://www.culturalequity .org/alan-lomax/friends/hurston. Transcriptions and some facsimiles of letters from Hurston to the Lomaxes can be found at the website of the Association for Cultural Equity. I've also benefited from Jessica Teague's discussion of Lomax and Hurston's relationship in *Sound Recording Technology and American Literature: From the Phonograph to the Remix* (New York: Cambridge University Press, 2021).

29. Teague, *Sound Recording Technology,* 57.

30. Leadbelly, "Take This Hammer," on *Lead Belly Sings for Children* (Smithsonian Folkways, 1999).

31. Ashon Crawley, *Blackpentecostal Breath: The Aesthetics of Possibility* (New York: Fordham University Press, 2017), 34.

32. John F. Szwed, *Alan Lomax: The Man Who Recorded the World* (New York: Viking Penguin, 2010), 63.

33. William Eleazar Barton, *Old Plantation Hymns* (Boston: Lamson, Wolffe, 1899), 34.

34. Hector Berlioz, *A Treatise upon Modern Instrumentation and Orchestration,* trans. Mary Cowden Clark (1844; London: Novello, Ewer, 1858), 198–233. My thanks to Bonnie Whiting for pointing me toward the Berlioz work.

35. A decades-old controversy continues over whether Gellert fabricated the protest songs in his collections. See, for instance, Bruce M. Conforth, *African American Folksong and American Cultural Politics: The Lawrence Gellert Story* (Lanham, MD: Scarecrow, 2013). Steven Garabedian has analyzed Gellert's original field recordings and persuasively refuted these charges. Steven Garabedian, "Lawrence Gellert, *Negro Songs of Protest,*" *African American Review* 49, no. 4 (Winter 2016): 297–311.

36. Alan Calmer, "A Part of Our Folk Literature," *New Masses,* November 6, 1934, 23–24, 23.

37. Szwed, *Alan Lomax,* 163.

38. Hortense Spillers, "Moving on Down the Line: Variations on the African-American Sermon," in *Black, White and in Color: Essays on American Literature and Culture* (Chicago: University of Chicago Press, 2003), 251–276.

39. Retman, *Real Folks,* 5–6.

40. Sean Patrick Farrell, "Last Word: Odetta," *The Last Word, New York Times,* December 2, 2008, video, 19:50, https://www.nytimes.com/video/arts/music /1194832844841/last-word-odetta.html.

41. Later in the story, Helen considers telling Carol that "emotion" is "a characteristic of the religion of all oppressed peoples, yes your very own great-grandparents." This strongly suggests that Helen and Carol have Jewish heritage because the profile the line presents—of a heritage that in the late nineteenth century involved oppressed status and emotionally expressive religious practice but that by the 1950s had shed both its oppressed status and the emotionally expressive elements of its practice, if it retained any religious practice at all—is one that fits the arc of assimilating Ashkenazi Jews in the United States during this period. The fact that Olsen, née Tillie Lerner, was descended from Ashkenazi Jews (her husband, Jack Olsen, was another assimilated Jew, having changed his name from Olshansky) and that she wrote the story "Tell Me a Riddle" explicitly about a Jewish-descended woman who has rejected her religion ("You are on the Jewish list.// Not for rabbis. At once go and make them change. Tell them to write: Race, human; Religion, none" [80]) further supports my claim.

42. Tillie Olsen, "O Yes" (1956), in *Tell Me a Riddle,* 39–62, 61. The story was initially published, under the title "Baptism," in *Prairie Schooner* 31, no. 1 (Spring 1957): 70–80.

43. Olsen, "O Yes," 41.

44. Spillers, "Moving on Down," 252.

45. Olsen, "O Yes," 41.

46. Olsen, "Tell Me a Riddle," 109.

47. Olsen, "O Yes," 47.

48. Tillie Olsen, "'My Tape-Recorder Ear': An Interview with Tillie Olsen," interview by Robin Dizard, *Massachusetts Review* 55, no. 2 (2014): 282–294, 291–292, 294.

49. Olsen, "O Yes," 43.

50. Olsen, 43.

51. Ashon Crawley's *Blackpentecostal Breath* offers a detailed elaboration on the practice and importance of whooping in Blackpentecostal worship.

52. Olsen, "O Yes," 45.

53. Olsen, 46, 48.

54. Olsen, 60.

55. Olsen, 60–61.

56. Olsen, 61.

57. Olsen, 61.

58. Marianne Noble, "The Ecstasies of Sentimental Wounding in Uncle Tom's Cabin," *Yale Journal of Criticism* 10, no. 2 (1997): 295–320, 295.

59. See Saidiya Hartman, *Scenes of Subjection: Terror, Slavery, and Self-Making in Nineteenth-Century America* (New York: Oxford University Press, 1997).

60. See, for instance, Glenn Hendler, "The Structure of Sentimental Experience," *Yale Journal of Criticism* 12, no. 1 (1999): 145–153.

61. Olsen, "O Yes," 61–62.

Chapter 3. "I Stand Mute"

1. Philip Scheffler and Sam Zelman, *The March in Mississippi*, CBS News special report, aired June 26, 1966, Paley Center for Media, 1:00:00.

2. Scheffler and Zelman.

3. Martin Luther King Jr., "Address to the Chicago Freedom Movement Rally," Soldier Field, Chicago, July 10, 1966, Series III, Box 278, Folder 2932, Chicago Urban League Collection, Special Collections, University of Illinois Chicago.

4. "Meredith May Join March Again Today," *Boston Globe*, June 8, 1966, 2; Aram Goudsouzian, "Three Weeks in Mississippi: James Meredith, Aubrey Norvell, and the Politics of Bird Shot," *Journal of the Historical Society* 11, no. 1 (2011): 23–58.

5. Akinyele O. Umoja, "The Ballot and the Bullet: A Comparative Analysis of Armed Resistance in the Civil Rights Movement," *Journal of Black Studies* 29, no. 4 (March 1999): 558–578, 558.

6. For more on the classical phase, see Bayard Rustin, "From Protest to Politics: The Future of the Civil Rights Movement," *Commentary* 39, no. 2 (February 1, 1965): 25–31.

7. Stokely Carmichael, *Ready for Revolution: The Life and Struggles of Stokely Carmichael (Kwame Ture)*, with Ekwueme Michael Thelwell (New York: Scribner, 2003), 504.

8. Carmichael, *Ready for Revolution*, 479; James Haskins, *Profiles in Black Power* (Garden City, NY: Doubleday, 1972), 190.

9. Carmichael, *Ready for Revolution*, 488, 489, 490.

10. Stokely Carmichael and Martin Luther King Jr., press conference on the March Against Fear, June 7, 1966, YouTube video, 18:20, https://www.youtube.com/watch?v=gcTwo_B9CV4.

11. Carmichael and King, press conference.

12. Martin Luther King Jr., *Where Do We Go from Here: Chaos or Community?* (1967; Boston: Beacon, 2010), 26.

13. Julius Lester, "The Angry Children of Malcolm X," *Sing Out!,* October / November 1966, n.p.

14. The quotation appears on its own in Guy Carawan and Candie Carawan, *Sing for Freedom: The Story of the Civil Rights Movement through Its Songs* (Montgomery, AL: NewSouth, 2008), 23, where it is credited as having initially appeared in a songbook from the Highlander Folk School.

15. See Shana L. Redmond, *Anthem: Social Movements and the Sound of Solidarity in the African Diaspora* (New York: New York University Press, 2013), chapter 4, "Women's Work: 'We Shall Overcome' and the Culture of the Picket Line."

16. James Farmer, *Lay Bare the Heart: An Autobiography of the Civil Rights Movement* (New York: Arbor House, 1985), 27.

17. In her definitive study of this song and its travels, Shana Redmond argues that the word *someday* replaces the celestial release heralded in the slavery-era spirituals with an anticipated victory on earth: "The use of the word 'someday' offers a vision into a future of brighter possibility, but this vision is not based on blind faith in things unseen—it is instead grounded in the action surrounding the performance of the song, whether that be on the picket line or in the jails that housed demonstrators during the Civil Rights Movement. . . . Whereas spirituals under slavery often relied on delayed redemption in heaven, 'We Shall Overcome' rose to prominence within the context of a lived labor battle in which the workers understood that their victory would be here on earth." Redmond, *Anthem,* 148–149. While her reading helps account for the early embrace of the song, I'm arguing here that by 1966, the "someday" of the lyrics was understood by some activists as acquiescing to a continued demand for performed patience with which they were no longer willing to comply.

18. Julius B. Fleming, *Black Patience: Performance, Civil Rights, and the Unfinished Project of Emancipation* (New York: New York University Press, 2022), 9.

19. Lester, "Angry Children of Malcolm X," n.p.

20. See, for instance, Robert Lipsyte, "Clay Refuses Army Oath; Stripped of Boxing Crown," *New York Times,* April 29, 1967, 1.

21. Carmichael, *Ready for Revolution,* 507.

22. Charles E. Cobb Jr., "From Stokely Carmichael to Kwame Ture," *Callaloo* 34, no. 1 (2011): 89–97, 89. See also Harvard Sitkoff, *The Struggle for Black Equality, 1954–1992,* rev. ed. (New York: Hill and Wang, 1993), 199.

23. King, *Where Do We Go,* 29.

24. Quoted in Carmichael, *Ready for Revolution,* 507.

25. King, *Where Do We Go,* 29–30.

26. David R. Underhill, "When They Ask, 'What Do You Want?' the Cry Changes to 'Black Power,'" *Southern Courier,* June 25–26, 1966, 1.

27. *Eyes on the Prize II: America at the Racial Crossroads, 1965–1985,* season 2, episode 1, "The Time Has Come: 1964–66," directed by James A. DeVinney, Julian Bond, and Henry Hampton, originally aired 1990 on PBS, Alexander Street Video, 2006, https://video.alexanderstreet.com/watch/the-time-has-come-1964-66.

28. DeVinney et al., "Time Has Come."

29. Frank Hunt, "'I Got So Darn Mad Nobody Could Talk to Me,' Mother of Three Tells AFRO: 'Lord, I Got All Shook Up,' Marcher Cries," *Baltimore Afro-American,* June 18, 1966, 13.

30. Goudsouzian, "Three Weeks in Mississippi," 53; Nicholas von Hoftman and George Lardner Jr., "March Enters Jackson amid Hostility," *Washington Post,* June 27, 1966, A1.

31. Scheffler and Zelman, *March in Mississippi.*

32. NAACP, "Negro Silent Protest Parade," flyer, July 1917, National Humanities Center, 2014, https://nationalhumanitiescenter.org/pds/maai2/forward/text4 /silentprotest.pdf; Barbara Maranzani, "The 'Silent' Protest That Kick-Started the Civil Rights Movement," History.com, July 27, 2017, http://www.history .com/news/the-silent-protest-that-kick-started-the-civil-rights-movement.

33. Kevin Quashie, *The Sovereignty of Quiet: Beyond Resistance in Black Culture* (Piscataway, NJ: Rutgers University Press, 2012).

34. Carmichael, *Ready for Revolution,* 511–512.

35. Sophia Hatzisavvidou, "Disturbing Binaries in Political Thought: Silence as Political Activism," *Social Movement Studies* 14, no. 5 (2015): 509–522, 520.

36. "Silence, in other words, can be constitutive. It can create identities and enable communities." Kennan Ferguson, "Silence: A Politics," *Contemporary Political Theory* 2, no. 1 (2003): 49–65, 59. See also Hatzisavvidou, who writes that silence "can function to unite a heterogeneous constituency around a fugitive commonality, thus constituting it as a political subject, demos." Hatzisavvidou, "Disturbing Binaries," 517. While I would question whether silence's constitutive function necessarily guarantees political subjectivity to the collectivity it coalesces, Hatzisavvidou's emphasis here on heterogeneity and fugitivity is very useful in thinking about the soundscape of the Meredith march.

37. Scheffler and Zelman, *March in Mississippi.*

38. Judith Butler, *Notes toward a Performative Theory of Assembly* (Cambridge, MA: Harvard University Press, 2015), 7–8.

39. Hunt, "'I Got So Darn Mad,'" 13.

40. Carmichael, *Ready for Revolution,* 512.

41. Carmichael, 490.

42. Martin Luther King Jr., interview on *Meet the Press,* transcript, National Broadcasting Company, April 17, 1960, Martin Luther King, Jr. Papers Project,

Martin Luther King, Jr. Research and Education Institute, Stanford University, http://okra.stanford.edu/transcription/document_images/Vol05Scans/17Apr1960 _InterviewonMeetthePress.pdf.

43. Martin Luther King Jr., "Letter from Birmingham Jail," April 16, 1963, Martin Luther King, Jr. Papers Project, Martin Luther King, Jr. Research and Education Institute, Stanford University, 4, https://kinginstitute.stanford.edu/king-papers/ documents/interview-meet-press.

44. Martin Luther King Jr., "I Have a Dream," August 28, 1963, address delivered at the March on Washington for Jobs and Freedom. See Martin Luther King Jr., *I Have a Dream* (New York: HarperCollins, 1993), 2–4.

45. This is one of the *American Heritage Dictionary*'s two definitions of the word. It's worth noting, however, that neither the *Oxford English Dictionary* nor *Merriam-Webster's* offers any version of this definition; both stick to the two main definitions of "to adapt for theatrical production" and "to represent dramatically." *American Heritage Dictionary*, s.v. "dramatize," accessed October 26, 2022, https://www .ahdictionary.com/word/search.html?q=dramatize; *Oxford English Dictionary*, s.v. "dramatize," accessed October 26, 2022, https://www-oed-com.proxy.library .nd.edu/view/Entry/57486?redirectedFrom=dramatize#eid; *Merriam-Webster's*, s.v. "dramatize," accessed October 26, 2022, https://www.merriam-webster.com /dictionary/dramatize.

46. "Here's What Dr. King Told Vast Thousands," *Chicago Daily Defender*, July 11, 1966, 1.

47. Bayard Rustin, "The Negro and Non-violence," *Fellowship* 8, no. 10 (October 1942): 166–167, 167.

48. See Amy Louise Wood, *Lynching and Spectacle: Witnessing Racial Violence in America, 1890–1940* (Chapel Hill: University of North Carolina Press, 2009).

49. Saidiya Hartman, *Scenes of Subjection: Terror, Slavery, and Self-Making in Nineteenth-Century America* (New York: Oxford University Press, 1997).

50. Martin Luther King Jr., "Nonviolence: The Only Road to Freedom," *Ebony*, October 1966, 27–30, 32, 34.

51. Martin Luther King Jr., "The Birth of a New Nation," April 7, 1957, sermon delivered at Dexter Avenue Baptist Church, Montgomery, AL, Martin Luther King, Jr. Papers Project, Martin Luther King, Jr. Research and Education Institute, Stanford University, 155–167, 162, https://kinginstitute.stanford.edu/king-papers/ documents/birth-new-nation-sermon-delivered-dexter-avenue-baptist-church.

52. "Negro War-on-Fear Trek in South: Meredith Hiking from Memphis to Jackson, Miss.," *Chicago Tribune*, June 6, 1966, 18.

53. I'm grateful to Daphne Brooks for encouraging me to take stock of the importance of improvisation in this episode.

54. Carmichael, *Ready for Revolution*, 490; Carmichael and King, press conference on the March Against Fear.

55. Aram Goudsouzian, *Down to the Crossroads: Civil Rights, Black Power, and the Meredith March Against Fear* (New York: Farrar, Straus and Giroux, 2014), 61–62.
56. Goudsouzian, 60.
57. Stokely Carmichael, "What We Want," *New York Review of Books,* September 22, 1966.
58. Goudsouzian, *Down to the Crossroads,* 83.
59. "Here's What Dr. King," 1.
60. Its tune, which along with its lyrics was originally written by George F. Root, was later used for "Jesus Loves the Little Children"; there's also a strong resemblance to "Go Tell It on the Mountain."
61. This connection likely registered with more than just Civil War buffs: in the same month that King gave his speech in Chicago, an article in the *Chicago Tribune* about a long walk through the Netherlands began with the sentence, "Tramp, tramp, tramp, the boys are marching, and the girls too, thru Holland's lovely countryside." "It's Tramping Time in Holland," *Chicago Tribune,* July 26, 1966, A3.
62. This latent affect rises even more pronouncedly to the top of the mix in the parody version that Industrial Workers of the World songwriter Joe Hill penned in 1913. That version is about an itinerant laborer; its chorus goes, "Tramp, tramp, tramp, and keep on tramping / Nothing doing here for you," and ends, "Keep on tramping, that's the best thing you can do."

Chapter 4. Senses of Solidarity

1. Audio recording of the Varied Voices of Black Women concert held at Medusa's Revenge, New York, November 7, 1978, Pacifica Radio Archives, 1:01:56, https://archive.org/details/pacifica_radio_archives-IZ1427.
2. Roadwork collaborated with a different group of women in each city on the tour to assist with local production tasks. The Boston concert's group, which named itself the Bessie Smith Memorial Production Collective, included many members of the Combahee River Collective. In addition to Parker, the tour's other co-headliners were the musicians Linda Tillery, Mary Watkins, and Gwen Avery. Like her tour mates, Parker was an Olivia recording artist; in 1976 the label had released a poetry LP with Parker on side 1 and the white lesbian poet Judy Grahn on side 2. Pat Parker and Judy Grahn, *Where Would I Be without You: The Poetry of Pat Parker and Judy Grahn* (Olivia Records, 1976, LF 909). I'm grateful to Amy Horowitz of Roadwork for sharing her invaluable insight into the coalition's history.
3. Three articles that address these presumptions directly are Annette Schlichter, "Do Voices Matter? Vocality, Materiality, Gender Performativity," *Body and Society* 17, no. 1 (2011): 31–52; María C. Lugones and Elizabeth V. Spelman, "Have We Got a Theory for You! Feminist Theory, Cultural Imperialism and the Demand for 'the Woman's Voice,'" *Women's Studies International Forum* 6, no. 6 (1983):

573–581; and Mikko Keskinen, "Her Mistress's Voice: Gynophonocentrism in Feminist Discourses," *Journal of International Women's Studies* 2, no. 1 (2000): 1–15.

4. Annette Schlichter's diagnosis of this lacuna is useful here:

    > What I refer to as "feminist phonocentrism" resonates in texts that construct "the female voice" as the representation of an authentic female self, while that self-representation is also contrasted with patriarchal misrepresentations of women, which it supposedly corrects. The phonocentric project assumes a "natural" relationship of the voice, the female body and female identity as the truth of the woman's self. Ironically, the material voice is banned from such arguments. Instead, a great number of feminist critiques of representation equate "speech" and "voice" as metaphors of agency and self-representation, which also reads as self-presence. . . . In other words, feminist critiques of representation tend both to participate in the tradition of western phonocentrism and are simultaneously phonophobic in the sense that they speak of the voice only figuratively. (Schlichter, "Do Voices Matter?," 37–38)

5. See Ginny Z. Berson, *Olivia on the Record: A Radical Experiment in Women's Music* (San Francisco: Aunt Lute, 2020), especially chap. 20, "Scars: Race Matters."

6. Parker recorded "Don't Let the Fascists Speak" for *Where Would I Be without You,* and her performance of the poem two years later at Medusa's Revenge was recorded as well. The poem appears in two editions of *Movement in Black* that were published in 1978 and 1999, and in *The Complete Works of Pat Parker,* ed. Julie Enszer (Brookeville, NY: A Midsummer Night's Press; Dover, FL: Sinister Wisdom, 2016). The text of the poem varies slightly from edition to edition. My discussion here will draw on the Medusa's Revenge recording and the version published in *Movement in Black: The Collected Poetry of Pat Parker, 1961–1978,* 2nd printing (1978; Trumansburg, NY: Crossing Press, 1983). The poem appears there without a title but has since come to be widely known as "Don't Let the Fascists Speak," which is also the title of the track from the LP *Where Would I Be without You.* For more on the lyric as an intermedial form, see Matthew Kilbane, *The Lyre Book: Modern Poetic Media* (Baltimore: Johns Hopkins University Press, 2024).

7. Parker saw herself as primarily a performance poet: according to her friend and fellow poet Cheryl Clarke, Parker was considerably less interested in setting her poems to paper than in performing them onstage. Cheryl Clarke, "Goat Child and Cowboy: Pat Parker as Queer Trickster," in *Movement in Black,* by Pat Parker, expanded ed. (Ithaca, NY: Firebrand Books, 1999), 15–21, 20. Thus the intermedial quality of lyric poetry generally is amplified in the case of Parker's work, and this poem, in its recorded and published forms, demonstrates the productivity of encounters between writing and sound making.

8. This anticipates bell hooks's 1994 assertion that "the classroom, with all its limitations, remains a location of possibility" for freedom, boundary crossing, and even, potentially, the creation of paradise. bell hooks, *Teaching to Transgress: Education as the Practice of Freedom* (New York: Routledge, 1994), 207.

9. Judy Grahn, "Coming on Strong: A Legacy of Pat Parker," in *The Complete Works of Pat Parker* (Dover, FL: Sinister Wisdom, 2016), ed. Julie Enszer, 15–21, 18–19.

10. Schenck v. United States, 249 U.S. 47 (1919).

11. Brandenburg v. Ohio, 395 U.S. 444 (1969).

12. The difference between the facts at issue in *Schenck* and *Brandenburg* actually supports the poem's main point about free speech being unequally upheld, more robustly than *Schenck* on its own does. The 1919 case dealt with Socialists distributing antidraft flyers during the First World War; this is the speech that the Supreme Court ruled sufficiently threatening to be worth proscribing. The 1969 decision, which loosened restrictions on free speech, took up the case of a Ku Klux Klan leader.

13. Nicholas Mirzoeff, *The Right to Look: A Counterhistory of Visuality* (Durham, NC: Duke University Press, 2011); Nicole Fleetwood, *Troubling Vision: Performance, Visuality, and Blackness* (Chicago: University of Chicago Press, 2011).

14. See Gregg Bordowitz, "Picture a Coalition," *October* 43 (Winter 1987): 182–196.

15. Audio recording of the Varied Voices of Black Women concert.

16. Cathy Lee, "Musical Politics," *Sojourner* 4, no. 4 (December 1978): n.p.

17. Lee.

18. Lee.

19. Bessie Smith Memorial Production Collective, "Responses to 'Varied Voices' Review," *Sojourner*, January 1979, 4.

20. Kiki Herold, "Positive Energy," *Sojourner*, January 1979, 4.

21. Amy Horowitz, interview by the author, August 3, 2022.

22. See Clare Hemmings, *Why Stories Matter: The Political Grammar of Feminist Theory* (Durham, NC: Duke University Press, 2011).

23. Verta Taylor, "Social Movement Continuity: The Women's Movement in Abeyance," *American Sociological Review* 54, no. 5 (1989): 761–775. A minor strain of scholarship attends to small-scale, local survivals of feminist activity in this period, but only as a nuancing addition to the narrative of a largely moribund movement, not as a facial challenge to that narrative's basic validity. See Nancy Whittier, *Feminist Generations: The Persistence of the Radical Women's Movement* (Philadelphia: Temple University Press, 1995).

24. Becky Thompson, "Multiracial Feminism: Recasting the Chronology of Second Wave Feminism," *Feminist Studies* 28, no. 2 (2002): 337–360; Kimberly Springer, *Living for the Revolution: Black Feminist Organizations, 1968–1980* (Durham,

NC: Duke University Press, 2005); Benita Roth, *Separate Roads to Feminism: Black, Chicana, and White Feminist Movements in America's Second Wave* (New York: Cambridge University Press, 2004).

25. Jennifer C. Nash's *Black Feminism Reimagined: After Intersectionality* (Durham, NC: Duke University Press, 2019) points out how narratives in which Black feminism exists to correct white feminism severely curtail the scope of Black feminism as a robust intellectual and political tradition in its own right, while ensuring that its proponents are always cast by white feminists as agents of disciplining and objects of anxiety.

26. See Marjorie Spruill, *Divided We Stand: The Battle over Women's Rights and Family Values that Polarized American Politics* (New York: Bloomsbury, 2017); Dianna Wray, "The 1977 National Women's Conference in Houston Was Supposed to Change the World. What Went Wrong?," *Houstonia,* January 30, 2018, https://www.houstoniamag.com/articles/2018/1/30/1977-national -womens-conference-houston; and Judy Klemesrud, "Equal Rights Plan and Abortion Are Opposed by 15,000 at Rally," *New York Times,* November 20, 1977.

27. California's Briggs Initiative was eventually defeated at the polls, but the initiative's launch, coming on the heels of the Dade County reversal, clearly demonstrated the strength and reach of right-wing backlash against feminism and the gay rights movement with which it was closely associated by the late 1970s.

28. Springer, *Living for the Revolution,* 61.

29. "The Combahee River Collective Statement," in *How We Get Free: Black Feminism and the Combahee River Collective,* ed. Keeanga-Yamahtta Taylor (Chicago: Haymarket Books, 2017), 15–27, 16–17.

30. This section of the Combahee River Collective statement mentions the National Black Feminist Organization as well, but without specifically discussing it as an object of disillusionment. In light of Barbara Smith's recollection quoted earlier, though, we can consider the possibility that along with disappointment in second-wave feminist and Black liberation movements, a "complicated" and difficult-to-express disappointment with previous Black feminist organizing played a role in the Combahee River Collective's founding.

31. "Combahee River Collective Statement," 21–22.

32. Carol Ann Douglas, "What If the Revolution Isn't Tomorrow?," *off our backs* 7, no. 7 (September 30, 1977): 10.

33. See, for instance, Janis Kelly, "Reflections," *off our backs* 6, no. 4 (June 1976): 13: "We haven't made much progress in the past two years. Either we squabble among ourselves (usually in the name of preserving 'real feminism' from the Philistines) or we keep saying the same things we've been saying for years, and

to the same people. In order to move beyond this stagnation and isolation, I think we need to start talking in more basic, human terms about the kind of society we want to build."

34. See, for instance, Janis Kelly, "Tolerance," *off our backs* 7, no. 3 (April 1977): 8; and Marcy Rein and Wendy Stevens, "Even Closets Won't Be Safe," *off our backs* 7, no. 6 (August 1977): 5.

35. Douglas, "What If the Revolution," 10.

36. Cherríe Moraga, preface to *This Bridge Called My Back: Writings by Radical Women of Color,* 2nd ed., ed. Cherríe Moraga and Gloria Anzaldúa (New York: Kitchen Table Women of Color Press, 1983), xiii–xix, xiii, xiv. The sections of the preface are all individually dated to specific days in July and September 1980.

37. Moraga, xiv–xv.

38. On this ongoing desire, see Robyn Wiegman, "Doing Justice with Objects," in *Object Lessons* (Durham, NC: Duke University Press, 2012).

39. Betty Friedan, *The Feminine Mystique* (1963; New York: W. W. Norton, 2001), 24. Subsequent page references will be given in the text.

40. Ann Rosalind Jones, "Imaginary Gardens with Real Frogs in Them: Feminist Euphoria and the Franco-American Divide, 1976–88," in *Changing Subjects: The Making of Feminist Literary Criticism,* ed. Gayle Greene and Coppélia Kahn (New York: Routledge, 1993), 64–82, 69.

41. Drucilla Cornell, "Las Greñudas: Recollections on Consciousness-Raising," in *Just Cause: Freedom, Identity, and Rights* (Lanham, MD: Rowman and Littlefield, 2000), 11–15, 11.

42. Aristotle, *Politics,* in *The Basic Works of Aristotle* (New York: Random House, 1941), 1127–1316, 1129.

43. On voice as a vehicle and metaphor for subjectivity, presence, and political participation, see Amanda Weidman, "Voice," in *Keywords in Sound,* ed. David Novak and Matt Sakakeeny (Durham, NC: Duke University Press, 2015), 232–245; and Laura Kunreuther, *Voicing Subjects: Public Intimacy and Mediation in Kathmandu* (Berkeley: University of California Press, 2014). The feminist embrace of voice also took shape in opposition to long-standing anxieties about women's voices and attempts to silence them: see Anne Carson, "The Gender of Sound," in *Glass, Irony, and God* (New York: New Directions, 1995), 119–142.

44. Hannah Arendt, *The Human Condition,* 2nd ed. (1958; Chicago: University of Chicago Press, 1998), 179.

45. Weidman, "Voice," 233. Adrienne Rich did engage with Arendt's work in the mid-1970s, though, which makes the lack of feminist reflection on Arendt's revisitation of Aristotle on voice even more striking. See Adrienne Rich, "Conditions for Work: The Common World of Women" (1976), in *On Lies, Secrets, and Silence: Selected Prose, 1966–1978* (New York: Norton, 1979), 203–214.

46. Kathie Sarachild, "Feminist Consciousness Raising and 'Organizing,'" in *Voices from Women's Liberation,* ed. Leslie B. Tanner (New York: New American Library, 1970), 154–157, 154; see also Kathie Sarachild, "Consciousness Raising: A Radical Weapon," in *Feminist Revolution,* by Redstockings (New York: Random House, 1978), 144–159. Sarachild, a key architect of feminist consciousness-raising, clearly saw her tactic as belonging to a lineage of political speech acts. According to Carol Hanisch, Sarachild made a poster spelling out this genealogy, which hung on the wall at New York Radical Women meetings in 1968. The poster read,

> *"Tell It Like It Is"*
> *—the Black Revolution*
> *"Speak Pains to Recall Pains"*
> *—the Chinese Revolution*
> *"Bitch, Sisters, Bitch"*
> *—the Final Revolution*

Carol Hanisch, "A Women's Liberation Tribute to William Hinton and the Women of Long Bow," 1999, http://www.carolhanisch.org/Speeches/Hinton Speech/HintonTribSpeech.html.

47. Adrienne Rich, introduction to *Voices: A Play,* by Susan Griffin (New York: Feminist Press, 1975), 5–13, 5–7.

48. Kunreuther, *Voicing Subjects,* 14.

49. Adrienne Rich, "Women and Honor: Some Notes on Lying," in *On Lies, Secrets, and Silence,* 185–194, 189.

50. Michelle Cliff, "Notes on Speechlessness," *Sinister Wisdom* 5 (Winter 1978): 8.

51. Rich, *On Lies, Secrets, and Silence,* 190.

52. Donald T. Critchlow, *Phyllis Schlafly and Grassroots Conservatism: A Woman's Crusade* (Princeton, NJ: Princeton University Press, 2005), 247.

53. Spruill, *Divided We Stand,* 11.

54. In their concerns about the potentially undependable or deceptive feminist voice, these US writers were operating on different assumptions from those of the French feminist Hélène Cixous, who in the mid-1970s was explicitly celebrating and encouraging feminist voice. Cixous's work was not often taken up explicitly in US feminist writing until the early 1980s, following the publication in 1980 of the anthology *New French Feminisms,* the first collection of translated works by French feminists, and a 1981 issue of *Yale French Studies* dedicated to feminism. Thus her ideas are not an integral part of the story of voice in US feminist thought in the 1970s, but her work resonates in intriguing ways with the US story, so I will address it briefly here.

(As one measure of the belated uptake of French feminist theory, including that of Cixous, in the US academy, Lynn K. Penrod notes that although Elaine

Showalter's 1981 essay "Feminist Criticism in the Wilderness" included four epigraphs from French feminists [including two from "The Laugh of the Medusa" alone], Showalter's 1978 essay "Towards a Feminist Poetics" didn't mention French feminism at all. Lynn K. Penrod, "Translating Hélène Cixous: French Feminism[s] and Anglo-American Feminist Theory," *TTR: Traduction, terminologie, rédaction* 6, no. 2 [1993]: 39–54.)

For Cixous, the central matter was less one of political participation and more one of voice's relationship to writing. In "The Laugh of the Medusa," which appeared in English in the summer 1976 issue of the US feminist journal *Signs*, she writes of a fusion between textual language and spoken voice, connected through embodied voicing, or voiced embodying: "Listen to a woman speak at a public gathering (if she hasn't painfully lost her wind). She doesn't 'speak,' she throws her trembling body forward; she lets go of herself, she flies; all of her passes into her voice, and it's with her body that she vitally supports the 'logic' of her speech. Her flesh speaks true. She lays herself bare. In fact, she physically materializes what she's thinking; she signifies it with her body. In a certain way she *inscribes* what she's saying, because she doesn't deny her drives the intractable and impassioned part they have in speaking." Hélène Cixous, "The Laugh of the Medusa," *Signs* 1, no. 4 (Summer 1976): 875–893, 881.

"The Laugh of the Medusa" is in deep conversation with Jacques Derrida's *Of Grammatology*, which itself became available to English-language readers (in a translation by Gayatri Spivak) the same year as Cixous's essay. Both works are concerned with rethinking the distinction in Western thought between spoken language and writing. Derrida, in his text, proceeds by reducing sonics out of the idea of voice, focusing instead on instances of thinking the voice as a purely internal monologue—the voice of conscience, the phenomenological occurrence of hearing oneself speak. This lets him argue that voice, rather than being prior to and distinct from writing, is already like writing insofar as it is communication shaped by the absence of an interlocutor.

By contrast, in constructing her conception of *écriture féminine*, Cixous brings us to a scene of voice as public utterance—"Listen to a woman speak"—casting us, her readers, in the role of listeners to a sonic event. It wouldn't be entirely accurate to say, just because Cixous envisages a relation of intersubjective listening, that she therefore sets up an instance of externalized voice in opposition to Derrida's scene of internal speech; it's more that she challenges the very division between internal and external, embodied and disembodied. If writing is supposed to sever language from the immediate presence of the person generating the language, Cixous responds by conjuring a writing that emerges so inexorably from the writer's body—akin to a woman standing up at a meeting or a rally to raise her voice—that the writing bears indelible marks of that physical reality, becoming sonic in the process. "Write your self," she exhorts, immediately continuing: "Your body must be heard" (880). When women speak in public, Cixous insists, "There is not that scission, that division made by the common man between the logic of oral speech and the logic of the text" (881). While Derrida's move in *Of Grammatology* is to argue that voice has only ever been writing, Cixous suggests that the most potent feminist writing incorporates the embodied, sonic voice.

55. Adrienne Rich, "Motherhood," in *On Lies, Secrets, and Silence,* 259–273, 259–260.

56. Rich, 271.

57. Rich, 259.

58. Parker, *Movement in Black,* 70.

59. Gloria Anzaldúa, "Foreword to the Second Edition," in *This Bridge Called My Back,* iv–v.

60. The passage's two linguistic tracks also diverge in their imaginations of what would take the place of talking: Anzaldúa institutes multiple slippages between the English and the Spanish in this passage, as if to emphasize both the difficulty of transparent communication and the potential of that very difficulty to be nevertheless productive. "Dejemos de hablar hasta que hagamos la palabra luminosa y activa," Anzaldúa writes, which translates literally as, "Let's leave off talking until we've made the word luminous and active." Yet the English she counterposes to the sentence introduces some significant changes: "*(let's work not talk, let's say nothing until we've made the world luminous and active).*" By adding the English phrase "*let's work not talk,*" which doesn't correspond to anything in the Spanish text, she suggests that her Anglophone readers bear a greater responsibility for working, while the first-person plural "let's" includes at least Anzaldúa herself in the exhortation. She also renders *palabra* as "world" rather than "word," suggesting again a potential disconnect between the possibilities of Spanish and those of English: she seems to propose a suspension of English speech until the whole world has been transformed, while Spanish speech is merely asked to transform itself. Enough empty words, the Spanish text exhorts, let's make our own language really count. Meanwhile the English text proposes ceding the microphone to the readers directly hailed in the Spanish phrases, suggesting this as one way to change the world.

61. Tillie Olsen, "Silences: When Writers Don't Write," *Harper's,* October 1965, 153–161.

62. Mainstream publications took notice, but often critically: Joyce Carol Oates tried her best to be sympathetic in the *New Republic,* but she confessed she found the book's thinking "simply glib and superficial" in comparison with Olsen's fiction, and she lamented the "busy, gnat-like presence" of "small, inconsequential footnotes" that "marred" most pages. Joyce Carol Oates, "*Silences by Tillie Olsen,*" *New Republic,* July 29, 1978, 32–34. Doris Grumbach, writing in

the *Washington Post,* was blunter, calling it "truly a terrible nonbook." Doris Grumbach, "Tillie Olsen's Scrapbook," *Washington Post,* August 6, 1978, F1.

63. Carol Ames, "Book Reviews," *Women's Studies* 6 (1979): 349–352, 350.

64. Sally McConnell-Ginet, "Intonation in a Man's World," *Signs* 3, no. 3 (1978): 541–559, 542.

65. Audre Lorde, "The Transformation of Silence into Language and Action," in *Sister Outsider: Essays and Speeches* (Trumansburg, NY: Crossing Press, 1984), 40–44, 40.

66. Lorde, 41.

67. Shortly after the conference, the panel's talks were published in *Sinister Wisdom* 6 (Summer 1978): 4–25, http://sinisterwisdom.org/sites/default/files/Sinister%20Wisdom%206_0.pdf.

68. Lorde, "Transformation of Silence," 42.

69. This aside appears in the *Sinister Wisdom* transcript, p. 14, and again when "The Transformation of Silence into Language and Action" is reprinted in Audre Lorde, *The Cancer Journals,* 2nd ed. (San Francisco: Spinsters / Aunt Lute, 1980), 18–23, 21. The sentence as published in *Sister Outsider,* though, omits the phrase "you can hear it in my voice," an omission that further underscores the textual instability of the sonic voice.

70. Lorde, "Transformation of Silence," 42.

71. Lorde, 42.

72. Sandra Lee Bartky, "Feminine Narcissism," in *The Second Sex—Thirty Years Later: A Commemorative Conference on Feminist Theory* (New York: New York Institute for the Humanities, 1979), 25–29, 28–29. There were no Black women on the "Her Silence, Her Voice" panel. Indeed, the lineup of the conference was overwhelmingly white—reflecting both the complexion of academic feminism circa 1979 and the conference organizers' failure to involve any women of color from the beginning of the planning process. See Jessica Benjamin, "Letter to Lester Olson," *Philosophy and Rhetoric* 33, no. 3 (2000): 286–290. This failure set the stage for Lorde's well-known rebuke to the conference, "The Master's Tools Will Never Dismantle the Master's House," which also centered on a call for vision—not literal visibility this time, as in Bartky's paper or in Lorde's Modern Language Association talk, but vision as a metaphor for conceptualizing a future for feminism that could incorporate and draw strength from difference. "Within the interdependence of mutual (nondominant) differences," Lorde said at New York University, "lies that security which enables us to descend into the chaos of knowledge and return with true visions of our future, along with the concomitant power to effect those changes which can bring that future into being." Audre Lorde, "The Master's Tools Will Never Dismantle the Master's House," in *Sister Outsider,* 110–113, 111–112.

73. Carole S. Vance, "Pleasure and Danger: Toward a Politics of Sexuality," in *Pleasure and Danger: Exploring Female Sexuality,* ed. Carole S. Vance (Boston: Routledge and Kegan Paul, 1984), 1–27, 16. Vance contrasts feminists' underdeveloped approach to images with the movement's more sophisticated take on literature. But literary scholars, too, were just beginning to take serious stock of "symbolic context and transformation" and to challenge straightforward ideas about experience, voice, politics, and representation in feminist literary criticism. See Toril Moi, "Sexual/Textual Politics," talk delivered at the 1982 Essex Conference on the Sociology of Literature and published in the proceedings *The Politics of Theory,* ed. Francis Barker et al. (Colchester, UK: University of Essex, 1983), 1–14; Elizabeth Abel, "Editor's Introduction," in "Writing and Sexual Difference," special issue, *Critical Inquiry* 8, no. 2 (Winter 1981): 173–178; and Jane Gallop, *Around 1981: Academic Feminist Literary Theory* (New York: Routledge, 1992).

74. Vance, "Pleasure and Danger," 16.

75. *Diary of a Conference on Sexuality,* self-published pamphlet by organizers of the conference "The Scholar and the Feminist: Toward a Politics of Sexuality," 44, http://www.darkmatterarchives.net/wp-content/uploads/2011/12/Diary-of-a -Conference-on-Sexuality.pdf.

76. Barbara Kruger, "No Progress in Pleasure," in Vance, *Pleasure and Danger,* 210–216, 210. The same issue is also raised, in remarkably similar language, in the other major early-1980s feminist anthology on sexuality, 1983's *Powers of Desire.* In E. Ann Kaplan's essay "Is the Gaze Male?," which draws heavily on feminist and Lacanian film theory, Kaplan asks, "Is the gaze *necessarily* male . . . ? Or would it be possible to structure things so that women own the gaze? Second, would women want to own the gaze, if it were possible? Third, in either case, what does it mean to be a female spectator?" E. Ann Kaplan, "Is the Gaze Male?," in *Powers of Desire: The Politics of Sexuality,* ed. Ann Snitow et al. (New York: Monthly Review Press, 1983), 309–327, 312.

77. Here I follow Hortense Spillers, who writes, "To speak is to occupy a place in social economy, and, in the case of the racialized subject, his history has dictated that this linguistic *right to use* is never easily granted with his human and social legacy but must be earned, over and over again, on the level of a personal and collective struggle that requires in some way a confrontation with the principle of language *as a prohibition,* as the withheld." Spillers, "'All the Things You Could Be by Now If Sigmund Freud's Wife Was Your Mother': Psychoanalysis and Race," in *Black, White, and in Color: Essays on American Literature and Culture* (Chicago: University of Chicago Press, 2003), 376–427, 400–401.

78. Adrienne Rich, "The Images," in *A Wild Patience Has Taken Me This Far: Poems 1978–1981* (New York: W. W. Norton, 1981), 3–5.

79. Audre Lorde, "Afterimages," in *Chosen Poems: Old and New* (New York: W. W. Norton, 1982), 102–105.

80. Marion Rust offers an excellent account of Rich and Lorde's long-running conversation and mutual criticism in "Making Emends: Adrienne Rich, Audre Lorde, Anne Bradstreet," *American Literature* 88, no. 1 (March 2016): 93–125.

81. Poetry readings by Adrienne Rich and Audre Lorde, recorded at Saint Peter's Church in New York City, March 7, 1979, first broadcast on WBAI, May 14, 1979, Pacifica Radio Archives, 43:45, https://archive.org/details/pacifica_radio_archives-IZ0809A.

82. Fleetwood, *Troubling Vision.*

83. Rust, "Making Emends."

84. Hortense Spillers, "Interstices: A Small Drama of Words," in Vance, *Pleasure and Danger,* 73–100, 84. In preparing this essay for republication in her 2004 collection *Black, White and in Color,* Spillers would alter this line to, "The subject is certainly seen, but she also *sees,*" downplaying the certitude of this countervisuality while further emphasizing its feminist implications. Spillers, "Interstices: A Small Drama of Words," in *Black, White and in Color,* 152–175, 163.

85. Saidiya Hartman's *Scenes of Subjection: Terror, Slavery, and Self-Making in Nineteenth-Century America* (New York: Oxford University Press, 1997) remains the classic exploration of this dynamic.

86. Audre Lorde, "Learning from the '60s," in *Sister Outsider,* 134–144, 135.

87. Susan Brownmiller, *Against Our Will: Men, Women, and Rape* (New York: Simon and Schuster, 1975), 247.

88. Hortense Spillers, "Interstices: A Small Drama of Words," in Vance, *Pleasure and Danger,* 73–100, 84. This passage was important enough for Spillers to update it slightly for inclusion in her collection *Black, White and in Color.* In the revision, she changed the first sentence to, "The subject is certainly seen, but she also *sees*"; for "This latter seeing," she substituted instead, "This return of the gaze." Spillers, "Interstices," in *Black, White, and in Color,* 163.

89. Fleetwood, *Troubling Vision,* 7; Mirzoeff, *Right to Look,* 4.

90. Spillers, "Interstices," in Vance, *Pleasure and Danger,* 86.

91. W. E. B. Du Bois, *The Souls of Black Folk,* Norton Critical Edition (1903; New York: W. W. Norton, 1999), 15–16.

Chapter 5. The Ancestors' Breath

1. Bernice Johnson Reagon, "Coalition Politics: Turning the Century," in *Home Girls: A Black Feminist Anthology,* ed. Barbara Smith (1983; Piscataway, NJ: Rutgers University Press, 2000), 343–355.

2. Reagon, 348.

3. Reagon, 352.

4. Reagon, 347.

5. The song was published in *Sing Out!* 28, no. 2 (1980): 12, without its final coda. An expanded score was later included in *Continuum: The First Songbook of Sweet Honey in the Rock,* comp. and ed. Ysaye M. Barnwell with Sweet Honey in the Rock; transcriptions by J. David Moore and Catherine Roma (Southwest Harbor, ME: Contemporary A Cappella, 2000).

6. Ysaye M. Barnwell, "Breaths," in *Continuum: The First Songbook of Sweet Honey in the Rock,* 4–8.

7. Julie Dash, "Breaths," music video, performed by Sweet Honey in the Rock, 1994, 3:53, https://juliedash.tv/2016/01/25/breathes-sweet-honey-in-the-rock/. I'm grateful to Nick Hallett for pointing me toward Dash's video.

8. Quoted in Deborah Gould, *Moving Politics: Emotion and ACT UP's Fight against AIDS* (Chicago: University of Chicago Press, 2009), 229, 228.

9. Douglas Crimp, "Mourning and Militancy," *October* 51 (Winter 1989): 3–18, 5, 18.

10. Dagmawi Woubshet's excellent book *The Calendar of Loss: Race, Sexuality, and Mourning in the Early Era of AIDS* (Baltimore: Johns Hopkins University Press, 2015) treats this issue in extremely useful detail.

11. See Nishant Shahani, "How to Survive the Whitewashing of AIDS: Global Pasts, Transnational Futures," *QED: A Journal in GLBTQ Worldmaking* 3, no. 1 (2016): 1–33; Jih-Fei Cheng, "How to Survive: AIDS and Its Afterlives in Popular Media," *Women's Studies Quarterly* 44, no. 1 (Spring 2016): 73–92; and Jonathan Bell et al., "HIV / AIDS and U.S. History," *Journal of American History* 104, no. 2 (2017): 431–460.

12. Gould makes this argument at several points in *Moving Politics.* Additionally, Steven Seidman writes that in the 1980s, "a backlash against homosexuality, spearheaded by the new right but widely supported by neoconservatives and mainstream Republicans, punctured illusions of a coming era of tolerance and sexual pluralism." Seidman, "Queer-ing Sociology, Sociologizing Queer Theory: An Introduction," *Sociological Theory* 12, no. 2 (July 1994): 166–177.

13. See Woubshet, *Calendar of Loss.*

14. Gould, *Moving Politics,* 338.

15. Douglas Crimp, "Right On, Girlfriend!," *Social Text,* no. 33 (1992): 2–18, 4–5.

16. Crimp, 8.

17. Crimp, 14.

18. Crimp, 15.

19. Crimp, 15, 12, 16.

20. Cathy Cohen, "Punks, Bulldaggers, and Welfare Queens: The Radical Potential of Queer Politics?," *GLQ* 3, no. 4 (1997): 437–465.

21. For *gay* and *lesbian* as mutually exclusive, see Gould, *Moving Politics,* 66–67.

22. See Joshua Gamson, "Must Identity Movements Self-Destruct? A Queer Dilemma," *Social Problems* 42, no. 3 (August 1995): 390–407; and Cohen, "Punks."

23. Cohen, 481.

24. My reflections here on listening are intended to sound in chorus with Elliott H. Powell's proposals about collective resonance and the sonic dimensions of Cathy Cohen's pathbreaking essay. Powell, "Coalitional Auralities: Notes on a Soundtrack to Punks, Bulldaggers, and Welfare Queens," *GLQ* 25, no. 1 (January 2019): 188–193.

25. On the inadequacy of the paradigm of "hearing the voices" of the marginalized, see Pooja Rangan, *Immediations: The Humanitarian Impulse in Documentary* (Durham, NC: Duke University Press, 2017); and Pooja Rangan, "In Defense of Voicelessness: The Matter of the Voice and the Films of Leslie Thornton," *Feminist Media Histories* 1, no. 3 (2015): 95–126.

26. Marlon T. Riggs, dir., *Tongues Untied* (Signifyin' Works / Frameline, 1989), 54 minutes.

27. In a keen reading of this scene, focused largely on queer appropriation of the obituary form and its powers, Woubshet sees an additive operation, evidence that "while a politics of recognition was central to this renaissance" of Black queer art of which Riggs was a part, "so too was a politics of mourning" (*Calendar of Loss,* 58–59). Without taking anything away from Woubshet's important theorization of the obituary's place in creative responses to AIDS, I'm highlighting how the insistent entry of death to the closing moments of *Tongues Untied* complicates and transforms the politics of recognition that constitutes the film's overt mission.

28. Marlon Riggs, dir., *Black Is . . . Black Ain't* (Signifyin' Works, 1995), 1 hour 28 minutes.

29. Christiane Badgley, interview by the author, June 30, 2021.

30. Jennifer Denise Williams, "Black Mourning: Readings of Loss, Desire, and Racial Identification" (PhD diss., University of Texas at Austin, 2006), 123.

31. Marlon Riggs, "Letter to the Dead," *Thing,* Fall 1992, 40–44. The essay was later reprinted, with substantial revisions, as "Letters to the Dead," in *Sojourner: Black Gay Voices in the Age of AIDS,* ed. B. Michael Hunter (New York: Other Countries, 1993), 141–147.

32. Riggs, "Letter," 43.

33. James Baldwin, "My Dungeon Shook: Letter to My Nephew on the One Hundredth Anniversary of the Emancipation" (1962), in *The Fire Next Time* (New York: Vintage, 1991), 1–10, 7.

34. This text, which is most often identified by its opening line, "When I put my hands on your body," appears, for instance, in Wojnarowicz's artwork *When I Put*

My Hands on Your Body (1990), which can be seen on pp. 82–83 of *David Wojnarowicz: Brush Fires in the Social Landscape,* 20th anniversary ed. (1994; New York: Aperture, 2014). Wojnarowicz also read it aloud as part of the multimedia performance work *ITSOFOMO (In the Shadow of Forward Motion),* which he created in collaboration with composer and musician Ben Neill and performed at the Kitchen in New York in 1989.

35. David Wojnarowicz, *Close to the Knives: A Memoir of Disintegration* (New York: Vintage, 1991), 91–92.

36. Cynthia Carr, *Fire in the Belly: The Life and Times of David Wojnarowicz* (New York: Bloomsbury, 2012), 410.

37. David Wojnarowicz, "The Compression of Time: An Interview with David Wojnarowicz," interview by Barry Blinderman, in *David Wojnarowicz: Tongues of Flame* (1990; Normal: University Galleries of Illinois State University; second printing copublished with Distributed Art Publishers, 1992), 49–63, 54.

38. David Wojnarowicz, 1988 Journal, Nov., Dec. #1 (Part 1 of 2), 1988; David Wojnarowicz Papers; MSS 092; Case 092.0465, access copy of Source 092.0218; Fales Library and Special Collections, New York University Libraries. Transcription also in Lisa Darms and David O'Neill, eds., *Weight of the Earth: The Tape Journals of David Wojnarowicz* (South Pasadena, CA: Semiotext[e], 2018), 73.

39. Wojnarowicz, 1988 Journal. Also in Darms and O'Neill, 78.

40. Wojnarowicz, 1988 Journal. Also in Darms and O'Neill, 78.

41. Wojnarowicz, 1988 Journal. Also in Darms and O'Neill, 77.

42. Wojnarowicz, 1988 Journal. Also in Darms and O'Neill, 84.

43. Charles Hirschkind, in writing about people's listening to Islamic sermon tapes in Cairo, observed that listening practices can nourish somatic and affective potentialities from which ethical dispositions draw sustenance. Charles Hirschkind, *The Ethical Soundscape: Cassette Sermons and Islamic Counterpublics* (New York: Columbia University Press, 2006).

44. Darms and O'Neill, 141–142.

45. David Wojnarowicz, *Cross Country: Tape Journals February–June 1988,* triple LP with digital download (Reading Group, 2018).

46. Tracy Chapman, "Fast Car," track 2 on *Tracy Chapman* (Elektra, 1988).

47. Reagon, "Coalition Politics," 352.

48. This idea of listening as a practice of caring for those who have come before is influenced by a talk Daphne Brooks gave at the School of Criticism and Theory at Cornell University in July 2019. This idea animates much of Brooks's *Liner Notes for the Revolution: The Intellectual Life of Black Feminist Sound* (Cambridge, MA: Belknap Press of Harvard University Press, 2021), where she writes, for instance, that "the archive of blues music, the art of a disenfranchised people, demands our scrupulous collective attention, our communal care" (180).

Coda

1. W. E. B. Du Bois, *The Souls of Black Folk,* Norton Critical Edition (New York: W. W. Norton, 1999), 162, 163.

2. Asali Solomon, *The Days of Afrekete* (New York: Farrar, Straus and Giroux, 2021), 122.

3. Solomon, 61.

4. Solomon, 77.

5. Solomon, 189.

6. "Stevie Wonder Offers to Perform Surgery on Stephen," *The Late Show with Stephen Colbert,* aired November 14, 2016, YouTube video, 5:42, https://www.youtube.com/watch?v=X6zRfQpYOwQ.

7. Solomon, *Days of Afrekete,* 189.

ACKNOWLEDGMENTS

It has been a joy to write this book within the structures of intense discussion and critique that define academic writing and publishing. I'm grateful for the many conversations I've had about this book over the years with peers, mentors, senior colleagues, and students, and for the generative feedback the project has received from editors and anonymous readers. *Political Disappointment* first took shape during my doctoral studies at Princeton, where the project benefited greatly from the generous advising of Daphne Brooks, Diana Fuss, and Bill Gleason, as well as important input from Sarah Chihaya, Andrew Cole, Jill Dolan, Devin Fore, Dirk Hartog, Josh Kotin, Russ Leo, Kinohi Nishikawa, Dan Rodgers, Britt Rusert, Gayle Salamon, and Alexandra Vazquez. Princeton's Interdisciplinary Doctoral Program in the Humanities, under the visionary leadership of Jeff Dolven, welcomed me into a community of creative scholars working between disciplines. Anonymous reviewers from *American Literature* and *PMLA* helped me refine Chapter 1. A conversation with Tavia Nyong'o in Montreal helped Chapter 2 find its shape. The Post45 meeting at Notre Dame in 2019, especially comments from Emily Lordi and Tom McEnaney, proved invaluable as I finalized Chapter 3. Alice Echols and Amber Jamilla Musser read and offered generative comments on Chapter 4; David Velasco and Derek Baron did the same for parts of Chapter 5. The coda builds on ideas first presented in "Listening in an Emergency," published in *Dissent* in 2020, and in "The Postdemocratic Novel," published in *American Literary History* (*ALH*) in 2023. Portions of Chapter 1 were first published as "'Time Enough, but None to Spare': The Indispensable Temporalities of Charles Chesnutt's *The Marrow of Tradition*," *American Literature* 91, no. 1 (March 2019): 31–58. Many thanks to the editors of these publications, especially Matthew Taylor and Priscilla Wald at *American Literature,* Josh Leifer and Nick Serpe at *Dissent,* and Gordon Hutner and Rachel Greenwald Smith at *ALH.* Josh Kun, Emily Lordi, and Anthony Reed generously read the entire manuscript at an earlier stage in its development and offered enormously helpful feedback that, among other things, helped me see how to turn a collection of chapters into something more cohesive. The book is much better thanks to all these readers' comments and suggestions. Of course, any remaining shortcomings of this book are mine alone.

ACKNOWLEDGMENTS

Thank you to the gracious organizers, audiences, and copanelists who hosted me and discussed these ideas at the New School, the Ohio State University, the Pop Montreal Symposium, the School of the Art Institute of Chicago, and the University of Massachusetts Amherst; to session organizers, copresenters, discussants, and attendees at the American Comparative Literature Association, Association for the Study of the Arts of the Present, Modern Language Association, Modernist Studies Association, Northeast Modern Language Association, Pop, and Sound and Affect conferences; to my students, especially those in English 40781: Decades of Disappointment; and to organizers of and participants in workshops at Princeton, the University of Chicago, Yale, and the Futures of American Studies Institute at Dartmouth, where I was lucky to be in the seminar that Soyica Diggs Colbert led with brilliance, precision, and warmth. I am grateful to Hortense Spillers for attending the seminar session where I presented and for offering incisive comments that greatly improved the book. Thanks also to Alexander Weheliye and the participants in the "Black Life" seminar at the School of Criticism and Theory at Cornell, especially Derek Baron, Andrew Belton, Kim Bobier, Seb Boersma, Rahma Haji, Clara Lee, Jessica Modi, Umniya Najaer, and Henry Washington Jr., for rigorous discussions on crucial questions that profoundly affected this book and the way I approached it.

At Harvard University Press, I thank Lindsay Waters for seeing the value in this project and bringing me on board, Joseph Pomp for editing the project with enthusiasm and rigor, Stephanie Vyce and Jillian Quigley for their logistical acumen, the anonymous readers whose insightful comments proved immensely helpful as I refined the book, and the copyeditors, designers, and production editors who shepherded the manuscript into concrete form, especially Cheryl Hirsch. Thanks to the Institute for Scholarship in the Liberal Arts, College of Arts and Letters, University of Notre Dame, whose support helped make this publication possible. Thanks as well to Philip Leventhal for his early support; to Ken Wissoker for a galvanizing early conversation; to anonymous readers from Columbia University Press and Duke University Press for their careful readings and critical questions; and to Charlotte Sheedy, always.

Special thanks are due to the librarians and archivists at the Cleveland Public Library Special Collections, Cornell University Radical and Labor Songbook Collection, Fales Library at New York University Special Collections, Fisk University Special Collections, Oberlin College Archives, Schlesinger Library at the Harvard Radcliffe Institute, Stanford University Special Collections, and University of Illinois Chicago Special Collections, as well as Rachel Bohlmann and the other librarians at Notre Dame, for facilitating access to rare and archival materials. Funding from Princeton's English Department, Program in American Studies, and Dean's Fund for Scholarly Travel made it possible for me to access many of these archives. Additional thanks to the P·P·O·W gallery, the Lester S. Levy Collection of Sheet Music at Johns Hopkins University, Joan E. Biren, and Amy Horowitz of Roadwork for connecting me with images for the book. Christiane Badgley, Sam Green, and Amy Horowitz also helped fill in some of the historical context for the more recent moments I discuss, and Marie Shelton contributed invaluable research assistance.

I'm grateful for the warm support and fellowship of current and past colleagues at Notre Dame, in the English Department, the Program in Gender Studies, the Initiative on Race and Resilience, and farther afield. Thanks to Laura Betz, Susan Blum, Dionne Irving Bremyer, Pam Butler, Pete Cajka, Nan Da, Ranjodh Singh Dhaliwal, John Duffy, Steve Fallon, Johannes Göransson, Barbara Green, Sandra Gustafson, Susan Harris, Romana Huk, Lionel Jensen, Cyraina Johnson-Roullier, Essaka Joshua, Matt Kilbane, Laura Knoppers, Jesse Lander, Tim Machan, Kate Marshall, Barry McCrea, Jarvis McInnis, Joyelle McSweeney, Orlando Menes, Ernest Morrell, Xavier Navarro Aquino, Ian Newman, Emma Planinc, Sarah Quesada, Mark Sanders, Valerie Sayers, Yasmin Solomonescu, Elliott Visconsi, and Laura Walls. Special thanks to my core South Bend crew of Korey Garibaldi, Chanté Mouton Kinyon, and Francisco Robles and Brandon Menke; the neighborhood squad of Allison Beyer, Melissa Christianson, Emily Holloway, Sheila McCarthy, Joy McCoy, Graínne McEvoy, Catherine Osborne, and Kathy Schuth; and Jeremy Brown, Valeria Slapak Brown, Amy Levin, Joel Mittelman, and Scott and Nechama Weingart.

Beyond Notre Dame, I am grateful for invigorating conversations over the years with Kimberly Bain, Hadji Bakara, Derek Baron, Mary Walling Blackburn, Stephanie Burt, Joshua Chambers-Letson, Dawn Chan, Sarah Chihaya, Amy Cimini, Peter Coviello, Anna Craycroft, Meehan Crist, Thomas Davis, Leah DeVun, Brittney Edmonds, Ren Ellis Neyra, Merve Emre, Gloria Fisk, rl goldberg, Mark Greif, David Hajdu, Jack Halberstam, Matthew Hart, Briallen Hopper, Sam Huber, Jess Hurley, Robin James, Brian Kane, Seth Kim-Cohen, Evan Kindley, Emanuela Kucik, Clara Latham, Andrea Lawlor, Jonathan Leal, Sarah Leonard, Karen Lepri, Heather Love, Khaela Maricich, Tom McEnaney, Eileen Myles, Julie Beth Napolin, Anahid Nersessian, Liora O'Donnell Goldensher, Dushko Petrovich, Hilary Plum, Ann Powers, Zach Savich, Shayna Silverstein, Rachel Greenwald Smith, Suzanne Snider, Stefanie Sobelle, Gus Stadler, Karen Tongson, Dayna Tortorici, Gayle Wald, Eric Weisbard, Gabe Winant, Johanna Winant, Douglas Wolk, Cookie Woolner, and Molly Zuckerman-Hartung. Princeton brought a new circle of colleagues and friends, including Anat Benzvi, Edna Bonhomme, Alice Christensen, Ian Davis, Jill Jarvis, Liz John, Emanuela Kucik, Ashley Lazevnick, Jesse McCarthy, Rosalind Parry, Kate Thorpe, Amelia Worsley, and Bora Yoon. A special acknowledgment of love and solidarity goes out to Jess Arndt, Sara Jaffe, and Jason Daniel Schwartz—dear longtime friends and coeditors in the indefinitely suspended but continually reverberating New Herring Press endeavor.

I started thinking about the texts and ideas in this book long before I started writing it. The seeds are present in some of my undergraduate work, in research I did at Yale in conversation with Michael Thurston and Jack Halberstam and then at Oberlin with Pat Day, Ron Kahn, and especially Sandra Zagarell, who advised my senior honors thesis on 1930s US Communist literary nonfiction and continually urged me to consider the potential downsides of doctrinal certainties. It has been a joy to remain in conversation with her.

The years I spent in nonacademic pursuits have left their mark on this project as well. In the early 2000s, I worked at the Jewish Fund for Justice (which has since merged with other organizations to become Bend the Arc), where Shona Chakravartty, Cindy Greenberg, Roz

Lee, Vera Miao, Marlene Provizer, and Lee Winkelman, as well as the many grassroots leaders with whom we collaborated and whose leadership we endeavored to follow, had a lasting influence on my thinking about how movements succeed and fail. My closest activist comrades during these years in New York—among them Guy Austrian, Ilana Berger, Jey Born, Jesse Ehrensaft-Hawley, Jo Hirschmann, Adam Horowitz, Abbie Illenberger, Evelyn Lynn, Ryan Senser, Sonja Sivesind, and Elizabeth Wilson—helped shape my understanding of the workings of whiteness, the importance of solidarity, and the possibility of fundamental change.

At Columbia University's School of the Arts, I was fortunate to receive mentorship and guidance from Margo Jefferson, Richard Locke, and Patty O'Toole, and to build friendships with Nitsuh Abebe, Stacey Cook, Marie Elia, Tupelo Hassman, Brendan Hughes, Saki Knafo, and Billy Merrell. Some years later, my work at *Artforum,* in the company of colleagues and writers including Melissa Anderson, Caroline Busta, Nikki Columbus, Sam Frank, Jeff Gibson, Tim Griffin, Michelle Kuo, Claire Lehmann, Elizabeth Schambelan, and Polly Watson, helped me think more deeply about connections between politics and the aesthetic practices of literature, art, and sound.

Many scholars engaged with my work following the publication of *Girls to the Front* and drew me into rich, rewarding conversations. I still remember with particular fondness engagements at the University of Tennessee, Wesleyan University, the University of Maryland, George Washington University, the University of Michigan, and Yale University. I am especially grateful to Lisa Cohen, Christina Crosby (z"l), Margaret Lazarus Dean, Mark Oppenheimer, Tara Rodgers, Lisi Schoenbach, Ilana Sichel, and Gayle Wald for facilitating these visits and conversations, which had the perhaps unintended but largely happy consequence of luring me back into academia. A fortunate convergence with Jack Halberstam, Wayne Koestenbaum, and Maggie Nelson at the Cabinet space in Brooklyn propelled me on this path, and Stephanie Burt, Mark Greif, and Stephen Squibb offered key early encouragement. I have been lucky to count Atossa Abrahamian, Josh Leifer (who got me into Big Thief for an assignment from *Dissent*), Laura Marsh (who, by assigning me to review a Greil Marcus book for the *New Republic,* set me off on research that would anchor Chapter 2 of *Political Disappointment*), David O'Neill, Lauren O'Neill-Butler, Joy Press, David Velasco, Lloyd Wise, and Mike Wolf as occasional editors of my work in addition to valued interlocutors.

My years in Brooklyn were made sweet, lively, and full of love by people whose friendship and comradeship still mean everything to me, including Bobby Abate, Becca Albee, Vanessa Anspaugh, Guy Austrian, Nicholas Boggs, Rebecca Brooks, Tova Carlin, JJ Chan, Mark Doten, Christy Edwards, Nicole Eisenman, Emily Farrell, Johanna Fateman, Keltie Ferris, Sheri Fink, Kira Garcia, Claudia Gonson, Sam Green, Bianca Grimshaw, Nick Hallett, K8 Hardy, Jo Hirschmann, Tennessee Jones, Alhena Katsof, Lauren Klein, Zach Layton, Karen Lepri, David Levine, Jess Loudis, Emily Manzo, Hedia Maron, Douglas Martin, Benny Merris, Brock Monroe, Itty Neuhaus, Jillian Peña, Litia Perta,

Cassie Peterson, Alissa Quart, Sabine Rogers, Thomas Rogers, JD Samson, Lauren Sandler, Bill Schuck, Ilana Sichel, Lauryn Siegel, Amy Sillman, Brooke Smith, Emilie Smith, Lanka Tatterall, Josh Thorson, and Elizabeth Wilson. I'm also glad to have had opportunities along the way to make music with Ginger Brooks Takahashi, Aileen Brophy, Alice Cohen, Lisa Corson, Ben Daniels, Zeke Healy, Lita Hernandez, Lauren Klein, Pete Leonard, Gerard Smith (z''l), and Tae Won Yu.

I did some of my earliest work on this project at MacDowell, a magical artists' residency in New Hampshire. My gratitude to the MacDowell staff, especially Michelle Aldredge, Emily Drury, David Macy, and Blake Tewksbury, knows no bounds. Fellow residents including Annie Baker, Brooke Berman, Dan Fishback, Sam Green, Gabriel Kahane, Wade Kavanaugh, Andrea Kleine, Jennie Livingston, Jena Osman, Brian Selznick, David Serlin, and Lynne Tillman continue to inspire me. Work I did at the Blue Mountain Center in 2012 was also germinal to this project, and I am particularly grateful for the company there of Blair Braverman, Joan Larkin, Jane McAlevey, Maureen McLane, and Basya Schechter. My too-brief time in Houston in 2016 brought me closer with Katie Anania, Andy Campbell, Lily Cox-Richard, Dean Daderko, Taraneh Fazeli, JD Pluecker, Risa Puleo, Cory Silverberg, and Zoë Wool.

My postdoctoral fellowship at the University of Southern California in 2019–2020 was effectively cut short by the arrival of COVID-19 on the scene, but I was grateful to intersect there with Alice Baumgartner, Ashley Cohen, Alice Echols, Kate Flint, Alice Gambrell, Devin Griffiths, Suzanne Hudson, Zakiyyah Iman Jackson, Hilary Schor, Thomas Seifrid, Sara Sligar, David St. John, and Karen Tongson, along with, farther afield in Los Angeles, Amanda Davidson, Lissa Gundlach, Maya Gurantz, Hilary Kaplan, Evan Kindley, Sarah Lehrer-Graiwer, Anahid Nersessian, and Michelle Tea. On a steep Highland Park hillside, Thom and Kate and Sonny Shelton started off as landlords and became friends, then pandemic podmates, filling those strange early months of the shutdown with companionship, wading-pool parties, living-room singalongs, and moments of sheer joy. Speaking of the pandemic, I would be remiss not to register my loving gratitude to the San Gabriel Mountains, the Santa Monica Mountains, the Pacific Ocean, Lake Michigan, and Love Creek County Park.

This book would have been logistically unthinkable without the labor and care of many preschool teachers, including those at Discoveries, the Silverlake Independent JCC, the Early Childhood Development Center, and our current school community, as well as the many babysitters who have helped over the years, most especially Brianna Dewey, Maria Everett, Angie Lorang, Riley McCoy, Berkeley Oceguera, Anne Malin Ringwalt, Nalani Stolz, and Eli Williams.

I'm grateful to my parents for their stalwart support of all my endeavors; to my aunt Susannah Sirkin and uncle Lawrence Harmon for many incisive discussions over holiday dinners in Boston and on the back porch in New Hampshire; to my in-laws, especially Theresa, Mary, and Mia; and to my brother, Jeremy, my delightful nieces and nephews, and my beloved cousins Leah, Ana, Naomi, and Sahara.

Roy Scranton has been here since the book started taking shape, and everything in these pages has been honed and sharpened by the many discussions, arguments, pep talks, and editing sessions I've been lucky enough to share with him over the past decade. Our ongoing life together serves as evidence that rigor and joy, love and critique, can not only coexist but amplify and transfigure each other. Reyzl came onto the scene about halfway through the project, and she immediately altered my understanding of how I and my work relate to those who have gone before and those who are yet to come. What I owe these two dynamic beings exceeds any words I could possibly use to express my gratitude and love—yet the words will have to do.

INDEX

Page numbers in *italics* refer to illustrations.